EVERYBODY IS WRONG ABOUT GOD

EVERYBODY IS WRONG ABOUT GOD

James A. Lindsay

Foreword by Peter Boghossian

PITCHSTONE PUBLISHING
Durham, North Carolina

Pitchstone Publishing
Durham, North Carolina
www.pitchstonepublishing.com

Copyright © 2015 by James A. Lindsay

Library of Congress Cataloging-in-Publication Data

Lindsay, James A.
  Everybody is wrong about God / James A. Lindsay ; foreword by Peter Boghossian.
    pages cm
  Includes bibliographical references.
  ISBN 978-1-63431-036-9 (pbk. : alk. paper)
  1. God. 2. Religion—Controversial literature. 3. Psychology, Religious. 4.
Atheism. 5. Theism. 6. Secularism. I. Title.
  BL473.L56 2015
  211—dc23
                          2015027515

To Sam Harris and Jonathan Haidt

CONTENTS

Foreword by Peter Boghossian   9

Preface   13

Introduction: The Next Rational Move   15

1. Exposing Theism   34

2. The End of Atheism   45

3. Post-theism   67

4. The Goodness of God   74

5. "God"   97

6. Okay, Now What?   175

7. Uprooting Faith   179

8. Secularism   196

9. Unthinking Atheism   203

10. Filling the Religion Gap   209

11. Going Post-theistic   227

Conclusion: The Future of Reason   241

Acknowledgments   245

About the Author   248

FOREWORD

I am inclined to think that the far greater part, if not all, of those difficulties which have hitherto amused philosophers, and blocked up the way to knowledge, are entirely owing to ourselves. We have first raised a dust, and then complain we cannot see.

—**George Berkeley**

For decades tobacco companies conducted and promoted research into the harms of tobacco, even though they knew smoking was deadly. Their objective was to persuade people that there was some question as to the toxicity of cigarette smoke. They reasoned that people would think the act of researching indicated there were questions that weren't answered—and that the more uncertainty there was around the question of whether smoking is harmful, the easier it would be for people to smoke.

A nearly identical mechanism is found in theology, apologetics, and religion. So many people spending so much time investigating the existence of God must mean that there's some*thing* to investigate. The act of researching indicates there are questions that aren't answered—and the more uncertainty there is around the question of God, the easier it is for people to believe in God.

This is obviously nonsense. The number of people—or the number of hours, or the length of time—spent researching a phenomenon is not an indication of the likelihood of the actual existence of the phenomenon. For over 100 years phlogiston theory dominated a branch of chemistry. It stated there was a combustible element in things, called phlogiston, that released when combusted. There is no phlogiston. A lot of intelligent, thoughtful people spent a lot of time pursuing a fiction.

And so too it is with God: *A lot* of intelligent, thoughtful people have spent *a lot* of time trying to prove the existence of something that can't be proven. The byproducts of this uniquely unprecedented, tragic waste of time range from the production of endless corpses to the creation of countless cultures that have been inimical to human flourishing. With *Everybody Is Wrong About God*, God—and with it atheism—is finally and unequivocally interred. James Lindsay is the undertaker.

Everybody Is Wrong About God shifts the way we understand an ages-old problem, while providing frameworks and mechanisms for a post-theistic world; it articulates how and why we've fundamentally misconceptualized theism. Theism is not a philosophy. It is not a *Weltanschauung*. It is not a symptom of an underlying social pathology. Theism is mythology. It looks to a fantasy as a method of characterizing reality. God is a psychologically satisfying idea believed in via mythology; Lindsay exposes the roots of the myth and thus argues for a psychological as opposed to philosophical or scientific understanding of the term "God." Treating theism on its own terms is a mistake that gave the title to this book—it gets God wrong.

Consequently, because theism does not merit consideration, atheism as a counterpoint is senseless. When atheism gets treated as its own kind of thing it becomes ridiculous. And while culturally it will be difficult to recover from millennia of moral and intellectual vandalism caused by theism, atheism is not even a nostrum: atheism is harmful to the goals of leaving God behind and constructing a post-theistic world. (This may seem like a contradictory statement coming from the author of *A Manual for Creating Atheists*. It's not. My objective has always been to create critical thinkers—atheism, or whatever word replaces it, is a byproduct of this.) Atheism, as a counterpoint, gets God wrong when it treats theism on its own terms, and in so doing tends to take on features that its critics rightly see as looking quite religious.

Lindsay argues that one of the gateways to herald the end of theism *and atheism* is leaving belief in God behind by changing the direction of the conversation. For centuries philosophers readily took the bait and positively ran with theism on its own terms as a philosophical position, and this doomed them to arguing endlessly in circles with theologians. No more. If we can identify what God means to people and look at it in terms of those real-world foundations, we can treat the problem differently and begin the process of burying God-beliefs. There's no reason to persist in asserting that the word "God" means something other than what it does, and seeing it as a psychosocial construct can take us post-theistic almost at once—absent atheism.

Everybody Is Wrong About God is a crucial book. It's a signpost at a crossroads. It takes a completely novel approach to understanding faith, religion, theology, and the psychology of belief, yet it builds upon multiple domains of literature before removing this scaffolding. As Wittgenstein writes, it allows readers to throw away the ladder after they've climbed up it.

Everybody Is Wrong About God is an opportunity to clear the dust, so that we can see.

Peter Boghossian
Portland, Oregon

PREFACE

I'm going to start this book by telling you a few things that do not seem to go together. Everyone will find these things controversial because everyone is wrong about God.

First, I want to tell you that "God" exists.

Second, I want to tell you that people who do not believe in God have it more or less right, and in fact, that at the level of ideas, their view has already rightfully won.

Third, I want to tell you that the key to getting "God" right, and thus getting over God and on with our lives and societies, is recognizing that belief in God itself is how we get God wrong.

Because "God" exists, when people say "God doesn't exist," they are not saying something intelligible to believers. In fact, what they're saying is worse than nonsense. The trick is that God doesn't exist; "God" does, and believers hear what they really mean by that word whenever they hear it. All that's needed is sorting out whatever "God" really means. That is an effort this book will set into motion.

This is not paradoxical. Believers are speaking mythologically about something real, so they all talk about their beliefs in the wrong way. They talk about them theologically, and that's really mythologically. Thus, they are wrong about God.

Very few nonbelievers understand this fact, and they also do not understand what "God" means. Lacking another way to talk about the topic, they argue in the same mythological language, and thus they are also wrong about God. While a lack of belief in the existence of God is the right position, theological terms are the wrong way to engage the topic. "Atheists," increasingly identifiable as a motivated subset of those who lack belief in God, are particularly keen to commit this error and do so at two major costs. First, they perpetuate the debate about theism on its own terms, and the continuation of that debate is all the intellectual defense that belief in God has going for it. Second, they set themselves up for a number of avoidable pitfalls, most notably becoming identifiable from the outside with being something that seems almost religious and, worse, actually becoming such.

Many atheist interest groups currently and ambitiously seek to "normalize" atheism, to make it a normal part of society. Once we understand "God," we will understand why atheism, as anything that could be misconstrued as a thing, cannot be normalized. As we will see, the first thing "God" means to almost every believer is nearly always "how I understand moral values." Second (or thereabouts), and intimately related, comes "how I contextualize myself in my culture/community."

Atheism, from the believer's point of view, is therefore always heard as a rejection of those values, hence we see rampant mistrust of atheists. We must understand that, alongside everything else it does, religion acts to form moral communities, which allow for a bypassing mechanism to our natural distrust of unknown others under the perception of shared moral and cultural values. Those values are grounded in the idea people call "God." Atheism stands in negation to those values, as understood by the believer, and so the "theism versus atheism" conversation is doomed.

In too-short summary, "God" means "my values," and so "atheism" is heard as "I reject your values." This is why "atheism" needs to die. This is why we need to drop it and go post-theistic. The first step in doing so is understanding how everybody is wrong about God and starting down the road to getting it right.

This book is meant to change how we understand the term "God," ending theism and theology in their entireties, and thus it will call for a complete rethink on atheism (*un*think would be a better word, in fact). In a way, it will be a call back to roots, and in another way, it will be an open door to the next stage of humanity's future.

INTRODUCTION: THE NEXT RATIONAL MOVE

The next rational move: Considering the entire theistic enterprise beneath serious consideration.

—Peter Boghossian

Philosopher and author Peter Boghossian tweeted this on June 18, 2014,[1] paraphrasing something extremely similar that I had just sent him in an email. We were having a discussion about the future of society, one focused on getting toward a goal we share with many others: helping our society become properly post-God and post-faith.

After the tweet, our email conversation continued, leading to the realization that this simple idea—considering the entire theistic enterprise beneath serious consideration—was the final step in getting rid of God for good, and Pete said so. He suggested "The Final Step in Getting Rid of God" as a first stab at a working subtitle for this very book, which was in the conceptual phases at the time. I completed his thought some hours later; the final step in getting rid of God *is getting rid of God*. This goal, however simply stated, is not easily achieved. The relevant questions are the usual big ones—why, when, and how? This book aims to lay the theoretical outline for why it should be done, explain why now is the time, and most importantly offer practical guidelines to make it achievable. In the process, it argues that a key part of getting rid of God is realizing that we've been wrong about "God" all along, maybe all of us.

Of course, to say that we should place "the entire theistic enterprise beneath serious consideration" is to declare victory for "atheism"[2] at the level of ideas. That is, whatever people believe, the ideas that present themselves under the banner called *theism* are intellectually bankrupt.

Theism means belief in the existence of gods or, especially, the God of the major monotheistic religions, and it is time that we put these superstitions away. Declaring complete and total defeat for theism at the level of ideas is the first of my goals, and the first part of this book is presented in its service. Once we understand that nonbelief has won, we will turn our attention to what we should do from here.

Atheism Victorious

Understanding how it is that atheism has won the war of ideas requires us to make sense of a number of different seemingly simple topics. On the one hand, we have to come to grips with the term "atheism." Many will object to the issues surrounding the meanings of "atheism" being raised at all, but we must be willing to admit that there are several divergent meanings of the term, these arising from a fundamental lack of clarity in what it means to be "without God." One can, for instance, lack a belief in God, consider belief in God irrelevant, or actively believe that there is no God, to name just three variations on what atheism means to different audiences. One can also assume, or not, that various additional ideas, like secularism, philosophical naturalism, or humanism (again, to name just three) are intrinsically a part of what atheism means.

The first part of this book seeks to bring the reader to embrace a clarified position on the term atheism, one that speaks back to the meaning originally put forward by the most prominent atheist writers of the beginning of this century, among them Sam Harris, Richard Dawkins, the late Christopher Hitchens, Daniel Dennett, the late Victor Stenger, and Jerry Coyne. It is this view that should best serve the goal of transitioning to a post-God world in which the word atheism becomes obsolete.

To do this, we will have to work with another unfortunate term, *theism*. Of course, atheism is a word that exists only in counterpoint to theism, so understanding what atheism is about requires getting to the bottom of theism as well. Alongside clarifying the term atheism, the next several chapters are presented also in service to this goal. The central contention of this book, however, is that we should no longer treat theism as a valid philosophical position at all, recognizing it as a *theological* one—this distinction[3] being nontrivial as theology is a kind of mythology. The chapters following the clarification of theism and atheism will detail exactly why everyone is wrong about God. They will also illustrate how theism is a gigantic mistake that attempts to make sense of the term "God" in a completely misguided way.

Before getting started, we need to understand myth. Myth doesn't just mean a misinterpretation of a phenomenon. At the core of myth is a blend of misinterpretation, obscuring ignorance, and yet clear apprehension, but what is most relevant about mythology is none of these. True, myths are built out of ignorance, often due in part to the complexity of the subject matter at their cores, and, true, myths are a kind of misinterpretation of that subject matter. On the other hand, and importantly, also true is that myths encapsulate some degree of understanding of what they represent—otherwise they'd be far less compelling than they are. What is most relevant about myths, however, is exactly what makes them most compelling: myths are culturally relevant narratives that simplify complex or unclear phenomena and that speak to people at the level of their psychological needs. Narratives of this kind, though, are exactly what religions provide for people, and it is therefore precisely this observation that illustrates why God, at the center of so many religious beliefs, is a mythological construct.

It is also necessary to pause to observe that the so-called New Atheism[4] succeeded. It won a key and decisive victory in an ongoing culture war about the roles of religion and faith in society. It defeated theism at the level of ideas and obliterated the taboo surrounding an open lack of belief in God, which was its main goal. In doing so, it followed and promoted the simple maxim that serves as an overarching theme for dealing with ideology: *don't believe because it's not true; speak out and work because it harms.* Speaking out and working, however, have to be done in particular ways to succeed against ideological belief structures. It isn't nearly enough to attempt to use reason to point out where ideologies go wrong because ideologies are held for reasons that aren't always reasonable.

At the moment I am writing this, the scuttlebutt around the Internet, and increasingly in significant journalistic outlets, keeps asking whether "New Atheism" needs to die. The answer is a rather heavily qualified "yes." In the West—though not yet elsewhere where it is sorely needed—atheism has done its job; it changed the conversation, or metaphorically, it opened the can. Just as we wouldn't scoop out the contents of a can of beans with the can opener, opting instead for a more appropriate tool, we need not continue with New Atheism. It has done its work. It is now time to go post-theistic instead.

That atheism has won, when construed rightly, still needs some defending. How could atheism have won the war of ideas if so many people still believe in God, including some who are very intelligent and highly educated? Put simply, wars of ideas are protracted affairs that are decisively won often long before everyone gets on board, sometimes decades sooner. Racism, to draw one notable example, is obviously still present in the United States, but few of us would deny that the *idea* of racism was defeated decades ago.

Over the idea of God, like with racism, there are two battles being fought at the same time, and they tend to get conflated. On one front, there is a war of ideas, which I claim has ended with the notion of God as the clear loser. On the other is a cultural fight, and that will endure for some time, maybe indefinitely. We saw the idea of racism collapse long before the culture started really catching on, a process lamentably still continuing today. The cultural fight is mostly distinct from the arguments over the idea, and it must be fought in a different way.

To take a simpler example, consider astrology (not to be confused with *astronomy*, which is an actual science). The idea of astrology is long since dead, but it still has acceptance in some corners of our culture despite our best efforts. Where it matters, alchemy has been left behind, though, and the argument here is that the same is now also true for the idea of God. It is just up to us to realize it and then move forward. If belief continues, and it will, we can work to help people learn to form a better understanding of the world than reliance upon faith and superstition. The second half of this book investigates how we might best approach changing our cultures instead of continuing to flog the dead horse that is theism.

The reasons we should understand that theism has lost the bid for intellectual credibility are numerous. Perhaps the most obvious is that while theism itself is a slippery idea, every religion founded upon it is transparently false from the perspective of every other religion. Indeed, it is often the case from within religions on their own. So patently false are so many tenets of religion that it is widely considered by the more sophisticated adherents to those faiths[5] to be unfair for people to criticize belief by taking the articles of faith literally. Indeed, much of holy scripture is so out of step with scientific knowledge that only the most throughly faithful can take it at face value. Given this pitiful state of affairs, it's difficult to conclude anything but that the world's religions have become parodies of themselves as accounts of the universe, albeit ones taken very seriously by those who believe them.

Another reason theism is beyond hope as an intellectual position is that while "God" is given as an answer to many questions, it answers nothing. In fact, it doesn't even try to answer the relevant questions. Where faith pretends to answer questions, it fails so miserably at going about it with reliable methods that it insists it doesn't need them.

Instead of answering questions, giving "God" as an answer simplistically tries to give a because to a why without attempting to address the more salient hows. To say "God created the universe" tells us exactly nothing at all about how it happened. In so doing, it lets "God" serve as unassailable stuffing for the curiosity. This is the hallmark of mythology.

One more clue, among countless, is that apparently straightforward questions like "does God exist?" and thus "is theism true?" only seem to have meanings, but it is not clear that they do. These phrases, and the terms in them, are best characterized by perpetually seeming to elude any clarity at all. What this tells us is plain and the subject of this book: we're talking about the whole thing the wrong way.

Sure, some philosophers, mostly philosophers of religion, try to nail down what "theism" or "God" means, perhaps using classical theism to do so,[6] and argue for or against it. But theism is plenty flexible to dodge all such efforts by little more than saying we fallible humans simply aren't correctly conceptualizing a perfect deity beyond our comprehension. Predictably, the utterly pointless discussion goes on and on.

For these reasons, at the least, we should see theism as bankrupt, and we should stop pretending it isn't, even for the sake of argument. Religious beliefs and conviction to those beliefs by faith are relevant matters in the world today, along with their consequences, but theism itself is not. We must stop pretending that the meanings usually given to words like "God" and "soul" should be taken on their own terms. Of course, it isn't that we don't have some idea of what people mean by these words. It's that the terms, as they are intended, are misleading and should be rejected as such.

I think it is fair to say that if the very terms of a philosophical position are grossly in error, any war fought on behalf of those terms has been lost.

When Did Theism Lose?

When did theism lose the war of ideas? This is harder to answer, though it is my personal suspicion that theism tacitly raised the white flag approximately at the same time as Richard Dawkins' famous book *The God Delusion* stopped being considered an outrageous controversy.[7] At the moment when it became a part of our cultural furniture to have the words "God" and "delusion" in neat juxtaposition, God, as an idea, no longer deserved to be given serious consideration. Of course, an idea becoming "part of the cultural furniture" does not imply anything like everyone accepting it. It merely means that it is no longer seen as scandalous, having become instead an irrevocable part of contemporary culture.

In writing this, I must point out something that I am *not* arguing. Richard Dawkins' book was not what won the war. The general acquiescence to its existence, along with what it symbolizes, stands as an emblem that the shift must have occurred. Though Dawkins' book unarguably played a role in this occurrence, other factors did as well.[8]

What about God?

We should wonder, if we are to feel comfortable with declaring the idea of theism dead, how we might give an account for widespread belief in God if the idea is bankrupt. That is, how can so many people believe so firmly in God if the idea is bogus? And this is an important question, one so important that a good deal of space in the middle of this book will be devoted to it.

One thought that may differentiate my thinking from that of many other nonbelievers is that I take very seriously the idea that people mean *something* when they say the word "God," and not only that, they also have some idea of what they mean by it. This implies that, contrary to the title of Dawkins' famous book, believers aren't exactly delusional when talking about and believing in "God." The insight shared in this book is just that *what they mean when they say "God" is not best accounted for by theism.* That is, belief in "God" mistakes something real, or real enough, for something mythological.

In this book, I will start the effort to account for that something, for "God," in a way that doesn't leave a shred of space left for theism, and in so doing we will really see that theism is a failed idea. Specifically, it seems that "God" is an abstract mental construction that people employ to help them meet or ignore various psychological and social needs. Chapters one, four, and five are devoted to developing this idea clearly, breaking the spell that keeps us pretending theism has any intellectual traction.

The Goal All Along

At least since the real dawn of the New Atheism, becoming post-theistic (a state in which even atheism is irrelevant) has been the obvious goal. Sam Harris wrote eloquently about this in his "An Atheist Manifesto," published in 2005, originally in *TruthDig*, and the words he spelled out then are the banner for this book. In that sense, the present work could be considered a call to return to the roots of what it means to break free of belief in God, among other bad ideas. In another, it can be seen as an attempt to become ready to hear, ten years later, what Harris intended from the beginning. Harris wrote,

> Atheism is not a philosophy; it is not even a view of the world; it is simply a refusal to deny the obvious. Unfortunately, we live in a world in which the obvious is overlooked as a matter of principle. The obvious must be observed and re-observed and argued for. This is a thankless job. It carries with it an aura of petulance and insensitivity. It is, moreover, a job that the atheist does not want.
>
> It is worth noting that no one ever needs to identify himself as a non-astrologer or a non-alchemist. Consequently, we do not have words for people who deny the validity of these pseudo-disciplines. Likewise, atheism is a term that should not even exist. Atheism is nothing more than the noises reasonable people make when in the presence of religious dogma.[9]

Not only is arguing for the obvious a job that the atheist does not want, it is an argument that she must let go when the time is right, leaving the obvious to argue for itself. In so doing, we will come to regard theism as a pseudo-discipline beneath serious consideration.

I insist that the time to drop this thankless job is either very near or upon us already. It is time to keep making the noises, beset by religious dogma as we still are, without pushing "atheism." It is time to make the situation Harris describes into the new normal, as it would be in any truly post-theistic society.

Before making a case that now is the time for us to make a cognitive shift in all discussions having to do with the idea called "God"—which I will continue to frequently refer to in scare quotes to indicate its status as an *idea*, not an entity—I want to state that I do not think Sam Harris was wrong in 2005. On the contrary, I think he was precisely right, but he was right too soon. The war of ideas hadn't yet ended then. Indeed, Harris was at the time instrumental in launching the campaign that would draw it to a close. As a result, people weren't ready to hear him, and based upon inherent ambiguity in what the term atheism means, as well as the intrinsic lack of clarity on everything theism, atheism became something, or rather many competing somethings. This, then, is a call back to our roots.

Why Now?

The loudest sign that tells me that now is the time, other than the plain fact that theism is dead as a philosophical object, is the growing hostility to atheism. This hostility has been a fixture from the religious from the beginning, particularly of the New Atheism turn (because that's when atheists started putting their feet down about this dangerous, outdated nonsense, saying that theism is not just unjustified and irrational but also pernicious and threatening), but it appears also from "within atheism," a phrase itself that needs unpacking and is an indication of the problem. This hostility toward atheism is likely to be a recognition that, as it has been proceeding, it has done much of what it can do. To continue doing something past the point of efficacy is a waste of time that can become counterproductive.

As the atheism of the last decade has run its course, people who do not identify as religious ache for a change. We see this manifesting—groups organize around "atheism plus" other social and political efforts, we have a rise in so-called faitheists,[10] others push for a philosophically enhanced "strong atheism," there are now "atheist churches,"[11] and creative folks like Alain de Botton are suggesting quirky next steps like "Atheism 2.0."[12]

These have all been popular on some levels and yet fairly significantly resisted by other self-identifying atheists, and something very akin to denominationalism seems to be occurring within people who increasingly see themselves as part of some broader "atheist community." Yet upon exactly what is this community based? Its lack of content, being that it is nominally based upon a lack of belief in God, is scant foundation for a rounded community, hence the subsequent add-ons.

These approaches are well-intended, and they are mistakes. The correct final step in this process is shifting to a fully post-theistic position, one where we consider theism beneath serious consideration. Certainly, the gaps left by the death of religion have to be filled, and so the second half of this book takes up the challenge of discussing what will hopefully be fruitful ways to do it. It is important to avoid the kinds of pitfalls that either will not grow roots or that become troublesome ideologies in their own ways.

At any rate, the evolution of these various approaches are a signpost telling us that it's time to move on, to do something different, and the growing hostility toward New Atheism lights it in vibrant neon. To put it simply, since the previous step—arguing against belief in God—is ending, it is time to take the next one, which is the last one. It is time to end theism entirely and start tackling other, often related, problems.

Why This Step?
Might it be that, while we should be moving onto a new dimension of getting rid of God, going directly toward a post-theistic state is too hasty? Might there be other steps that are more appropriate to take first?

Bear in mind that, whatever steps we take, the one advocated here is certainly the last one as it leaves "God" behind entirely. Still, there are three primary contenders for other options. First, we could carry on with "atheism" as we have been. Second, we could double-down on the philosophical assault on theism on its own terms, heading toward something like "strong atheism" in which people actively disbelieve in a God. Third, we could aim to soften what often gets called "New Atheism" into something more "faitheistic," or otherwise interfaith and ecumenical, in which we recognize the value of religion and give it the kind of berth that its adherents seem to want from us.[13] People are pursuing all three of these efforts, to be sure, but each has considerable difficulties.

Carrying on as we have will continue to be productive for a time, though facing a law of diminishing returns, and as it progresses we will continue to face increasingly entrenched belief systems that are resistant to it. What entrenches them is a kind of developed immunity to our best efforts to overcome them. In other words, this atheistic medicine will probably run its course without finishing the job, leaving us with a faith-based superbug that is even more difficult to contain and overcome.

Additionally, the present course seems to be alienating many younger people, people who finished growing up in a world that already sees *The God Delusion* as part of their cultural furniture. This state makes it hard to see the relevance of a fight, one often divisive and ugly, they seem to wish would just go away. They, with many others, want something different, particularly something less argumentative, and this trend seems marked by a desire for less conflict and by a general apathy to theistic nonsense. Getting "God" right would open this path, whereas continuing to argue as we are is unlikely to.

Worse, continuing as we have been runs the risk of denominationalizing "atheism" even more than has already begun. Various groups, as we will discuss later, rally around various conceptions of "being a good atheist," and then use that to form implicit moral codes that slowly spiral toward becoming moral communities and then ideologies. Arguably, in fact, some of these already have and are increasingly recognized as quasi-religious in nature.[14]

Some of this behavior can be accounted for by realizing that theism has lost the war of ideas, and for lack of something else to do with it, groups cobble other goals onto it. Many of these goals are shared, often coincidentally, with other nonbelievers. These groups miss the point entirely. "The atheism movement" and "atheist communities" are results, missing the fact that the goal isn't to form identifiable communities rallied around "atheism," defined as some kind of sociopolitical ideal, but rather to go post-theistic. We should want to place belief in God beneath serious consideration and thus remove the significant part of its influence upon society while helping people out of "bad ideas, held for bad reasons, leading to bad behavior," as Sam Harris aptly put it.[15]

When it comes to turning our eyes to more ecumenical approaches, there are two main reasons for hesitance. One is that there commonly tends to be, later in life, a boomerang effect whereby people who have left religion in their young adulthood come back to it as they start to settle, raise families, and realize their mortality.[16] It is therefore very important not to set ourselves up to have to fight this fight again in a generation, as seems to have happened with previous ebbs and flows in the predominance of religious beliefs.[17]

One of the last things we want is to let the current pushback against New Atheism set the stage for another intense religious revival cycle, not least because we very well may be on the threshold of getting past this pernicious aspect of our superstitious past. A second is that religion tends to maintain itself during times of challenge by lying quietly under the radar, reaching out "ingratiating" and "unctuous,"[18] as Christopher Hitchens put it, only because it has to. We should not encourage that. In order to get to a post-faith society, we should and must delegitimize faith. Getting over "God," not "living and letting believe," is integral to that effort.

When it comes to pushing toward strong atheism—actively disbelieving in God—we run at least three risks. One is becoming fully ideological about what should be the default, null position regarding belief. It is often said that "atheism is a conclusion," but this is just an artifact of theistic indoctrination and its cultural prevalence. Absent those, nonbelief just is what is. Another is that, while it is not as ridiculous to robustly deny the existence of God as it is to embrace it, actively believing in no God still relies upon, as Peter Boghossian might word it, "pretending to know something we do not know."[19]

It is enough that we have no reasons to believe in a God and to see belief in God as irrelevant and beneath serious consideration, and we should always remain open to having our minds changed. We don't need a philosophical doctrine to reject belief in God, and adopting one invites us into making the mistake of taking theism seriously on its own terms. This, of course, is a third risk: perpetuating theism by letting people maintain a belief that its terms deserve serious consideration.

Of course, arguments for belief or disbelief, usually found in the philosophy of religion, are enticing, forming interesting puzzles with an apparently strong historical and academic pedigree. For a time, too, these arguments were important—before the war of ideas was won. No longer. Alluring though these philosophical puzzles may be, getting involved with them inadvertently legitimizes much of the theistic enterprise by pretending they are worth taking seriously.[20] Much of the philosophical puzzle presented, and thus any interest theological arguments might deserve, arises merely because the arguments are slick and are commonly peddled by apologists, not because they have philosophical merit. This situation justifies little more than a niche archive of rebuttals to stock theistic arguments, not a (somewhat) respected academic subdiscipline.[21] This book will expose exactly why this controversial assertion stands by revealing exactly how everybody is wrong about God.

As we will see, the next rational step is to stop treating the idea called "theism" seriously at all. That war of ideas is over. The goal is not to create an *atheist* society so much as to create one that has left belief in "God" behind in its superstitious past. By dwelling on atheism, we dwell on the debate, and by dwelling on the debate, we perpetuate its counterpoint, theism, as something debate-worthy instead of something that already lost. The ideas of theism are fallacious, and the religions that base themselves around them, measured as claims to truth about the world, are as absurd—in fact, they're mythology. Since they are absurd in their own terms, they should be treated as such, and deference to their claims should be considered a mistake, a virtue that never was. It's time to move on, and the path we should follow is to stop pretending that theism deserves serious rational consideration.

The Move Is Strategic

It could be misunderstood that placing theism beneath serious consideration is just an attempt to shut down discussion, but it is, in fact, a strategic maneuver designed to facilitate productive conversations that move us forward. The goal isn't to shut down any discussion, particularly not in an authoritarian way. Instead, we should shift our mentality and admit that the terms of theism aren't serious and are therefore not owed serious consideration.

In order to discuss theism on its own terms we must first make the mistake of pretending that it has something to discuss, but why keep up this pretense? The goal of arguing for theism, of course, is to provide a sense of legitimacy to certain cherished beliefs, but if those beliefs were based upon actual legitimacy, such as the kind provided by evidence, the kinds of discussions it has wouldn't even be necessary.[22] When we understand what these beliefs represent, we can do away with twisting words into pretzels in the service of defending mythology. The discussions about religious beliefs that will follow naturally will be more helpful and worth our time. In the process, we spare ourselves the tedium of arguing again and again for the obvious, to borrow again from Sam Harris.

Furthermore, treating theism beneath serious consideration is strategic for the same reason that indifference is more fatal to love than is hate. Theism is mythology, and as such, taken as a proposed explanation for the world, it isn't even wrong. By ceasing to pretend that theism has intellectual force behind it, we expose it for the quaint, old-fashioned, superstitious set of psychosocial mechanisms that it represents.

Doesn't This Let the Disease Fester?
It is reasonable to be concerned that giving up atheism will let theism win by default, but giving up atheism is the natural consequence of theism falling out of fashion. Fighting against something that has already lost, which is often how atheism is construed, isn't something to hold onto.

One might worry that theism will "win" simply by its refusal to go away—rather like we must continually address certain kinds of medical infections to prevent them from festering. If we were just dropping the matter entirely and walking away from culturally relevant discussions, there is little doubt that this would be the case. Giving up isn't the goal. Instead, we are moving away from treating theism as if it has any theoretical legs to stand on in serious discussions, such as in academics and politics.

We shouldn't continue to conflate the debate over the idea of theism, which is over, with the needed cultural shift away from it, which is not. The thing is, it seems unlikely that continued arguments will cause a cultural shift with the potency that *social pressure* will effect. Of course, it would be an error to use social pressure to sway our thinking before the ideas are sorted out, but they have been. Theism is the clear loser. If we start to acknowledge and act upon this fact by going properly post-God, we can expect the resulting social pressure will push our cultures in the right direction.

Again, the issue of racism makes a poignant example. When racism was decisively beaten as an idea, in the United States probably by the Civil Rights Movement in the 1960s, social pressure took over, aided greatly by satirists who deftly helped people realize that the idea is, indeed, laughably bad and inappropriate. Something similar is already starting where it comes to theism with more and more satire arising around lampooning the ridiculousness of religious beliefs. This activity should be encouraged. It is not inherently insulting,[23] and it will be effective.

As for how we might promote the idea that there is no God and no supernatural if we leave atheism behind, just looking at it this way asks the wrong question. It is more relevant to ask how we might get people to stop promoting these ideas and how to help people walk away from them. The idea that there is no God and no supernatural takes care of itself once we reject faith-based thinking and replace it with informed skepticism.

Achieving the Goal

If our ambition is a post-theistic society that has left faith behind, we must drop theism from the list of possible explanations for anything. We should aim to get to where belief in God and faith-based thinking are considered so obsolete that they bear no relevance on the functioning of our societies and our academies. In service to this goal, we need to engage in a number of activities—helping people uproot their reliance on faith, securing secular societies, creating and consuming educational materials in the right subjects, modifying our thinking and our behavior to match, and finding ways to fill the needs currently filled by religion. The second half of this book offers discussion and practical suggestions on every one of these points.

It is possible, of course, that we have a bit more work to do before we can move on. Nonbelief may need to become more comfortable as cultural furniture than it is now. (Here, of course, I'm talking mostly about the United States, though much of Europe faces elements of this challenge in addition to the problem of an influx of Islamism.[24]) We have organizations that are successfully working in those directions, though, such as the Freedom From Religion Foundation,[25] the Clergy Project,[26] American Atheists,[27] the Out Campaign,[28] Openly Secular,[29] and others. These others include many humanist organizations, like the International Humanist and Ethical

Union[30] and the American Humanist Association,[31] as well as the related push for informed skepticism, such as is presented by the James Randi Educational Foundation[32] and its annual The Amazing Meeting!.[33] Leaving theism, and thus atheism, behind does not obviate the need for these efforts, though it may modify their approaches. Also, of course, these organizations along with many others are currently doing excellent work that enables us to take the steps recommended here, starting essentially immediately.

Many people still adhere to faith-based thinking, including belief in "God." This needs to be remedied, and by drawing upon the contributions of the many talented individuals who have worked for this goal, we can do it. The seventh chapter gives some specific suggestions for how it might start being done. Further, secularism must be demanded and maintained. The eighth chapter addresses that topic. We also need to change what we argue about—and how we do it—when it comes to the role of religion in society, particularly dropping any respect for the idea of theism. This will change the fights that we should be fighting and the way in which we undertake them, and in the ninth chapter, this topic will be covered in detail. The tenth chapter is dedicated to offering suggestions on how we might fill the psychological and social gaps that people use "God" to ignore or fill. Cultivating ways in which we can help people learn how to fill those gaps is likely to be very helpful, if not necessary, to creating and maintaining a stable post-faith society. The eleventh chapter makes a call for how we might service these goals and handle some issues that are likely to arise as we shift to a post-faith, post-theistic society.

Notes

1. Peter Boghossian, [@peterboghossian], The next rational move: Considering the entire theistic enterprise beneath serious consideration. @GodDoesnt, [Tweet], 18 June 2014.

2. The reader should note my disdain for the use of the term *atheism* in this context. The reasoning is that atheism is technically approximately a philosophical position, the negation of the pseudo-philosophical position called *theism*, and yet it has often come to stand for so much more than that. When I say that atheism has won at the level of ideas, all I mean is that theism is exposed as bankrupt at that level, not anything more.

3. A brief summary of the distinction is that theology is pseudo-philosophical in that it treats the object of its efforts, which is a fiction, as if it is not a fiction. It is better seen for what it is, a kind of sophistry, than as a legitimate philosophical pursuit.

4. "New Atheism" is a term here grudgingly used for the style of presentation of ideas that stand in opposition to theism, religious belief, and faith, mostly following the attacks of September 11, 2001. It is often identifiable with an enough-is-enough attitude, a clear indication of the reliable harms that evolve from ideological thinking, concern with the fact that religions are actually false, and a marked pro-science attitude where it comes to making sense of the world.

5. Biologist Jerry Coyne has made a fairly well-known habit of referring to complex theological obscurantism by the pejorative "Sophisticated Theologians™," satirizing claims by theologians that those criticizing theology are insufficiently sophisticated in their theology to do a decent job of it.

6. Classical theism usually assumes that God is omnipotent, omniscient, and morally perfect (perfectly good), and though this serves as a basis for classical theism, the matter is unsurprisingly not settled. Some theologians insist that transcendence is required as well, including total transcendence, and others assert that God must be ultimately simple. Timelessness, or eternalness, and immutability are other assumptions sometimes included in the formulations that get called "classical theism." Anyone wishing to debunk classical theism has quite a job on their hands, then, given that, besides many of these being unfalsifiable, all an adherent has to do is assert that one or both parties involved in the discussion simply must have the conception of God somehow mistaken. Further strengthening my point, not all religious believers accept this view, including prominent theologians, though it is probably the predominant philosophical conception of theism, rejecting or taking in carefully parsed degrees various ones of these seven fantastic properties. Because theism is utterly bogus, none of this is surprising in the least. It is exactly what we should expect from getting the whole idea of God wrong and then treating it with central importance and pseudo-philosophical gerrymandering for centuries.

7. Richard Dawkins, *The God Delusion* (Boston: Houghton Mifflin, 2006).

8. Of note, shortly after Dawkins' book became another part of contemporary culture, philosopher Keith Parsons, widely understood to be a philosopher of religion, abandoned and disparaged the case for theism on the grounds that it has absolutely no merit. See Julia Galef, "A Philosopher of Religion Calls It Quits,"

Religion Dispatches, 5 January 2011, where Parsons is quoted as writing, "I have to confess that I now regard 'the case for theism' as a fraud and I can no longer take it seriously enough to present it to a class as a respectable philosophical position—no more than I could present intelligent design as a legitimate biological theory." The opening decade of this millennium also happens to be when the Center for Inquiry, founded by philosopher and author Paul Kurtz, started to fully mature, along with Kurtz's publishing imprint, Prometheus Books. Since 1969, Prometheus has given voice to many nontheistic points of view, and in the early 2000s it enjoyed a boom coincident with the waning of the long-standing disinterest by major trade publishers in nontheistic and antitheistic books. Now, many of the titles published by Prometheus make a backbone of valuable published literature standing in opposition to belief in God.

9. Sam Harris, "An Atheist Manifesto," *TruthDig*, *Web*, 7 December 2005, accessed at http://www.truthdig.com/dig/item/200512_an_atheist_manifesto on 12 May 2015.

10. See Chris Stedman, *Faitheist: How an Atheist Found Common Ground with the Religious* (Boston: Beacon Press, 2013).

11. There is a subtle difference between an "atheist church" and a secular "Sunday assembly" that prevents me from mentioning the latter here. These will be discussed in a later chapter.

12. See Alain de Botton, "Atheism 2.0," *TED Talk*, July 2011, accessed at http://www.ted.com/talks/alain_de_botton_atheism_2_0?language=en on 11 May 2015.

13. I consider well-meaning approaches like Alain de Botton's "Atheism 2.0" to fall beneath serious consideration on this matter, though it would be considered broadly under being more ecumenical and faitheistic since it makes atheism rather explicitly into a quasi-religion.

14. Though they deserve very little commentary, the group and social movement styling itself as Atheism+ is a noteworthy example.

15. Sam Harris, "A Response to Controversy," Blog, *Web*, 4 April 2013, accessed at http://www.samharris.org/site/full_text/response-to-controversy2 on 11 May 2015.

16. Ralph W. Hood, Jr., Peter C. Hill, and Bernard Spilka, *The Psychology of Religion: An Empirical Approach*, 4th Ed. (New York: Guilford Press, 2009), pp. 238–241.

17. Consider the religious revivalism cycles in the United States in the nineteenth and twentieth centuries.

18. Christopher Hitchens, god *Is Not Great*, (New York: Twelve, 2007), p. 67.

19. Peter Boghossian, *A Manual for Creating Atheists* (Durham, NC: Pitchstone Publishing, 2013), p. 23.

20. Isn't this a position in the philosophy of religion, though? Maybe, or maybe it's meta-philosophy, but who cares about such a trivial technicality? Even if it is, it would do nothing to justify delving into theism like it might mean something of any real worth.

21. The philosophy of religion, incidentally, is a sub-discipline within philosophy that arose after the Second World War apparently mostly in service to giving a veneer of academic respectability to Christian theologians. (See Taylor Carr, "Armchair Atheism, Ep. 2 —Why the Philosophy of Religion? With Graham Oppy," YouTube [Video], 23 July 2014, accessed at https://www.youtube.com/watch?v=Yv3DVvxgo5E on 19 June 2015.) As philosopher Keith Parsons put it, "One of the things the really active conservative Christians covet enormously, more than anything else, is intellectual respectability. And they think they have found it in some of the arguments from these philosophers of religion." (See Dan Fincke, "Atheist Philospher of Religion Keith Parsons Abandons Theism Debate and Calls Theist Positions Frauds," *Camels With Hammers* Blog, *Patheos Network*, 5 January 2011, accessed at http://www.patheos.com/blogs/camelswithhammers/2011/01/atheist-philosopher-of-religion-keith-parsons-abandons-theism-debate-and-calls-theist-positions-frauds/ on 11 May 2015).

22. If theism had real evidence to support it, it would never make arguments for why it doesn't need evidence, relying instead on other kinds of nonepistemic warrant, for example, as is claimed by Reformed Epistemology.

23. The difference between satire and direct ridicule is of such huge significance that it's a marvel that it gets so easily confused. A satirist mocking a set of beliefs is not mocking an *individual*. The individuals who hold those beliefs may feel insulted, embarrassed, sheepish, or humiliated for holding those beliefs, but that is the very point of satire and the reason it is effective (besides taking the over-serious edge off topics that are often taken too seriously). Of course, this is a bit more complicated than stated because satirists can mock an individual, but we need not get lost in this complication and pretend that satirical jousts are the same thing as malicious personal insults. Further, we'd do better to stop letting people with over-serious beliefs bully us into pretending that we should maintain such confusion,

especially under the guise of some kind of perverted moral "enlightenment."

24. Islamism on its own, even without its influx into otherwise mostly secular Western European society, is a significant problem, and both it and its creep into Europe lie mostly beyond the scope of this book. The topics presented here, of course, do actually apply on a theoretical level, and some of the practical suggestions reach to those problems, but the issue of Islamism is so deeply entrenched that other approaches are genuinely likely to be needed before they are at a point where leaving theism behind is the right *next* step, even if it is the right *last* step and the eventual goal. Generally speaking, the sign that dropping theism is the appropriate next step is likely to be that its negation becomes part of the cultural furniture. In cultures where nonbelievers are forced to convert on pain and threats of death, and in which apostates are murdered for leaving their faiths, other work is necessary first. The cultures in which it is possible to change should, then, partly as a hopeful beacon and model for cultures that cannot.

25. See ffrf.org.

26. See clergyproject.org.

27. See atheists.org.

28. See outcampaign.org.

29. See openlysecular.org.

30. See iheu.org.

31. See americanhumanist.org.

32. See web.randi.org.

33. See www.amazingmeeting.com.

CHAPTER 1

EXPOSING THEISM

Theism means belief in the existence of God or gods, but the term is loaded a bit more heavily than that bare definition. Usually, theism entails believing in a god that is the creator of the universe, the grounding for all sorts of important ideas like morals, purpose, knowledge, truth, and justice, and, most importantly, that can intervene in the universe while sustaining a personal relationship with his creations—this mainly meaning human beings.[1] Theism is a term that still enjoys the pretense of being technical and interesting in the lexicon of philosophers. The central contention of this book is that theism, being a kind of mythology, isn't technical or interesting; it's the wrong model for making sense of the myriad ideas caught up in the word "God," which is the only reason it's discussed at all.

Though theism is a kind of mythology, the word "God" definitely means something, and that something is important. Nearly the entirety of humanity's immense squabbling about anything to do with beliefs in God testify to this fact. What essentially everyone involved in this argument gets wrong is treating the term "God" in accordance with the assumptions of theism. Because we perennially get this wrong, we continuously talk past each other in the wrong ways about the wrong things, and because we talk past each other under the fog of such confusion, the conversation about "God" keeps going.

This is the central irony of taking theism seriously. Lacking anything like proper evidence for belief in God, only the perpetuation of this hopelessly misguided conversation constitutes intellectual support for theism. Among the serious—not to be confused with the sincere—the conversation about whether God exists perseveres by little more than being taken in by the terms of theism. It is time to reject these terms, and it is time to end this conversation.

To be sure, the conversation about "God" need not be put in terms of theism at all, although this statement is likely to seem profoundly controversial. In fact, it is the other way around. It is rather astounding that we seem unable to see where to place the terminology of this conversation if not in theism. There is no mystery whatsoever to where we should look to make sense of the word "God." The term is personal, and the term is cultural. Psychology—which is to say the working of the human mind— is the obvious locus for the actual, nonmythological meaning of the term "God."

To a degree that is hardly trivial, people are consequences of the cultures in which they grow up and live. The prevailing culture around a mind sets many of the social, and thus psychological, conditions in which it comes to know the world, including others and itself. Religions form a major component of cultural identification, and given the role that religion plays in forming, defining, and reinforcing moral communities,[2] it's hardly surprising that religions therefore play a major role in helping people define themselves and their relationships with one another. The term "God" takes on varied meanings according to different religions (and subdivisions within religions, and so on from there), and these nearly tautological[3] differences are the source of much unnecessary human strife.

The cultural dependence of religious beliefs[4] show us that theism is, and always has been, an all-but-hopeless way to get at anything like universal, timeless, and absolute truths, and any hope that exists is dashed to pieces in any religion that claims to be "revealed." Unsurprisingly, "God" seems worthless for finding out much of anything that the culture believing in it doesn't already assume about the world. To put it plainly, "God" doesn't tell people anything they don't already know because "God" is a kind of mythological stand-in for psychosocial phenomena peculiar to the times, people, and cultures that talk about it. "God" is an abstract emblem for the cultures themselves, and thus for the beliefs of the people who believe.

We have to bear in mind that even if our cultures do not necessarily determine everything about us, they do form the basis for the way we conceive of the world and our places in it. Many of these elements are difficult to see and powerfully self-reinforcing. To that point, Daniel Quinn, the author of a novel, *Ishmael*, that captured my attention in my youth, referred to this invisible, self-reinforcing nature of our parent culture as "the whispering of Mother Culture."[5] Voltaire referred to the same idea when he said, "Every man is the creature of the age in which he lives; very few are able to raise themselves above the ideas of the time."[6]

Indeed, as moral psychologist Jonathan Haidt puts it, "A dictum of cultural psychology is that 'culture and psyche make each other up.'"[7] Research done by social worker Brene Brown[8] reinforces this fact—we see ourselves in terms of how we perceive others will perceive us, which is a cultural phenomenon with deep roots in morality and social relationships. It is very difficult to escape one's culture and see the world properly in another way, and it is far harder when there are perceived rewards for thinking the "right" way and punishments for thinking otherwise. The sacred and the taboo—these being expressly morally charged terms—lock people into beliefs they already hold.

Let's be fair, though. Of course, it is possible that God does exist and, given the cultural dependence of beliefs about it, people could all just be partially wrong about something that is ultimately true in some sense. For years I thought exactly this way myself, that the variety of conflicting religions is a consequence of guessing at something too big to get right. Idealist though I was, I wasn't too far off base except in the fact that theism is not true. The seemingly timeless and absolute grains of truth hiding within religious beliefs speak only to the fact that all of our cultures and religions have something in common: human beings.[9] It is much more concise simply to accept that mythological attempts, including theism, to make sense of the various psychosocial aspects of our human lives are just myths.

A significant problem is that theology, as a kind of "investigation" into theism, is utterly unreliable for figuring out—well—anything, really. I strongly suspect it is true that for any (philosophical) proposition given in the language of theism, there can exist a theology that defends its validity. Worse, there appears to be no real way to determine which theology is doing a better job than any other since each is a model based, at some point, upon unfalsifiable and unexaminable elements.

To get some scope of how off-the-track theism and theology are, let's borrow from Sam Harris's famous analogy that religion, in its capacity to offer comforting beliefs, is comparable to a belief that there is a diamond the size of a refrigerator buried in one's backyard.[10] Taking this metaphor at face value, if religion is believing that there's a diamond the size of a refrigerator buried in one's yard, theology is arguing over the brand of the refrigerator. This problem is exactly what we should expect from thinking about "God" in completely the wrong way.

If "God" is ultimately some kind of idea that operates on a psychosocial level, it is in those terms, not nonsense about the divine, that we should be talking about it. When we start talking about "God" as a kind of idea—as a mental construction, a notion, an imaginary thing employed to a specific purpose, that being a way that we try to make sense of the world we live in—then we can start to address the "mysteries of faith" in ways that completely demystify it. "God" is not an element of this world or any other, and it is not a living, breathing entity that has something to do with creation and the fate of the universe or the judgment, reward, punishments, and concerns of people. "God" is an abstraction utilized to pretend something exists that does those things because that pretense allows people to meet or ignore certain important psychosocial needs.

Ideologies, thus religions, thus theism, thus "God" have to be understood as ways in which we see and interpret the world, ourselves included. I had considered calling "God" a "worldview axiom," a basic assumption about how the world works on all levels, and thus each take on theism could be understood as a philosophical position based upon the acceptance of the relevant "God" axiom.[11] But God is a *mythological* object and thus emphatically *not* best treated philosophically because philosophy takes the idea too seriously in the wrong way. Philosophical terms should be jettisoned, then, and we should address "God" in terms of what it actually seems to do for people. We should also recognize theism as a *pseudo-philosophical* position instead of a properly philosophical one.[12]

It is vastly more accurate to view "God" as what we might call an *attributional framework*, a set of connected ideas and assumptions employed to attempt to make sense of the world. Thus we see God as a mythological extension of something that is, in a way, real. People use their "God" attributional frameworks to meet or ignore certain psychosocial needs. These needs are common, it seems, to all human beings as part of our evolutionary heritage, and "God" is one way we've tried to help ourselves deal with them.[13]

Forensic psychiatrist J. Anderson Thomson, Jr., in his short gem of a book, *Why We Believe in God(s)*, reinforces this line of thought. He writes,

> religion, while not an adaptation in itself, derives from the same mind-brain social adaptations that we use to navigate the sea of people who surround us. These adaptations formed to solve specific social and interpersonal problems as humanity evolved. Almost incidentally, but no less powerfully, they come together to construct the foundation of every religious idea, belief, and ritual. Religious beliefs are basic human social survival concepts with slight alterations.[14]

He goes on to note that for all their differences, "still, [gods] are all remarkably similar."[15] A potential explanation for this observation waits a few pages later, where Thomson notes,

> Religion uses and piggybacks onto everyday social-thought processes, adaptive psychological mechanisms that evolved to help us negotiate our relationships with other people, to detect agency and intent, and to generate a sense of safety. These mechanisms were forged in the not-so-distant world of our African homeland. They are why we survived.[16]

It is hardly a leap at all to assume that gods, which are "all remarkably similar," are objects invented by people specifically to serve some function related to the kinds of needs that human beings have always faced.

Of particular importance are the challenges we have faced in our social universes. This is a major insight, then, into understanding the idea of "God." The abstraction is one we employ to manage psycho*social* needs. Again, we can turn to Thomson for a compelling explanation.

> Because we need to work with other people to survive, our brains evolved the ability to make assumptions about others, to create conjecture to help us coexist in social settings. We are born accepting that others are like

us, intentional agents with minds like ours, even though we are unable to literally see their minds.

One aspect of this is called the *mind-body split* or *dualism*, the view that the mind and body function separately, without interchange. We cannot conceive of souls unless we see mind as separate from body. And we do, because our brains are wired that way.[17]

He goes on to add, "Religious ideas are influential and endure because they fit neatly with this structure, this mind-body split."[18] Thus, "understanding . . . the mind-body split is just the beginning of understanding the ways in which the mind can be tricked into [theistic] belief."[19]

Philosophy since time immemorial has occupied itself with the mind-body split and dualism, and few make more use of this philosophical construct as a metaphysical underpinning than theologians. Of course, the goal of this book isn't about claiming to know for sure what makes up the ultimate nature of reality. Fewer quests are more full of folly than that academic sinkhole. This book is about creating plausible alternatives to theism as an account for the meaning caught up in the word "God." That "God" is an idea that human beings use to manage their psychosocial needs is one such option.

Some may still wonder how we can *know* that "God" is just an idea instead of a part of reality, and technically we cannot know this to be the case. We can, however, make a very convincing case that requires very few assumptions that people use the word "God" to mean something that can be captured more or less in its entirety by a variety of attempts to meet psychosocial needs, plus a bit of mythology in how it is expressed.[20]

An objection that believers might offer here is that their feelings of "God" are legitimate indications of a relationship with some higher power. Thomson explains this too:

We humans have the remarkable ability to create and implement a complex interaction with an unseen other—boss, spouse, friend—in our minds, regardless of time or place, in the past or future. . . . This is called *decoupled cognition*, and it is key to religious belief. . . . Interacting in our minds with unseen others is natural. Many people mentally converse with recently departed loved ones. A natural extension of this—a leap of faith, if you will—can become ancestor worship and belief in gods. Our mind's ability to create a complex relationship with unseen others simply expands.[21]

Thomson goes on to note other psychological phenomena throughout his book that contribute to the feeling that "God" is more real than idea.[22] Since God seems not to exist and "God" so clearly serves a psychosocial role for believers, they are left with little to protect theism from the charge that it is, indeed, a form of mythology metaphorically representing abstract ideas applied to our psychosocial needs.

Is this circumstance reciprocal, though? That is, is it fair to say that atheism represents something of the same thing—a reflection of underlying psychosocial needs—and thus that the same criticisms I extend to theism apply also to atheism? The answer is no. Atheism is not a mythology or even a construct of any kind, even if certain nonbelievers seem to mistake it for such by cobbling on other concepts like skepticism, humanism, secularism, science, and, too often, a certain intellectual arrogance that's unbecoming in pretty much everyone. Beliefs help people meet their needs; atheism is the lack of a certain kind of belief. Theism is a mythological structure; atheism provides nothing that could be considered mythological in any way. Indeed, people who reject theism tend to understand mythology exactly as it is, a kind of metaphorical story used to attempt to make sense, often with moral overtones, of phenomena in the world. The closest thing to a defining belief that atheism possesses is the profoundly parsimonious idea that we shouldn't believe in what we don't have truly good reasons[23] to believe in.

Of course, religious philosophers seek reasons to warrant belief in God—that is, to make their belief seem rational. Seeing that "God" acts primarily as an attributional framework, belief in the ideas the word "God" represents *is* rational. For believers, then, it seems natural to believe in God, and the reasons supporting that belief seem obvious. This confusion lies at the heart of perpetuating belief.

What we cannot ignore, then, is that the word "God" does mean something, and that something has nothing to do with theism. Something that nonbelievers are sorely missing when it comes to handling the fact of religious belief in our world is a nontheistic account of the term "God."

It is one thing to say that "God" is a mythological entity, but it is entirely another to do so while explaining what it mythologizes. Once that is done, theism falls apart, an embarrassing, infantile mistake that we cannot seem to grow out of any other way.

We have spent thousands of years trapped in religious thinking. The reasons that people get stuck into religious thinking are myriad, but ultimately they all boil down to one reason that manifests in a number of very complicated ways:

Every time someone says that he believes in God, he's saying that he has psychological or social needs that he doesn't know how to meet.

One of the major goals of this book is to lay out in one place a first effort at exposing what some of these needs are, thereby exposing the myth plainly. Elaboration will wait until chapter five, however. For now, it will suffice to mention that many of these needs are rooted in culture because these are especially difficult to see for what they are.

Theism, then, is exposed. It makes no sense to attempt to study via "theology" something that is ultimately psychological and sociological in nature. Furthermore, to the dismay of many thinking nonbelievers, it isn't even really appropriate to study it by means of philosophy, unless we are casting the philosophical net widely enough to cover all of careful thought, particularly including the social and psychological sciences.

In light of the fact that we cannot take theism seriously on its own terms, then, we should have a harder time taking "atheism" seriously as well, given that it has effectively adopted the terms of theism in order to defeat it. Ironically, the result of doing so is *perpetuating* theism, since the ongoing nature of the debate about whether there is a God is all theism has to its credit. Before delving more deeply into the meaning of "God," we will turn our attention to "atheism" and examine it under the light of theism's obituary.

Notes

1. Definition adapted from the one given for *theism* by Google.

2. Moral communities are a very important concept for understanding religion, and thus "God," because *religions are moral communities*, that is, communities organized around like-mindedness in moral intuitions. Renowned sociologist Émile Durkheim, in fact, defined religions as moral communities. In 1915 he wrote, "A religion is a unified system of beliefs and practices relative to sacred things, that is to say, things set apart and forbidden—beliefs and practices which unite into one single moral community called a Church, all those who adhere to them." Religions are a subset of a particular kind of moral community, then, in that they are ideologically motivated. By "ideological motivation," all that is meant is that certain aspects of the moral beliefs of such a moral community are elevated in importance (or sacredness) beyond being able to be questioned—those moral attitudes become "supertrue." Ideologically motivated moral communities are the central target of any discussion that seeks to understand or undermine faith-based thinking and moral authoritarianism, religions being the most glaring example of such sociological objects.

3. Each use of the term "God" is so intrinsically dependent upon the presumptions (most of these being moral) of the culture promoting it that to argue over this detail or that about what "God" really means is really to argue "my culture is different from your culture," usually in terms of the moral frameworks defining the moral communities that form the backbones of the things we call cultures anyway. The degree of this dependence is effectively complete, in fact, since religions are always moral communities. In light of that equivalence, understanding that "God" is an intrinsic core of what such moral communities profess to stand for reveals the tautology in cultural disagreements about the "nature of God." (Citation reference available in note 3, p. 436, of Jonathan Haidt's *The Righteous Mind*, see note 7 in this chapter for full reference.)

4. John W. Loftus, *The Outsider Test for Faith: How to Know Which Religion Is True* (Amherst, NY: Prometheus, 2013), chapters 2 and 3.

5. Daniel Quinn, *Ishmael: An Adventure in Mind and Spirit* (New York: Bantam, 1995).

6. Voltaire is widely credited with having said this.

7. Jonathan Haidt, *The Righteous Mind: Why Good People Are Divided By Politics and Religion* (New York: Vintage Books, 2012), p. 115, note 9 indicates the internal quote is from cultural psychologist Richard Shweder.

8. Brené Brown, "The Power of Vulnerability," *TED Talk*, *Web*, June 2010, https://www.ted.com/talks/brene_brown_on_vulnerability?language=en.

9. To the undoubted woe of many philosophers, saying that human beings are something held in common by all cultures and religions means that all cultures and religions operate in service to a particular constrained system: human psychology. Many philosophers, though perhaps not very many good ones, seem to fail to appreciate that the human mind is not a *carte blanche* but is actually a thing apparently wholly dependent upon the human brain, which was itself shaped by biological evolution. This error, incidentally, is likely to be the central failure of most moral philosophy as well.

10. Sam Harris, *The End of Faith: Religion, Terror, and the Future of Reason*, (Norton: New York, 2004), p. 62.

11. My first book, *God Doesn't; We Do: Only Humans Can Solve Human Challenges* (CreateSpace, 2012) was the first place that I attempted to make a case that whatever "God" means, it's probably axiomatic, or at least a kind of abstract presumption. I developed this theme in a particular vein in my second book, *Dot, Dot, Dot: Infinity Plus God Equals Folly* (Onus Books, 2013), where I argue that the connection between the concept of the infinite and the concept of "God" is a strong hint that "God" is indeed some kind of idea, not an entity.

12. Richard Carrier, "Is Philosophy Stupid?" published 2013 at http://www.richardcarrier.info/philosophy.html.

13. We cannot lose sight of the fact that religions are based upon ideas that are false and reliably damaging. Many of the ideas have their roots in culture, and culture is important. Still, it has been tried and tested that cultures can change for the *better* by becoming secular and even post-theistic. The least religious cultures on Earth at present—the Nordic countries, some of Western Europe, and Japan—score highest on many widely recognized metrics of societal health (such as the Social Progress Index), and the most religious ones—Afghanistan, Pakistan, and others—score near the bottom. However important cultural reasons for belief may be, they are not robust justifications for believing the false and the harmful when we know how to do better.

14. J. Anderson Thomson, Jr., MD, with Clare Aukofer, *Why We Believe in God(s): A Concise Guide to the Science of Faith* (Charlottesville, VA: Pitchstone Publishing, 2011), p. 31.

15. *Ibid.*, p. 32.

16. *Ibid.*, p. 38.

17. Thomson, *Why We Believe in God(s)*, p. 50

18. *Ibid.*, p. 51.

19. *Ibid.*, p. 53.

20. The application of mythology to notions of "God" could be a holdover from a more superstitious past or could be a way to make the ideas caught up in theistic beliefs seem more real. Either or both of these suggestions, among possible others, could be operating at the same time.

21. Thomson, *Why We Believe in God(s)*, pp. 54–56.

22. Other phenomena listed by Thomson include attachment theory, theory-of-mind mechanism, intensionality (an "awareness of what other people think, and what other people might think about what we might think," Thomson, p. 58), transference, hyperactive agency detection (cf. Michael Shermer, *Why People Believe Weird Things: Pseudoscience, Superstition, and Other Confusions of Our Time* [New York: Holt 1997]), inferential reasoning, minimally counterinuitive worlds (an "optimal compromise between the interesting and the expected," Thomson, p. 66), overread determination, outright self-deception, deference to authority, and so on and so forth. All of these contribute to religious belief and thus strongly suggest that "God" is best understood in psychosocial terms, not philosophical ones, and certainly not theological ones.

23. It seems a waste of time, but some people might argue that there are "good" reasons to believe in God even if there's no God in existence—comfort, community, purpose, and so on. Those may be satisfying reasons to believe, and they may even be somewhat beneficial, but they are not good *epistemologically*, which is the relevant sense of "good" where the statement "good reasons to believe" is concerned. To have a good reason to believe something, we have to have robust reasons to think that it is true, not merely comforting or convenient.

CHAPTER 2

THE END OF ATHEISM

If theism is invalid, and thus has already lost the fight of ideas, then why should atheists keep fighting the battles that have already been won? They shouldn't. In fact, it perpetuates theism for atheism to keep being a thing, so it's time for atheism to end.

Understanding the term "God," and thus what theism represents to people, should make it obvious why anyone should be very cautious to label herself an atheist. One of the most significant concepts attached to the word "God" is a representation of a believer's core values. Many of these values are intimately concerned with his sense of person, self-esteem, context in society, and cultural and moral values. Understanding this point is crucial: *for believers "God" means something critical to their core values.* So important is that which "God" means to them that it often isn't even allowed to be questioned, in times and places on threats of torture and death for daring to.[1]

Theism, for those who accept it, is simply an acceptance of certain core values, and so atheism sets itself, by definition, as a rejection of those values. That is, "I am an atheist" to a believer literally means "I reject your core values" (on some level determined by how much secularism the believer embraces). The term atheist, then, besides other intrinsic problems, is poison both to the goals of being accepted as a normal part of wider society and of moving society to a post-theistic status.[2]

Of course, we can look to much of Western Europe and see an apparent challenge to what I have just said. Many Western Europeans, majorities even in some countries, do not believe in God and yet are accepted. I want to contend that the reason is that Western Europe did not go "atheistic" so much as it went *post-theistic*, where religious status became mostly irrelevant.

The difference is subtle but critical, and sorting through it requires understanding the variety of meanings caught up in the term "atheist." Especially relevant is whether or not "atheism" is being used as a term of rejection and defiance or more as a bland and unfortunate term of description. Being post-theistic means that the questions and arguments about "God" are only relevant when someone makes them relevant; being atheistic seems to mean that they matter all the time.

It certainly seems that "lacking belief in God or gods" should cover the entirety of what "atheism" means, but there are serious problems with that meaning. The most glaring, and thus most commented upon, is that it is very odd to describe oneself in terms of what one doesn't believe. (I lay the blame for this confusion directly at the feet of philosophers who, in their well-meaning attempts to parse out the meanings of everything, come up with an -ism for both everything and its negation, which gives substance to some negations that need none.) Another is the eagerness with which many who lack belief, especially if they have escaped from it, wish to identify with the term in a kind of active rejection of beliefs.

"Atheist" is a label, then, that many people readily take upon themselves despite the fact that it seems not properly applicable. Because atheism is a term of negation, once someone takes the term upon herself, often in pride, she must also seek what that label means for herself. "Becoming an atheist," then, is a process of conflation built upon a central confusion that one can actively *be* an atheist at all. The best it seems anyone (other than some philosophers) manages in this vein is to cobble other identities together[3] and decide that those identities constitute being an "atheist."

It would be as though all of the people who play tennis but not golf decided that to truly be doing not-playing-golf correctly, a person must play tennis. "I'm not a golfer; I play tennis!" we can imagine such a confused individual saying. This may sound ridiculous, but "I'm not a Christian; I'm a secular humanist!" falls under the exact same illogical umbrella.[4] We can also imagine such a confused nongolfing zealot declaring, "Joe is not a real nongolfer because if he were, he would take up tennis in order to get it right about sports involving hitting balls with specialized equipment." Again, this may sound ridiculous, but "Joe would be a better atheist if he were a social progressive" falls in the same universe of self-righteous bafflement.

What seems to be happening in these cases is that taking atheist—a null term—upon oneself causes a search for what it means about oneself to ensue. Since this quest is guaranteed to fail to be fulfilling, coincidentally like-minded nonbelievers will begin to coalesce together around causes and beliefs that are important to them, and they will reliably form moral communities. This process is fundamentally human, and yet this process is the foundation of every religion that ever has or ever will exist.[5] We really should tread carefully, then. Ending "atheism" is a good way to inject some care into this situation.

And here we can reliably expect bellyaching from philosophers, et alia. There is, of course, an apparent problem with ending atheism, they will tell us. Atheism is, technically, the rejection or denial of theism, and so it is the default position regarding the matter of the existence of gods. That means anyone who doesn't believe in God is automatically an "atheist" by default. Because it's the default, we can't really "end atheism." Obviously, this isn't what I mean.

I like to think of it this way. If theism were to go away, technically everyone would be atheists, so the term would be utterly obsolete because of its lack of providing useful information about anyone. If everyone on earth rejected theism, we wouldn't call anyone atheists because we wouldn't need to. We'd just call them people. "Atheism," then, is a word that shouldn't exist.

The term "atheism," though, does exist, and it seems like it needs to. This sense arises because at present a majority of the people in the world believe in some kind of god. Christianity and Islam together represent almost half the world's population, and they cannot be ignored. As "atheist" means someone who rejects all of this, it seems like we just can't ditch the term yet. The feeling is that the term is very important in that regard, and in a way, it is. It is a linguistic and philosophical counterpoint to what is probably the most influential pseudo-philosophical position in the world, one that is incorrect and harmful effectively beyond any doubt. Maybe it's better to say, then, that "atheism" is the most important word that shouldn't exist.

Take a moment, though, to fully appreciate what is going on here. Because nonbelievers are branded with this unfortunate word, they are suddenly expected to defend a lack of belief, a burden that isn't theirs and yet that they routinely accept for themselves. This is a mistake, one Sam Harris has identified as having all of the markings of a "trap," one that may have been "deliberately laid for us."[6] Part of the nature of this trap is that it enables religious people to misunderstand atheism as a thing like a religion, which they reliably do.

In this way, atheists not only set themselves up but also ensnare themselves into seeking an identity in something that cannot provide one, and their success in this search is their tragedy. By creating an identity out of being atheists, they, being people, create moral communities around that banner, and there has been no shortage of this behavior in recent years. But then, moral communities are *a thing like a religion*, and so the trap springs itself and catches a prey that thinks it cannot be caught.

That the term "atheist" has always had a negative connotation—and rightly, since it ultimately means what will be heard as "I reject your core values"—only makes the trap uglier. Ugly though it is, it is also cunningly elegant. The atheist is caught between defining herself, being defined by others, or refusing to do so. By defining herself, she traps herself, as just noted. By accepting the definitions of others, she lets them trap her. By rejecting any such definition, she perpetuates the misleading trope that "atheism stands for nothing," which gets repeated *ad nauseam* and allows her opponents to define her anyway, in this case as being inhuman or morally deficient.

The conflation of "atheism" with things atheists frequently stand for defines this trap and is unfair, and it is rife and unavoidable. It will not go away until the label does. This sticky situation—one that could be sidestepped easily by rejecting the need for the meaningless label at all—often leads atheists to choose to tilt at windmills in an attempt to define for themselves what an atheist must stand for.

Some attempts atheists use to define themselves are more benign than others, and at times they can be representative of many nonbelievers, and thus they, like Sancho Panza, often go along for the ride, even if they know better. For instance, most, if not all, nonbelievers are secularists, believing in the separation of church and state, freedom of belief, thought, speech, and conscience, and desiring no special legal or societal privilege for any belief system, or for none. There is a common tendency, therefore, to conflate atheism with secularism, perhaps on the observation that secularism is naturally necessary to protect the interests of those lacking a religion. Many nonbelievers are also humanists, grounding their sense of morals in the human experience, along with that of other sentient beings. Fewer, though still a fair proportion, are (informed) skeptics, doubting that which sounds dubious and requiring strong reasons, usually evidential, before conferring belief. None of these stances are actually "atheism," though; they are secularism, humanism, and skepticism, respectively. Conflating them with the rejection of belief in gods does not help matters, and taking that conflation as part of one's individual identity compounds the unfortunate problems with understanding what nonbelief really entails.

What, Then, Is an Atheist?
The atheist is a strange kind of animal. Upon discovering that someone is an atheist, we will, upon reflection, realize we know next to nothing about her. We know nothing about her political attitudes, her favorite sports teams (and whether she even has any), or the particulars of any interests she may have. We know nothing about foods she may enjoy or dislike, not a hint about her hobbies, no clues about her sexual preferences or predilections, not one of her biases, almost nothing about the culture she was born into, very little about her moral sensibilities, and certainly nothing about how she handles many of the great psychological and social challenges faced by all people in their unique settings and circumstances. Broad statistical statements may apply, of course, and provide us with some guesses about her, but given the variety of spectra of possibilities that characterize these and other aspects of human existence, knowing that a person is an atheist tells us staggeringly little.

All we know for sure about an atheist is that, of the countless ways that we as human beings reliably mislead ourselves about the nature of the world and our lives in it, the atheist has put one—just one—of these ways aside or somehow managed to avoid picking it up in the first place. Atheism is a nonposition, or more accurately a pseudo-position, a position that pretends to exist, a word that pretends to mean something, only because so many people insist on embracing a belief in a God that isn't there. And this is the best that can be said for atheism.

That means there's worse that can be said. Because atheism is a position only defined in counterpoint to theism, there is an inherent lack of clarity in what that term describes. There are atheists, for instance, who merely reject theism. They lack belief in gods, and that's it. There are also atheists who subscribe to atheism. They, sometimes called *strong atheists*, actively believe there are no gods, and most of them are philosophers or philosophy enthusiasts of some kind. Some strong atheists work very hard to argue that all atheists who have considered whether God exists are technically strong atheists too, and many other atheists reject this claim. The thing is, "there isn't enough evidence to convince me to believe in any deity" is really all atheism takes.

There are also other kinds of people who do not accept theism as well. There are people who are genuinely apathetic to the matter, and, as they technically lack belief, they're a kind of atheist.[7] They have already placed theism beneath rational consideration, so they're really a step ahead of their time. Additionally, there are people who do not think the term "God" is defined clearly enough to say anything about belief at all, often called *ignostics*. Of course, there are also *agnostics*, those who claim that they don't know whether God exists, and thus, though not all realize it, tacitly admit that they do not actually believe in God. Furthermore, many pagans and New Age adherents don't exactly qualify as theists, even if they have beliefs that border on the theism spectrum.[8]

There are also people who seem genuinely confused because they have adopted the label "atheist" as part of their identity without realizing that it doesn't represent anything (unless they're strong atheists). Some of them, having adopted the identity, seem to think it must stand for something and cobble on to the brand a variety of other ideas and agendas that they feel are important to any—and here we have the seeds of a major problem—"good atheist." They organize communities around skepticism, humanism, rationalism, atheistic religious philosophy, or other various ideals they feel are right and proper for atheists to hold[9] and then conflate those with "atheism." If we wished to concoct a better recipe for quasi-religious ideological behavior to develop within a moral community branded with the term "atheism" than this unfortunate and confused situation, we'd be hard pressed to come up with a way to do it.

Saying that it is time for atheism to end, then, is tantamount to saying that all of those interpretations of atheism should end, and they should end because they're obsolete or consequential errors. "No, I don't believe that," is more than enough.

Movements and Philosophies That Aren't Atheism

Skepticism about the question of God's existence leads pretty reliably to nonbelief, but skepticism is not synonymous with atheism.

Abandoning religious ethical frameworks when people lose their faith in God often leads to them seeing that ethics can be understood in terms of human experience, along with that of other sentient creatures, leading nonbelievers to become humanists. Still, humanism is not the same as atheism, and religious people who believe in God can certainly be humanists.

Keeping erect a firm wall of separation between church and state (secularism), fighting for equal social and political rights for nonbelievers in societies dominated by believers, and challenging religious privilege and bullying are all worthy goals that interest many who believe in no gods, but these, which we might broadly classify as "freedom from religion,"[10] are not atheism either.

Encouraging people to be open about their nonbelief, secularism, or humanism, as with the Out Campaign and Openly Secular, while beneficial for nonbelievers in almost every conceivable way, is also not part of atheism.

Even developing communities for camaraderie and support for non-believers, particularly in communities that are predominantly religious, doesn't constitute an activity that is identifiable with atheism, even if the only people who engage in it are all self-identifying atheists.

All of these are valid, worthy efforts, and many of them are reasons that people decide to question their religious beliefs and leave them, but none of them *are* atheism. Atheism is an unfortunate term describing a particular kind of lack of belief, and that's all.

The conflation of these various *things* with atheism—a null position— is a problem because it gives people the impression that atheism, hence not believing, is something it isn't. All social and political movements and all communities based upon "atheism" are better seen as being based upon some combination of other things while being pushed for predominantly by people who happen not to believe in gods. Endlessly these days we hear about "the atheism movement" and "the atheism community," along with what is and isn't good for "our movement," "our community," or "our atheism." None of this makes sense, and so it predictably leads to squabbling and outright fighting. What is the fighting over? Well, to religious believers, whatever it might be over is what "atheism" is, and how religion-like it looks as a result from their perspective.

In the case of an alleged "atheism community" or an "atheism movement," we're left wondering exactly what and who are being talked about. The atheism movement is little more than a loose confederation of disparate, motivated, and disagreeable moral communities that have the diminution of religious belief and influence as the only thing like a goal held in common, and that only roughly. Seen this way, as it is, immediately makes clear why it's such a horrible idea. Much worse still is the apparent fact that taking pride in being an atheist often seems to manifest in people believing themselves smarter, more advanced, more moral, or better because of their lack of belief. This, though, is the nearest second to a unifying feature of the people making up the so-called atheism movement. This arrogance and the attitudes of condescension and moral righteousness behind it do not go unnoticed, nor do they help anyone, really.

Atheistic Philosophy of Religion
Strong atheists keep fighting a philosophical fight that has already been won and that cannot end until we simply give it up. This fight is the pseudo-philosophical atheism fight, and the atheists who engage in it join their religious peers in calling themselves philosophers of religion.[11] Their tactics are not terribly effective because people don't often believe in God for philosophical reasons (or care about philosophy at all). The philosophical defenses of theism exist to satisfy the inner lawyers of believers so that they can feel rational about maintaining beliefs held for other reasons.[12]

At the philosophical level, the argument about God has descended into something resembling embarrassing ruins, presently unable even to find its own purpose. Prominent nonbelieving philosophers working in the philosophy of religion, such as Graham Oppy and Keith Parsons, seem to agree that the philosophy of religion should no longer focus upon the defeated case for theism and certainly shouldn't keep playing favorites to the Christian (and sometimes Islamic) ideas for which the philosophical subdiscipline seems to have been invented and continues to exist.

Oppy, in fact, wrote a book in 2014 titled *Reinventing Philosophy of Religion: An Opinionated Introduction*.[13] Following an interview Oppy gave on the book,[14] John W. Loftus summarized and criticized a number of his points, writing,

> Oppy offers his criticism, saying, "Most of the people who have done philosophy of religion have been theists." So it stands to reason "it has had an extremely narrow focus. . . . It hasn't really been the philosophy of religion but rather Christianity with a very great emphasis on theism." . . . Oppy offers a solution to this malaise. He argues the discipline must be reinvented. . . . To reinvent the philosophy of religion Oppy argues, "it must address questions that apply to the phenomena of religion in general." That's it.[15]

We might wonder what exactly Oppy has in mind, and we gather some hints by considering the next book he published. In November 2014, Oppy published an authoritative book through the prestigious Cambridge University Press called *Describing Gods: An Investigation of Divine Attributes*.[16] The description for this volume on Amazon.com reads,

> How do religious believers describe God, and what sort of attributes do they attribute to him? These are central topics in the philosophy of religion. In this book Graham Oppy undertakes a careful study of attributes which are commonly ascribed to God, including infinity, perfection, simplicity, eternity, necessity, fundamentality, omnipotence, omniscience, freedom, incorporeality, perfect goodness and perfect beauty. In a series of substantial chapters, he examines divine attributes one by one, and relates them to a larger taxonomy of those attributes. He also examines the difficulties involved in establishing the claim that understandings of divine attributes are inconsistent or incoherent. Intended as a companion to his 2006 book *Arguing about Gods*, his study

engages with a range of the best contemporary work on divine attributes. It will appeal to readers in philosophy of religion.[17]

This book, scholarly as it is, is very difficult to see as anything but a perfect example of how seriously human beings can entertain ideas that we shouldn't. Given the existence of such explorations, we are left wondering why philosophers don't also produce painstakingly detailed academic tomes upon the unique and special qualities of dragonfire, be damned if there exist dragons to produce it. Put another way, we need exactly zero books written on any level of academic expertise to tell us that Superman's superpowers aren't real.

Divine attributes are properties applied to a mythological fiction called "God" so that "God" can be believed to satisfy psychosocial needs, largely including needs for attribution and control. Exploring the attributes to a deity completely misses the point—people need their needs met and will pretend if doing so seems to get the job done. "What are divine attributes?" and "Are they coherent philosophical objects?" are the wrong kinds of questions to be asking. The right questions are "What needs cause people to give the myth they call 'God' these attributes?" and "How can we help them meet those needs without relying upon the mythology of theism to do it?"

By focusing on "the divine" instead of what it symbolizes for the people who believe in it—which we will soon see has pretty much everything to do with moral valuation instead of magic beings outside of the universe—endeavors of this kind have little hope of moving forward any conversation of substance. Simply being honest about theism establishes this fact beyond much doubt and tells us how we can do better: focus on finding better ways to address the needs, not on trifling over details of the obvious fictions people use to pretend they're already met.

Perhaps it is something along the lines of this recognition that led philosopher Keith Parsons to declare the case for theism dead in 2010, writing on his blog at the *Secular Outpost,*

I have to confess that I now regard "the case for theism" as a fraud and I can no longer take it seriously enough to present it to a class as a respectable philosophical position—no more than I could present intelligent design as a legitimate biological theory. [By the way], in saying that I now consider the case for theism to be a fraud, I do not mean to charge that the people making that case are frauds who aim to fool us with claims they know to be empty. No, theistic philosophers and apologists are almost painfully earnest and honest.... I just cannot take their arguments seriously any more, and if you cannot take something seriously, you should not try to devote serious academic attention to it.[18]

What, then, exactly is the philosophy of religion anyway? I'd like to offer a functional definition. *The philosophy of religion is a type of academic puffery centrally concerned with pretending theism is worth taking seriously on its own terms.* Given that this description seems to fit, and that the terms of theism are mythological, it is very difficult to comprehend why anyone not employed by it should continue to treat this subject with the slightest amount of real concern.

If the philosophical case for theism is dead, and the main reason that religious philosophers engage in the philosophy of religion is in service to trying to keep its academic respectability "on life support"[19] or, as it more likely is, to resurrect it, then we should drop it. The entire field could be dismissed as beneath serious academic consideration, and, as would be fitting, philosophy departments could start to treat it as the academic poison that it is. As philosopher Peter Boghossian controversially put on Twitter, serious philosophy departments could get to a place where they recognize that "being published in the philosophy of religion should disqualify one from sitting at the adult table."[20]

In recognition of this fact, John W. Loftus has penned a passionate series on his blog, *Debunking Christianity*, calling for the end of the philosophy of religion as a serious academic discipline, spurring an important debate in moving toward the future of nonbelief.[21] Biologist Jerry Coyne has indicated his agreement with Loftus's position,[22] as have I.[23] It is our assessment that theology, even dressed up in academic regalia, has no place in a secular university, and that everything else covered by that field is better covered by other courses like psychology, sociology, anthropology, and so on. Even if we are overreaching, it will be far more harmful to theology than to the pursuit of actual knowledge to remove the philosophy of religion from serious academic consideration.

One thing strong atheists may fail to realize is that the philosophical fight itself is the only thing that lends religious belief the slightest shred of academic respectability. Another is that the whole of academic theology is an attempt to keep this discussion alive. It feels very important, particularly to smart, newly minted atheists (especially if they become activists) to rebut philosophical theism, but the rebuttals are done, and by continuing, they create the illusion that there is still a debate to be had where there is none. The meaningful replies have already been made, and they are copiously available in books and all over the Internet, easily and freely accessible to anyone looking for them or wanting to share them.

Of course, familiarizing oneself with these debates isn't completely devoid of merit, particularly when overcoming one's own religious beliefs. It isn't necessary to being a nonbeliever, or really a "good atheist," to know the ins and outs of the endless philosophical debate about theism. It, after all, is talking about the "God" question in entirely the wrong way, and all that's required to abandon belief in God is intellectual honesty anyway, no complicated, sophisticated arguments needed.

Being "Good at Atheism"

For people who have taken atheism as a label or as a meaningful part of their personal identities, there is a natural drive to be "good at atheism." Atheism, however, is best understood as a null position, as a term that shouldn't exist and, hopefully, eventually will not exist. For those of us who see atheism this way, the very notion of being "good at atheism" seems ludicrous, but we shouldn't overlook the value-laden nature of the expression.

All of the ways to be "good at atheism" boil down to tacking something on as an essential part of what "atheism" means and trying to be good at those things. Science is something many atheists consider a part of atheism, for example, as are the many ideas, movements, goals, and positions discussed earlier in this chapter. Getting better at science, however worthy an effort, though, makes one better at science,[24] not at "atheism."

A useful exercise to test yourself for incidental conflations between not believing in gods and other ideas is to imagine that the world has already left theism behind completely (whether this might ever actually occur is immaterial to this exploration). In such a world, one where nobody believes gods exist, ideally one where no one has believed it for a long time, what would we see?

There would be people who are skeptical and people who aren't. There would be people whose ethics are humanist and people whose ethics align with various political ideologies or agendas that see things differently. There would be people who are socially progressive and people who aren't. There would be scientists and those who completely fail to grasp the subject. We wouldn't automatically assume any set of social, political, or philosophical positions of anyone. Incidentally, no one would be called an "atheist" either; everyone would just be a person.

When this chapter calls for "the end of atheism," then, as it does, it does so in the sense that we should move beyond anything called "atheism" that we could be good or bad at.

Othering the Otherers

Perhaps most curious among the side effects of atheism being treated as a thing is a tendency to identify those who believe in God by the general philosophical term for them, *theists*. I recommend strongly against using this word[25] and consider it one of the significant problems with considering atheism as a thing, particularly with taking it as a part of one's personal identity.

To explain, it seems unclear who exactly is a "theist." Obviously, there are billions of Christians of thousands of different stripes in the world, and nearly as many Muslims and half as many Hindus. In addition to these, there are all sorts of other people who believe in gods or God in some sense or another, so much so that it might be accurate to describe a majority of the world's population as being theists. The problem is that no one, except perhaps a few philosophers and argumentative religious crusaders (mostly on the Internet), identifies as a "theist," and those who do are doing so typically in expressed othering to "atheist."

It seems that calling people *theists* is done largely to distinguish them from *atheists*, and to the degree that this is true, doing so therefore reinforces the sense of identity that can get tied up in "being an atheist." If there is a *them*, there must be an *us*, and if there is an *us*, we must stand together for something, particularly not what *they* stand for.

Consider the following observation by forensic psychiatrist J. Anderson Thomson, Jr., upon whom we relied significantly in the last chapter to make proper sense of theism:

> If you arbitrarily divide a room full of people into two groups for a game, they will invariably begin to identify with the group to which they've been assigned. They will consider those in their group as "in," and those in the other as "out." There likely will be strong competition between the two groups, even if the people in them were strangers to each other when the game began. The strangers have become teammates. Hasn't this ever struck you as odd? Probably not, because it is quite literally natural. You most likely would do the same thing. This "groupishness" is hardwired and helped our ancestors survive the worlds in which they evolved.... So, you ask, what does this have to do with religion? Everything.[26]

In Thomson's scenario, he asks us only to consider the situation where a room full of strangers is arbitrarily divided into two teams for the purpose of a game. With religion, and its opposition, the purposes in question are the direction of society, human and individual rights, and life itself. Groupishness of this kind is known to exhibit parochial altruism[27]—in-group prosociality and out-group hostility—and using labels to brand each other with is an effective means for identifying teams.

What Thomson is referring to is a phenomenon explained in social psychology by *social identity theory*, proposed in 1979 by social psychologist Henri Tajfel. Tajfel observed that human beings have a strong tendency toward in-group and out-group behavior because identification with such groups is a source of pride and self-esteem along with a sense of belongingness and thus social identity.[28] Social identity theory predicts exactly the kind of behavior that Thomson describes and yet goes further, identifying that in-groups will eventually discriminate against out-groups in order to enhance self-image.[29] If "atheists" can represent an us, then we have to carry some concern that it will see "theists" as a them.

This is the very process of creating the kinds of moral communities that have difficulty talking to one another, reaching one another, and avoiding becoming ideologies in their own rights. It strikes me that the use of the term "theists" to refer to people who believe in God, while technically correct, seems more as an antiatheist brand than anything, and I recommend against it.

Generally—and although it may be criticized as a semantic point—I think we would do well to avoid the terms "theist" and "atheist" as labels for people. It is my guess that the terms "believer" and "nonbeliever" are better terms, though "nonbeliever" still isn't good. People who do not believe in God are people, just like people who do not play golf. People who do believe in God are people who additionally have a belief in God, just like people who play golf are people who additionally play golf. Notice that there's no difficulty in answering the question "Is Janet a golfer?" with "No, she doesn't play golf," despite the lack of a specialized term to describe those who do not play golf. In fact, calling her a "nongolfer" is both awkward and pointless.

To further drive that point, believers across all faith traditions are united by *believing* the tenets of their religions. This point stands even if it makes very little sense to say so without qualifying it with what they believe (even terms like "Christian" and "Muslim" are hardly descriptive enough to reveal what individual believers actually believe in most cases). It isn't clear that we need a term of negation. If Bill isn't a Christian, we can simply say that he isn't. Still, if we must use a term for certain purposes, "nonbeliever" seems to fit without the attendant problems of "atheist" because it is softer, less negative in connotation, and less likely to be conflated with other concepts.

Atheism Maintains Theism

Atheism paradoxically maintains theism. This surprising effect is strongest with philosophical (strong) atheism, but it is true simply by the fact that atheism only really exists as a counterpoint to theism. In order for atheism, as the kind of thing one can hold or be good at, to have real meaning, theism must have something going for it. That is, just as theism implicitly defines atheism by negation, this kind of atheism implicitly defines theism by negation too.

Consider, by analogy to "God does not exist," the statement "dragons do not exist." In order for this statement about dragons to be intelligible, one must at the very least pretend to have an idea of what a dragon is. The sentence, otherwise, is utterly meaningless. Thus, this quintessentially "a-dragonist" statement, "dragons do not exist," implicitly causes us to seek meaning in the term "dragon."

Atheism, by asserting, "God does not exist," immediately causes us to seek meaning in theism. This invariably leads to trying to understand "God" as a kind of being. This sense of meaning to theism is all theologians and other believers need to keep their end of the conversation about belief going, and that's bad because the enduring conversation is all they have.[30] By saying that "God doesn't exist," we force enough meaning into the term "God" to keep people able to believe in it and argue that it does.

Many believers, especially theologians and apologists, will argue that theism has evidence supporting it, but that is false.[31] If there is no God, any alleged evidence for God is evidence misattributed to God. On the other hand, if there is a God—presuming the usual theistic assumption that God is the Creator of everything—everything is evidence for God. Anything that doesn't seem to fit with what we think about God, in these cases, is easily interpreted as our failure to correctly understand God's inscrutable ways. If this is the case, nothing at all stands out as particular evidence for God's existence, and so far as we know, we're left in the same boat as if nothing were evidence for God.[32] In both cases, evidence is immaterial, and nothing and everything as evidence boil down to what we assume.[33] Perhaps the most straightforward conclusion to draw from these observations is that "God" is an *idea*, not a being, assumed into existence by the force of mythological thinking and pseudo-philosophical sophistry.

Philosophers, though, often like to point out that philosophy, not science or any other field of human inquiry, offers humanity the best defenses against theism. Put another way, philosophers can be quick to credit philosophy with the best defenses of atheism, but that is a problem. Philosophical atheism goes to great lengths to take the terms of theism very seriously in an attempt to defeat them, and this is the exact opposite of placing them beneath serious consideration. The existence of an ongoing academic debate—with academic journals and academic positions in philosophy departments at major universities dedicated to it—provides academic believers with a pretense of academic respectability that they covet and yet do not deserve. Consider the words of philosopher Keith Parsons, when he was abandoning teaching philosophy of religion, the academic field being referred to:

One of the things the really active conservative Christians covet enormously, more than anything else, is intellectual respectability. And they think they have found it in some of the arguments from these philosophers of religion.[34]

All philosophical atheism makes a solitary and devastating mistake: it treats theism on its own terms and thus perpetuates those terms, adding more pretense at authority to keeping them alive.[35] This must end if we are going to get over God for good.

The End of Atheism

If we want to get over God, we have to get over God, and that means getting over being explicit about being "without God." In contrast, where we want to get is where God, as conceived of by theism, is an irrelevant antique belonging to humanity's infancy. So long as we can be "good at atheism," however, and so long as we treat God in theistic terms, this cannot happen. We need the end of atheism, and it is time to bring it about.

Notes

1. It needs nothing more than a casual mention that these abuses aren't merely historical—they occur in the world *now*—to illustrate that this horrific problem may actually be a feature, not a bug, of serious religious belief.

2. It is my guess that the term "nonbeliever," which in one technical sense means the same thing as "atheist," is likely to be a better term than "atheist," but even that term need not be used. Questions like "how do you identify yourself religiously?" can be answered simply with "I am not religious." Questions like "do you believe in God?" need only to be answered with a plain "no." It is difficult to see what is gained by adding "I'm an atheist" to either of those kinds of questions, but it isn't difficult at all to see what is lost by doing so. Declaring oneself an "atheist" in such situations immediately suggests belonging to a separate and opposing camp, one that easily can be construed as (or become) a moral community with a competing moral framework defining it.

3. These identities are often drawn from social movements and other moral communities that *currently happen to be* common among many, though by no

means all, people who lack belief in God at present. Since there is a fairly strong connection between social conservatism and being strongly religious, often these identities are strikingly far to the left in the social politics arena, usually being drawn from social progressivism in that it stands most powerfully opposed to social conservatism and much of the oppressive social structures that social conservatives tend to seek to maintain.

4. Google defines *secular humanism* as "humanism, with regard in particular to the belief that humanity is capable of morality and self-fulfillment without belief in God," and Christians certainly can believe in God and simultaneously believe that human beings are *capable* of morality and self-fulfillment without that belief. Just as there are people who play neither tennis nor golf, and people who play both, there can be people who are neither Christian nor secular humanists, and people who are both.

5. This slope need not be slippery. This is a call to caution, not an argument that "atheism" will become a religion if people insist in misapplying the label to themselves as though it describes something that they do believe.

6. Sam Harris, "AAI 2007—The Problem with Atheism," *YouTube*, video, 29 December 2010, https://www.youtube.com/watch?v=ODz7kRS2XPs.

7. These are sometimes referred to as *apatheists*, a portmanteau of "apathetic" and "atheist." I don't think this term needs more circulation.

8. Pantheists, those who believe God is synonymous with everything, and panentheists, those who believe God "interpenetrates and goes beyond" everything (*Wikipedia* definition, http://en.wikipedia.org/wiki/Panentheism), are two examples. It is not my intention to discuss anything to do with the specific vagaries of paganism, although many, at least in the West, are nearer in practice to pantheism or panentheism than the term "pagan" lets on.

9. One such group, called *Atheism+* (read: Atheism Plus), defines itself as "atheism *plus* a core set of basic humanist values and goals and a skepticism applied to everyone, even ourselves" (see Richard Carrier, "Atheism+: The Name for What's Happening," 14 January 2013, http://freethoughtblogs.com/carrier/archives/3018), though it might more accurately be defined as atheism cobbled together with skepticism and a brand of humanism that is an amalgam of rather fringe social justice activism, particularly with regard to promoting a specific type of feminism, and even more particularly with regard to fighting perceived sexism in "the atheism community," especially at "atheism movement" events and conferences. Many of its representatives seem consistently surprised and affronted

that not all atheists share these ambitions or perceptions and do not like to be branded among them by association with the "atheism" label.

10. With a hearty and cheerful nod to the Freedom From Religion Foundation (www.ffrf.org) while we say so.

11. By "philosopher of religion," in this context, I mean both the professionals who write and publish in that field and the amateur enthusiasts who engage in attempted robust philosophical argumentation in defense of atheism.

12. One important *apparent* exception to this claim is that people often adopt religious beliefs after being defeated by an argument to complexity, deciding that something like life or consciousness or the universe is so complicated that only a deity could be responsible. This, though, is one of the most classic philosophical errors in thinking, an appeal to ignorance. In a later chapter, we will discuss how this ties into a fundamental underlying psychological need for attribution for phenomena that lie outside of the befuddled believer's understanding.

13. Graham Oppy, *Reinventing Philosophy of Religion: An Opinionated Introduction* (London: Palgrave Pivot, 2014).

14. Taylor Carr, "Armchair Atheism, Ep. 2—Why Philosophy of Religion? with Graham Oppy," *YouTube*, video, 23 July 2014, https://www.youtube.com/watch?v=Yv3DVvxgo5E.

15. John W. Loftus, "I'm Calling for an End to the Philosophy of Religion as a Discipline in Secular Universities," *Debunking Christianity*, blog, 24 July 2014, http://debunkingchristianity.blogspot.com/2014/07/im-calling-for-end-to-philosophy-of.html.

16. Graham Oppy, *Describing Gods: An Investigation of Divine Attributes* (Cambridge: Cambridge University Press, 2014).

17. See the Amazon product page for Oppy's *Describing Gods*, http://www.amazon.com/gp/product/110708704X.

18. Parson's original post on *Secular Outpost* no longer exists after the website was reorganized, and it is here quoted from *Religion Dispatches* instead. Julia Galef, "A Philosopher of Religion Calls It Quits," *Religion Dispatches*, 5 January, 2011, http://religiondispatches.org/a-philosopher-of-religion-calls-it-quits/.

19. This phrasing is courtesy of Jeffrey Jay Lowder, founder of the *Secular Web* and *Secular Outpost*. Citation: Jeffrey Jay Lowder, "The Evidential Argument from Moral Agency Revisited: A Reply to Jerry Coyne," *Secular Outpost*, blog, Patheos

Network, 3 July 2014, http://www.patheos.com/blogs/secularoutpost/2014/07/03/the-evidential-argument-from-moral-agency-revisited-a-reply-to-jerry-coyne/.

20. Peter Boghossian, [@peterboghossian], Being published in the philosophy of religion should disqualify one from sitting at the adult table, [Tweet], 14 June 2014, https://twitter.com/peterboghossian/status/477980921711583232.

21. John W. Loftus, "On Ending the Philosophy of Religion Discipline," *Debunking Christianity*, blog, 31 July 2014, http://debunkingchristianity.blogspot.com/2014/07/on-ending-philosophy-of-religion.html.

22. Jerry Coyne, "Let's Stop Teaching Philosophy of Religion in Secular Colleges," *Why Evolution Is True*, blog, 29 July 2014, http://whyevolutionistrue.wordpress.com/2014/07/29/lets-stop-teaching-philosophy-of-religion-in-secular-colleges/.

23. Three essays on my own blog: (1) James A. Lindsay, "Don't God-Bother. Philosophy of Religion is Dead," *God Doesn't; We Do*, blog, 9 July 2014, http://goddoesnt.blogspot.com/2014/07/dont-god-bother-philosophy-of-religion.html; (2) "Christian Apologist and Theologian William Lane Craig Explains Why the Philosophy of Religion Is a Waste of Time," 13 July 2014, http://goddoesnt.blogspot.com/2014/07/christian-apologist-and-theologian.html; (3) "The Moral Angle of Apologetics for the Philosophy of Religion," 4 August 2014, http://goddoesnt.blogspot.com/2014/08/the-moral-angle-of-apologetics-for.html.

24. This is a little bit complicated, in fact. Getting better at science could mean learning lots of scientific facts, in which case one has merely become more knowledgeable. It could mean getting better at scientific reasoning or engaging in the scientific methods, in which case it could be said that someone has gotten better at doing science or thinking scientifically. Neither of these qualifies as getting better at *atheism*, however, even if it does provide a superior attributional schema for natural phenomena than do most religious beliefs.

25. From my own blog: James A. Lindsay, "Don't Say the 'Th' Word," *God Doesn't; We Do*, Blog, 13 December 2013, http://goddoesnt.blogspot.com/2013/12/dont-say-th-word.html.

26. Thomson, *Why We Believe in God(s)*, p. 38.

27. Haidt, *The Righteous Mind*, p. 308.

28. Herni Tajfel and John C. Turner, "An Integrative Theory of Intergroup Conflict," in *The Social Psychology of Intergroup Relations*, ed. William G. Austin and Stephen Worchel (Pacific Grove, CA: Brooks/Cole Publishing, 1979), pp. 33–47).

29. A particularly dramatic example of this kind of behavior was demonstrated (perhaps unethically) by social psychologist Muzafer Sherif a quarter century earlier than Tajfel formulated social identity theory. Sherif took a number of (well-adjusted, middle-class) adolescent boys to a Boy Scout campground known as Robber's Cave. The experiment began with the boys being split into two nearly equal groups, with each ignorant of the existence of the other group. He then had the groups engage in a competitive phase in which the boys became aware of one another, competed against one another for limited prizes and privileges, and frustrated one another via actions that Sherif engineered, like having one group eat all of the food at a picnic before the other group arrived, delaying the later group's mealtime. The two groups quickly came to use very positive language to describe their own groups and negative language for the other, a tendency that quickly escalated to such violence that the boys had to be completely separated from one another for their own safety. This example isn't included here to suggest that violent hostilities are likely to arise between "atheists" and "theists" (though there are some reasons to be concerned, especially where militant strains of religious beliefs are concerned) but rather to demonstrate that the human tendency to groupishness can be quick and powerful. See Muzafer Sherif et al., *Experimental Study of Positive and Negative Intergroup Attitudes Between Experimentally Produced Groups: Robbers Cave Study* (Norman, OK: University of Oklahoma Press, 1954).

30. They certainly have a lot of social and cultural momentum as well, but that simply constitutes people in the believing camp keeping their end of the conversation alive. The goal of this book is to shift our attention away from the conversation about God's alleged existence in favor of more fruitful ones.

31. Indeed, few believers actually assert that *theism* has evidence supporting it unless they're really pressed onto the ropes first. Instead, they argue that their particular belief system, Christianity or whatever, has various evidences in support of it, and because that system is theistic, therefore we can conclude that God exists. This is a fundamental and hilarious problem for philosophers of religion who argue for theism rather in general: even should they succeed, it remains all but impossible to get from there to whatever religion they actually mean to defend. Imagine, for instance, that a completely robust and valid philosophical (and evidence-free) proof of God's existence were given. Only a few minutes of thinking about what the Protestant Christians, Catholics, Sunni Muslims, and Shia Muslims would do with such a fact makes my point. Just ask yourself, from what would they be able to conclude that they are the only ones who are correct? Arguments for the existence of some generic philosophical God are all but worthless to any religionist

at all. The chances remain nearly perfectly stacked against them being right even in such a case.

32. Unfortunately, what exactly is meant by "evidence for" something isn't as clear-cut as we might hope. For a rather long-winded discussion on what "evidence for" does and doesn't mean, readers can see a post I made on my blog on this very topic titled "A Problem With Evidence," June 2, 2014, http://goddoesnt.blogspot.com/2014/06/a-problem-with-evidence.html.

33. The thrust here does not apply to *specific* conceptions of God, but note that those are easily just interpreted as human failures to succeed at understanding the Divine. Specific conceptions of God, like the God depicted in the Christian Bible, has very specific claims made about how it interacts with the world, and we have every reason to believe that those fail and no good reason to believe that they succeed. One may notice, however, a certain tendency among believers not to care very much about these sorts of facts most of the time, which gives birth to a willingness to let what they're calling "God" slip into a vague state that can't be understood or dismissed, leaving the idea that God exists, in one way or another, intact for later when the specific defeasible beliefs slide back into the picture. For a longer discussion of this phenomenon, see Lindsay, *God Doesn't; We Do,* chapter 4. Of note, the actual concept of God *believed in* is unlikely ever to change, illustrating that philosophy (rather, sophistry) is being used as a tool to maintain belief, not to get to truth regarding the beliefs, as is very often the case.

34. Dan Fincke, "Atheist Philosopher of Religion Keith Parsons Abandons Theism Debate and Calls Theist Positions Frauds," *Camels with Hammers,* blog, January 5, 2011, http://www.patheos.com/blogs/camelswithhammers/2011/01/atheist-philosopher-of-religion-keith-parsons-abandons-theism-debate-and-calls-theist-positions-frauds/.

35. To be fair, philosophical rebuttals to theological arguments *were* important, right up until theism lost at the level of ideas. To give credit, in fact, philosophical atheism had a great deal to do with that. The arguments for theism, though, have been successfully addressed, insofar as they really need to be, and their rebuttals are now easily available all over the Internet in both print and video format, to say nothing of the many good books published on these topics. They are no longer important except in archive or as material for new and creative presentations designed to reach broader audiences.

CHAPTER 3

POST-THEISM

Since I was a teenager, I have been fascinated with understanding what people mean when they talk about "God," and while this book represents what I believe is the culmination of that effort, one of the most pressing insights I've had in the process of seeking answers to that question is that theism is, itself, the problem. Theism is the wrong way to think about the meaning being conveyed by the most mysterious and captivating syllable most people ever bother to contemplate. Thus, atheism, as a counterpoint to theism, is the wrong way to think about dealing with theism.

Before addressing what "God" means without relying upon theism, I want to point out in this chapter that even if we are willing to accept the terms of theism, they don't make sense. Particularly, the object of theism, God, is generally not a sufficiently clearly defined concept to work with. "Do you believe in God?" is an inherently confusing question because theism does not specify a clear enough meaning for "God" to allow us to give an adequate answer.

Ignosticism

As briefly indicated in an earlier chapter, there are several ways to approach the question posed by theism without believing. After atheism, agnosticism is by far the most famous, and it is, in fact, a kind of nonbelief. By saying "I don't know" one is also implying ". . . and so technically I lack belief." Saying "I don't know" entails a certain kind of open-minded nonbelief.

Less well-known than agnosticism is *ignosticism*, and its take on the matter is a complaint that it seems impossible to know what "God" actually means. Given the question about belief in God, where theism says, "yes"; atheism says, "no"; and agnosticism says, "I'm not sure"—ignosticism says, "I don't know what you're asking me."

Formally speaking, being ignostic means that every theological position assumes too much about God, and thus it is one of the most intellectually honest positions one can hold about theism. For the ignostic, it is impossible to properly answer any question about belief in God because it isn't clear what the term "God" means. The problem is attempting to understand God under theism, which confuses mythology and reality.

It seems that the primary attribute that allows belief in God to be "rationally" defended is precisely the inherent ambiguity ignostics identify in the term "God."[1] The issue, in summary, is that someone defending his belief in God can mean one thing and then slip the meaning to something very nebulous and vague—what I call a "soft" definition—to avoid criticism, only to have it slide right back to the "harder" (less defensible) meaning the moment scrutiny is removed. We see this when a defense of some take on the God of the Christian Bible switches instead to philosophical topics like the alleged fine-tuning of the universe. Once the audience has been sufficiently blinded with bafflement, an apologist using this technique slides surreptitiously back to Christianity and thus to the character who, the story goes, ordered the wholesale genocide of the Amalekites right after insisting upon doing honest business via fair and accurate weights and measures.[2]

Not only does this happen, it is the religious apologist's bread and butter. Their business is little more than using highly technical and Sophisticated™ philosophical God-concepts to decorate the intellectual ruins in which their beliefs reside with curtains made of the finest invisible cloth.[3] We can easily surmise, then, critical to the survival of the theistic God as an idea is that it lacks clear meaning. In other words, that everybody is wrong about God is a *feature*, not a bug, of theism. The ignostic senses this problem acutely and cuts through the murk by calling theism on its vagueness. Ignosticism, then, is little more than a refusal to answer an unclear question in a misguided way.

It seems, then, that ignosticism would be advisable except for two flaws. The first is that people clearly do mean *something* when they say "God," and (even if using the mythological terms of theism to get there) most people have some sense of what that something is. In other words, ignosticism, for all its intellectual honesty, comes off a bit disingenuous. The second is that ignosticism is inherently poorly equipped to handle situations where people are being quite clear with the type of theism on the table, say one of the many variants of classical theism.[4] Maintaining the argument that the concept still lacks clarity at that point seems strained and damages the credibility of the ignostic position. Theism, after all, does sometimes bother to attempt to make itself clear enough to work with.

Not Caring

I completely sympathize with the desire not to care at all about anything called "God," particularly theistic conceptions, and there are people who do this who are, in a significant way, also ahead of their time.[5] If theism were to fall utterly into intellectual ruins, and that fact were recognized by the majority, no one would feel compelled to care about what anyone says about deities or any other mythologies. Those who already do not care about anything theology has to say realize this fact now and live it. They are people who not only consider the matter of theism meaningless but also irrelevant to their lives, just like Poseidon.

Not caring about theism can follow naturally, though not entirely reliably, from ignosticism. One can only brood for so long upon the fact that, whatever "God" means, everything theological is so fuzzy that one simply stops caring about it. Here, then, we are dealing with a principled and justified lack of interest in arguments about God's possible existence.

The major flaw with not caring a whit about theism is the obvious one: almost anywhere this book might be read, theism is still highly prevalent and likely to be affecting the people who live there in significant ways. Theism spreads like a virus if it is allowed to, and it infects its hosts with tremendous tenacity. When it goes wrong, which seems to be always if given enough time, its rigid demand for conformity and focus on ultimate and infinite ends reliably lead to problems that apathy is not equipped to repel.

Additionally, like with ignosticism, not caring at all about theism comes off as a bit disingenuous, and it smacks of being particularly selfish. Most people are religious and accept theism, and simply not to care about the matter is to miss that the widespread acceptance of theism has profound impacts on almost everyone's life. For most people, not caring just isn't a viable option. Belief in God is too in their faces.

Shooting Bull
We have every right and a duty to shoot down bullshit when we encounter it, including theistic bull. Nonbelievers seem to recognize this need fairly widely, and the particular brand of crap sniping that targets theism is probably the most recognizable meaning currently ascribed to the term "atheism."[6] So long as believers peddle nonsense, someone will need to shoot it down, even if we shouldn't lose ourselves in the weeds in the process.

Figuring out when we should ignore and when we should address piffle is a perennial problem, particularly with its religious brands. Engaging it legitimizes it in a way, even if doing so eventually embarrasses it. Ignoring it enables it to fester and spread unchecked, a problem for infectious ideas, especially ones that prey upon vulnerability. The matter is also context dependent: a conversation with one's cousin or mother, for instance, might admit a different threshold for engagement than impersonal discussions on national or international stages. Deciding when to expose crap for what it is can be a difficult problem.

Theism sometimes bothers to be specific enough to shoot at, and the circumstances sometimes warrant it. In those cases, we should sometimes take aim and fire. Note, however, that taking theism seriously enough to shoot it down has to have a shelf life. As theism becomes less and less meaningful culturally, antitheism becomes less and less appropriate. There is little reason to argue against something that most of us don't take seriously. Ignoring it, scoffing at it, and outright making fun of it[7] are sufficient to the task at that point.

Putting These Together
These approaches can be combined into a single picture that is suitable for post-theism. It combines the central ideas of ignosticism, not caring about

theism at all, and shooting down religious nonsense when it manages to be clear enough to bother with. Those espousing this position recognize that the theistic term "God" doesn't mean anything clear in general and yet often is given various theistic meanings in specific. Of note, many self-described atheists are already post-theistic.

People in this position realize that the vague, hence meaningless, general use of the term "God" is best ignored as unclear and irrelevant while the specific uses of the term are to be rejected for being incorrect and misleading. The post-theistic position recognizes that theism is not even wrong except when it bothers to be.

An Example Worth Mentioning

On Friday, February 21, 2014, theoretical physicist Sean Carroll and evangelical Christian theologian William Lane Craig met in New Orleans for a debate in the Greer-Heard Point Counterpoint forum, discussing "God and Cosmology." While I do not intend to make extensive remarks about their debate to belabor my point, I want to point out that by many accounts, Carroll did an outstanding job over Craig. I encourage my readers to watch this entire two-hour debate in full so that they can see for themselves exactly how Carroll did it, and I want to point out that it was by employing the post-theistic position—along with a lot of very robust understanding of cosmology—that Carroll caught Craig completely (and figuratively) with his pants down.

Carroll expressed a position I would describe as post-theistic because he kept many of his arguments centered on what theoreticians are ultimately concerned with: models. Theologians, as a kind of theoretician (to speak very loosely), are centrally concerned with creating models of the universe, though, as Carroll pointed out, they're not doing so in a mature way. At one point in the debate, while talking about whether we can have eternal models of the universe, he makes this point in a particularly strong way that also happens to illustrate my point about his taking a post-theistic position.

> What you should be doing is trying to build models, like I said. The question is, "Are there realistic models of eternal cosmologies?" Well, I spent half an hour on the Internet; I was able to come up with about

seventeen different plausible-looking models of eternal cosmology. I do not claim that any of these is the right answer; we're nowhere near the right answer yet. But you can come up with objections to every one of these models; you cannot say that they're not eternal.... Meanwhile, theism, I would argue, is not a serious cosmological model. That's because cosmology is a mature subject. We care about more things than just creating the universe; we care about specific details.... A real cosmological model wants to predict what is the amount of density perturbation in the universe, and so forth. Theism does not even try to do this because, ultimately, theism is not well-defined.[8]

This is precisely the post-theistic position being exhibited by Carroll. He directly states that theism is "not well-defined," and his attitude is that because it isn't well-defined, it isn't a serious (cosmological) model. He does, however, take pains before, during, and after this set of comments to shoot down Craig's arguments where they were specific enough to be commented upon. In this debate, Carroll gave us a perfect example of how post-theistic people, especially highly qualified ones, should handle the sophistry of theism.

Notes

1. See Lindsay, *God Doesn't; We Do*, chapter 4.

2. Deuteronomy 25.

3. Philosophers of religion who argue against these smarmy dodges help to deploy the very smokescreen that allows the God under scrutiny to escape the kind of rigorous examination that would expose it as a fraud. Also, another hat tip to biologist Jerry Coyne for the capitalized "Sophisticated" followed by the trademark symbol.

4. It isn't actually clear that any of the many varied definitions of classical theism escapes the ignostic's razor, but I do enjoy being charitable. Even so, just as I do not endorse using "atheist" as a label, I also do not endorse using "ignostic" as a label. Once we've gotten over God, neither term will matter.

5. These people are sometimes referred to as *apatheists*. It is my impression that this word is not widely used as a label, although a growing number of people

seem to be taking the position it represents. I don't encourage the use of this term either.

6. The point that arguing *against* theism is more accurately described as *antitheism*, not atheism, shouldn't really need to be made, but here it is.

7. It is of tremendous importance to realize that mocking an idea and mocking an individual person for holding the idea are not the same thing. This nuance is easy to see by considering the work of satirists who are very effective at lambasting ideas and generalized, faceless people that hold them versus grinding specifically upon an individual (public figures get some exception to this rule). The difference may be subtle but it is clear. A comedian will often rapidly lose her audience by rounding viciously upon an individual in mockery using effectively the same content that is hilarious and thought-provoking when executed in general. Readers are, of course, encouraged to mock bad ideas and discouraged from mocking individuals in the vast majority of situations. Also, apply decency and basic respect for human dignity liberally when doing so.

8. "'God and Cosmology' William Lane Craig and Sean Carroll—2014 Greer Heard Forum," *YouTube*, video, 3 March 2014, https://www.youtube.com/watch?v=X0qKZqPy9T8.

CHAPTER 4

THE GOODNESS OF GOD

Maybe the most important idea in this book is that the word "God" means something that theism doesn't account for. Still, when people say the word "God," they mean something, and that something is real. This chapter and the next will attempt to begin in earnest a conversation about what the term "God" really means.

That meaning is extremely important. No word has commanded so much reverence and intentional irreverence as the term "God." No term has generated more controversy—not even "sex"—than has "God," and for many billions of humans throughout history and today, no concept is considered more profound and significant. In all, no other word has come remotely close in generating the quantity of misguided human effort, much of it an astonishing font of blood, misery, and suffering, with much of the rest just an abysmal waste of time. Whatever "God" means, it is something of central significance to humanity, past, present, and likely future.

Even those who do not believe in a deity cannot escape the word "God" and thus its significance. It is easy, and not far from correct, to write it off as a kind of delusion, held en masse, but the danger in doing so is forgetting that the people using this word are *normal* ones. They also mean something so important by it that it can prove nearly impossible to free them from their beliefs, however delusion-like they may be.

It is time to lay the groundwork so that we can understand what this word means in how it is used, and to do so, we need to understand some of the basics of the psychology—not philosophy—of religion. To understand what good "God" might be to all of these people, we must start by trying to understand what religion does for them. As all theistic religions have "God" at their centers, it would be sheer pretense to imagine that the idea of the deity isn't directly connected with what religion is doing for them.

The Trinity

According to psychologists of religion Ralph Hood, Jr., Peter Hill, and Bernard Spilka, in their textbook *The Psychology of Religion: An Empirical Approach*, fourth edition, whatever it may be that defines religion (and they do not attempt to pin down what that is, noting that it may not even be possible to provide a blanket definition that covers all of what religion is[1]), three broad factors seem to characterize what religion does for people. All three are attempts to satisfy psychosocial needs, and they are needs for *attribution*, *control*, and *sociality*.

They note that these needs are significant, writing, "Simply put, religion is a central feature of human existence," and going on to say, "many of the research findings reviewed in this book speak strongly to the idea that religion is a powerful factor in meeting human needs for meaning making, control, and sociality."[2] Meaning making can be summarized under the term "attribution," which means "the process by which individuals explain the causes of behavior and events."[3] Sociality often has at its base at the individual level a core need for esteem, which Hood, Hill, and Spilka define as "a personal sense of capability and adequacy, which is a central part of sociality and is reflected in our relationships with others."[4] These needs are at once psychological and social, and so they will be referred to as human *psychosocial* needs throughout.

As simple as it is to state these three categories of psychosocial needs, each is very complicated, and they are often interrelated. For example, morality is a central feature of how our communities and cultures define themselves, and so a need for moral attribution lies also at the heart of our social need for effective, stable, mutually beneficial communities. Indeed, moral psychologist Jonathan Haidt directly refers to religions as a kind of *moral community* and refers to them as "moral exoskeletons" that leave us "enmeshed in a set of norms, relationships, and institutions that primarily work on [our intuitions] to influence [our] behavior."[5] None of this works unless we have an apparently solid way to make sense of what a moral exoskeleton is. Thus, attribution, at least where morality is concerned, is tied up with sociality.

Likewise, the sense of control many people derive from their religious beliefs relies upon both sociality and the various attempts people make to attribute causes and effects in the world. Specifically, attributing an earthquake to an angry God in hopes that its propitiation will prevent future tremors utilizes attribution (the God who can be propitiated and his wrath as the causes of earthquakes) and sociality (community rituals, acts of propitiation, and ethical standards that prohibit behaviors believed likely to anger the deity) to enable the sense of control (prevention of future calamity). The sense of control depends upon an attributional schema, then, and upon social mores.

Hood, Hill, and Spilka note, "Our theoretical position asserts that attributions are triggered when meanings are unclear, control is in doubt, and self-esteem is challenged. There is, as suggested, much evidence that these three factors are interrelated."[6] Thus, any attempt to parse these various needs is doomed to failure, and so with that proviso, I note that the presentation here and in the next chapter, by necessity, oversimplifies by being too narrowly reductive. That shouldn't be a problem in communicating the basic ideas, however, and the reader is trusted with being able to realize many more connections between these elements than are documented.

Attribution

The term "attribution" refers to attempting to explain. The goal here will be to outline the ways in which religious attributions arise as attempts to explain aspects of the world. The connections between these religious attributions and the proposed meaning of the term "God" will be discussed more fully in the next chapter. Quoting again from Hood, Hill, and Spilka,

> an individual may attribute the causes of events to a wide variety of
> possible referents (oneself, others, chance, God, etc.). For the psychologist
> of religion, these referents may be classified into two broad categories:
> "naturalistic" and "religious." The evidence is that most people in most

circumstances initially employ naturalistic explanations and attributions, such as references to people, natural events, accidents, or chance.[7] Depending on a wide variety of situational and personal characteristics, there is a good likelihood of shifting to religious attributions when naturalistic ones do not satisfactorily meet the needs for meaning, control, and esteem.[8][9]

This observation is of particular importance and should be salient for anyone who has ever taken the time to discuss religious beliefs from the perspective of the nonbeliever. Almost all such conversations, when not committed to condemning the nonbeliever to a fictional hell, inevitably run over a theme best summarized by, "Well, how do you explain *this*?" Of course, the "this" in the preceding question may range from the very mundane (say, tides) to the stunningly elaborate (say, the complexity of the living world) to the expressly human (say, love) to the profoundly mysterious (say, the ultimate nature of reality) to the statistical (say, luck) to the bizarrely misguided (say, some grand, transcendental, and ultimate purpose of human life). In every case, though, the religious person is relying upon his religious beliefs to try to make sense of something that he doesn't know how else to make sense of.

Of course, many of us recognize these questions for what they are: appeals to ignorance, sometimes referred to as God-of-the-gaps arguments. But this is exactly what psychologists of religion like Hood, Hill, and Spilka are indicating. Most people, most of the time, prefer to make sense of the world in terms of the world, but when they can't and yet need to, they tend to turn to religious attributions to do it. "God" is one such religious attribution.[10]

Incidentally, it is my opinion that whatever religious fundamentalism means—this being its own topic of important and complicated research—a key feature by which it can be distinguished is *a preference for religious attributions over natural ones when naturalistic ones are available*. It is not hard to see, if this conception of religious fundamentalism holds some merit, how it constitutes a kind of psychopathology, hopefully one that could be treated. It specifically manifests as adhering to a set of false beliefs about the world with such tenacity that established and available countervailing attributions are denied or rejected in an attempt to prevent revision of the beliefs. That these beliefs are maintained in order to meet or ignore psychosocial needs that can certainly be met in other ways should qualify it as a kind of pathological mental state, fundamentalism as a subtype of delusion.[11]

If we want to make sense of "God" without theism, we need to do little more than realize that the "how do you explain *this*?" questions believers so often ask are telling us a great deal about what the term "God" means for them: a need to understand the world and their lives in it. That is, a significant part of what "God" means for them is a kind of functional backbone to a superstitious[12] attributional schema. What takes that summary under the confused umbrella of theism is the ages-old process of personifying and mythologizing each of those attempted explanations in the form of a deity.

To quickly make a list that will be developed in the next chapter, it seems that the major attributional categories that "God" stands in for include at least these:

- Moral: the attempt to explain moral values.[13] This obviously has major overlaps with sociality since social engagements are largely contextualized in moral language.

- Teleological: the attempt to make sense of purpose in the world and human life.

- Phenomenological: the attempt to explain phenomena. This obviously has major overlaps with needs for control.

- Abstract: the attempt to make sense of abstractions and ideals.

- Spiritual: the attempt to make sense of what often gets called "spiritual" or "transcendent."

- Psychosocial context: the attempt to make sense of the self and others in the context of the cultures we live in. This obviously is largely done via the moral attribution, but it is significantly different enough to warrant its own treatment. It is also on the edge between attribution and sociality and difficult to tease apart.

Control

It is beyond question that the world operates in a way that is largely well beyond our control. We do not choose the machinations of nature, but we are subject to them sometimes in calamitous ways. We hope to exert control over our fellow human beings, whether for security, prosperity, or other purposes, and often we face the apparently grim reality that we cannot—and even when we can, often we should not. At times we even struggle for control over our own bodies and minds and are left unable to find it, as any sufferer of chronic pain, neuropathy, depression, or a host of other ailments will readily attest. And thus many of our hours and resources are squandered uselessly in one of the oldest of human errors, feeding the charlatans who are eager to sell us bogus cures for our desperate problems, from talismans to rituals to magic "secrets" to snake-oil potions to deities.

Gods have always been one such example of a fraudulent product sold on the pretense of offering control. The gods throughout history were imagined to control various aspects of nature, including ourselves and each other. If only propitiated the right way by the right superstition, we believed we could curry their favor to work our individual or collective wills. Little in this regard has changed, even if many of the old myths are seen clearly for what they are.

So long as we feel powerless—and in many regards we always will be—we'll turn to whatever we can to seize a sense of control if we become desperate enough. Poignantly, Hood, Hill, and Spilka note, "Though the ideal in life is *actual* control, the need to perceive personal mastery is often so great that the *illusion* of control will suffice"[14] (emphasis in the original). At the phrase "illusion of control," "God" conspicuously enters.

They go on to write,

> Religion's ability to offer meaning for virtually every life situation—particularly those that are most distressing, such as death and dying—also provides a measure of control over life's vast uncertainties. . . . An argument can be made that religious ritual and prayer are mechanisms for enhancing the sense of self-control and control of one's world.[15]

They continue,

> Gibbs claims that supernaturalism arises when secular control efforts fail.[16] Vyse further shows how lack of control relates to the development of and belief in superstition and magic.[17] Indeed, the historic interplay of magic and religion has often been viewed as a response to uncertainty and helplessness. When other attempts at control are limited (e.g., when a death is impending), religious faith alone may provide an illusory, subjective sense of control to help people regain the feeling that they are doing something that may work.[18]

Making sense of "God" without theism means, in part, realizing that people's mythological God-construct is what makes the illusory sense of control work. And it is important to note that it *does* work. Hood, Hill, and Spilka note, "[Welton, Adkins, Ingle, and Dixon][19] not only found that God control was independent of belief in chance and powerful others, but that it was also positively related to well-being—benefits normally only associated with internal control."[20][21] Furthermore, they note that "This enhanced subjective feeling of control is often capable of offering people the strength they need to succeed."[22]

My point here, of course, is not to argue that theism is something we should take seriously because of its potential for benefit as a coping mechanism. Theism is bogus, and there are efficacious nonbogus coping mechanisms available, so of course we shouldn't. Developing more realistically grounded coping mechanisms and helping people learn to accept powerlessness can suffice. There is a great deal of importance, though, in recognizing that whatever it is that "God" means to people, a hugely significant part is having a sense of control in life.

There are three main categories, it seems, in how religious appeals to a sense of control are relevant to religion. Two of these are important to making sense of the term "God" without theism. First is what I will term *active control*. These are routes by which we seek to exert control over our world and its circumstances. Second is what I will call *passive control*. This is a sense that we need not do anything really to feel secure because of a belief that the world is already controlled for us. The third category relevant to religious beliefs is *self-control*, which related to the meaning of the term "God" via moral attribution and sociality.[23] A feeling of self-control is expressed with regard to holding to one's moral framework over other desires.

Sociality

As Hood, Hill, and Spilka put it,

> "sociality" refers to behaviors that relate organisms to one another, and that keep an individual identified with a group.[24] Included here are expressions of social support, cooperation, adherence to group standards, attachment to others, altrusism, and many other actions that maintain effectively functioning groups. Faith systems accomplish these goals for many people, and in return the cultural order embraces religion.[25]

Immediately, they go on to note that

> Religion connects individuals to each other and their groups; it socializes members into a community, and concurrently suppresses deviant behavior. As Lumsden and Wilson put it, religion is a "powerful device by which people are absorbed into a tribe and psychically strengthened."[26][27]

The fact is simple. Religion plays a major role for many people in satisfying many of their social needs (and thus needs for esteem, as noted previously), most apparently by providing a sense of psychosocial context to individuals, including by means of a sense of extended fictive kinship (the "tribe" referred to by Lumsden and Wilson). As discussed earlier under social identity theory, we can see that these communities can form tight bonds that foster in-group sociality and carry the potential for out-group hostility. This phenomenon can be summarized both most clearly and in the most important way by remembering that *religions are moral communities.*

As religion is undoubtedly a social phenomenon, what is left to us in the present discussion is making sense of what role "God" plays in meeting these needs. "God" is an emblem of the social order and all of the moral and cultural ties that bind people unified in belief. That makes "God" something like a symbolic object that enables people to circumvent a great deal of otherwise necessary discourse when it comes to understanding each other—and thus being able to trust one another.[28]

Of note, essentially all of the sociality needs satisfied by religion can be met without assuming a theistic religion of any kind. That few, if any, nonbelievers feel unable to meet their social needs is clear evidence of this fact. Furthermore, the existence of, for example, Jewish atheists—people who engage in much of the social activity of the Jewish people and identify as such and yet who do not believe in any god—indicate that it can even be done in a religious context *without theism*.

Untangling Moral Thinking

Among all of the topics mentioned in this chapter so far, morality bears special mention because it is especially complicated and uniquely situated in the religious and theistic context. Of course, it would be ridiculous for me to attempt to simplify the whole topic of morality in just a few pages, but some clarity is necessary to proceed with its entanglement with the term "God." However, I will not attempt to engage significantly with moral philosophy or its literature, feeling it goes well beyond the scope of this book (and rather misses the point anyway).

First, we must note again that sociality and morality are intrinsically tied together, and the reason is that morality really seems only to make sense in terms of its impact on social structures. If we were to suppose a lone individual on a desert island somewhere with absolutely no possibility to in any way impact any other sentient being in his present or future, we have staggeringly few good reasons whatsoever to talk about his behavior in moral terms. The closest we might come would be with regard to goal-directed behaviors on his part, including the goal of living out this bleak existence as well as might be possible (which arguably could include making the decision *not* to keep living it out).

Further, it is my suspicion that the processes that we might call society-formation or culture-formation have to be understood in moral terms. People gather by some set of coincidences such as geographical proximity, genetic relation, or like-mindedness, and as they interact, rough codes of conduct that govern the group, often implicitly at first, start to take shape. As these become more obvious and concrete, they start to define the group itself, and by a dynamic feedback system, the group can be best characterized by the moral code that defines it. These communities united along *moral frameworks*—sets of moral attitudes and intuitions that define a particular community's moral code—are referred to as moral communities, and as we have discussed, religions constitute *moral communities* with "God" as a symbolic figurehead.

As a worthy aside, moral communities often become ideologically motivated. It seems that the operative difference between a moral community and an ideologically motivated moral community (IMMC, which could be read: "immcee") is that certain elements of the moral framework defining that community have become *unquestionable*. Unquestionable moral attitudes[29] seem to be the defining characteristic that distinguishes a moral ideology from a moral framework. Once a moral framework takes on unquestionable elements, an IMMC is born. Religions are often naturally ideological in nature because part of the very meaning of "God" is "beyond questioning," and so religions often aren't just moral communities; they are often IMMCs. Indeed, a working definition of a religion could be an IMMC that expresses itself in mythological language.

The facts, then, are that we cannot extract morality from sociality, that we have to recognize religions as a kind of social structure known as moral communities, and that moral attribution is attempting to make sense of what morals are and where they come from. In that sense, "God" is probably most readily thought of as an object of moral attribution. Thus, we need to understand morality on some level to understand what "God" means, and morality is about evaluating ourselves and others in terms related to "good" and "bad."

Turning to the research of moral psychologist Jonathan Haidt,[30] we see that psychosocial valuation—how we evaluate ourselves and others—is at least a three-dimensional phenomenon, meaning that there are at least three independent factors that come into play when it comes to evaluating people, including ourselves.[31]

The three dimensions of psychosocial valuation that Haidt identifies are (1) closeness of kin, (2) reputation, and (3) an apparently mysterious third dimension he refers to as "divinity," though he explicitly divorces this idea from being dependent upon any gods.[32] In Haidt's conception, "divinity" refers to that sense of goodness we attribute to people that is pretty much everything else that cannot be explained by kinship or reputation. While I'm not sure this characterization is complete,[33] what Haidt intends by the term "divinity" is not at all mysterious or fictional; it's adherence to a specific moral framework,[34] often measured in goodness, "spiritual" quality, or purity, typically as indicated by engaging in or refraining from certain kinds of behaviors.

Before elaborating upon these topics further, let's be clear on what these terms mean. Closeness of kin literally means family relationships, at one level, and then something that goes beyond that at another. We naturally tend to evaluate our own children, parents, grandparents, brothers, and sisters on a subjectively biased scale, with more distant relations, aunts, uncles, and first cousins getting more benefit of the bias than more distant relatives. We extend this same bias to our friends and, importantly, to our "fictive kin," our brothers and sisters, even parents and grandparents, in some something we identify as important. This behavior is rampant in religion and may even constitute a significant purpose of religion in society.

Reputation is obvious and needs little elaboration other than a brief observation that we often turn to our favorite athletes, actors, and actresses to comment on a topic, even when we have no reason to believe they have any especially valuable insight on the matter. The reason is because their reputation confers upon them a perception of being valued, which is to say "good," in many respects.

"Divinity," which I feel permanently needs scare quotes around it, is a bit more complex. Haidt introduces the concept in his book *The Happiness Hypothesis* by discussing his voyage to an Indian ashram.[35] By being flung into a world with an obvious sense of "divinity" and a moral code built up around it—notably one that is very different from his own, a point he bafflingly seems to mistake for his own culture *not having one*—he became aware of this third dimension in how we evaluate ourselves and each other. He noted especially that the people there would have inner sanctums in their temples into which no one but properly purified religious adepts could enter. Furthermore, there was a requirement to maintain purity of these spaces by being sufficiently spiritually "clean" and by removing one's shoes. That moral code and the sense of purity conferred by attending to it is an excellent example of the phenomenon that Haidt elucidates under the term "divinity."

Closer to home, if you have ever called someone a "douche"[36] for behaving in a way you deem socially unacceptable, you know about "divinity." That's how we arrive at that kind of evaluation, and it is precisely the way in which we make sense of the slang use of the word "douche," which is unlikely to be either coincidental or overtly misogynistic (as sometimes gets implied). Haidt identifies the negative end of the "divinity" scale as being *disgust*, and that emotion is the appropriate one associated with cleaning out any orifice of any human body. (Don't believe me? Imagine sharing a toothbrush with someone. That feeling you just felt while imagining it is disgust, and the social evaluation you would extend to anyone engaging in that behavior is the "down" direction in the "divinity" dimension of psychosocial valuation.)

More generally, we all evaluate people in these ways, positively and negatively, all the time, and since we're usually not as explicitly aware of "divinity" as we are closeness of kin or reputation, much of it seems invisible and, indeed, almost inexplicable from our own perspectives when it comes to sorting out just how and why we made these evaluations.[37] Our moral lives, though, are thoroughly infused with exactly these kinds of judgments, and we use them to evaluate ourselves and others. We use such ideas to place ourselves and those we have some interaction with somewhere in the landscape of social valuation that we constantly use to navigate socially and to like ourselves. Notice how it is irrelevant if we dress up our "divinity" dimension in ideas of magic, transcendence, rituals, and either sensible or arbitrary taboos and compulsions for us to be engaging in it all the time.

As mentioned, "divinity" seems to be best understood in terms of adherence to or rejection of an operating moral framework, and moral frameworks are defining characteristics of cultures, subcultures, and moral communities, including religions. This is why that person you called a "douche" does not evaluate himself as a "douche" but sees you, who evaluates him exactly that way, as a "freak." Each belongs to a different subculture with a slightly different take on the moral framework defining the overall culture they are a part of, and those frameworks don't line up exactly.

Of greatest importance to realize about "divinity" is that it is a significant component of moral valuation, it being the aspect of how we evaluate ourselves and others according to our moral intuitions. As its given name implies, it is often tied up with notions of the sacred or the divine, though this seems only to add a veneer of mystery and undeserved gravitas to a very mundane phenomenon. Still, "God" has a lot of room to hide in "divinity," and since we see it has nothing to do with theism and everything to do with very human moral frameworks, it is to those that we we will now must turn our attention.

To understand moral frameworks, again we should turn to Jonathan Haidt, who along with Craig Joseph has put forward an intriguing model called moral foundations theory.[38] Haidt and Joesph identify (at least) six fundamental axes that characterize how people's moral values manifest. These dimensions are care/harm, fairness/cheating, liberty/oppression, loyalty/betrayal, authority/subversion, and sanctity/degradation.[39]

Moral foundations theory gives us a compelling way to make sense of *moral frameworks*, which would be ways that particular cultures, subcultures, communities, and individuals exhibit moral values and moral reasoning. The idea of a narrowly applied framework-moral system is all we need to make sense of the moral aspect of what people mean when they say "God," so even if Haidt and Joseph's theory doesn't withstand scrutiny, the idea that there are culture-specific sets of values is sufficient.

According to their model, as I interpret it, individuals, informed by the moral communities they are parts of, will adopt particular moral frameworks and engage in psychosocial evaluation in the "divinity" dimension according to those. Religions, denominations, and churches form a fantastic hierarchy on which this effect can be seen to play out in regard to moral beliefs attached to the idea called "God." Christianity, for instance, asserts certain moral points of view; Baptists interpret those in a particular way; the First Baptist Church in Anywhere, USA, interprets those according to their own take on them; and John and Jill Churchgoer in the middle of the seventh pew each have their own ideas that are variations upon what their pastor is preaching.

It would make sense to talk about the moral frameworks involved at each level in this tower, and in many cases, each would be a slight variation on the level above it. Importantly, John's and Jill's moral frameworks, though individual, would be strongly informed by the First Baptist Church (along with other influences), and those would be strongly informed by the set of beliefs that define the Baptist denomination of Christianity, all of which can be understood under the umbrella of Christian moral frameworks.

Importantly, because of this fact, at each level there would be a real sense of community to which John and Jill feel they belong. They are individuals who are members of a church of like-minded people who are members of a denomination of extended brothers and sisters who are connected to all Christians by some sense of relation "in Christ." As a result, we would have no reason to be surprised if John or Jill evaluated Bill, a Catholic who they do not know, as "probably a good person," because Catholics are Christians, and yet with more reservation than Sally, another Protestant with views nearer in line to those of the Baptists.

The chief weakness of moral foundations theory, however descriptive it is of how people's moral values take shape, is that it lends itself naturally to some degree of moral relativism. If moral community A has these framework-moral values, and moral community B has these other framework-moral values, how might we determine who is doing better at being moral? Is it even possible?

Enter again into our discussion neuroscientist Sam Harris. His 2010 book *The Moral Landscape*[40] effectively bulldozes moral relativism and, among other things, argues that all attempts to make sense of moral reasoning should, in principle, be able to be evaluated upon a metric somehow tied up in what he refers to as "well-being and suffering." Haidt rejects Harris's case as overly simplistic and overly compatible with only two of the (at least) six moral foundations: "harm/care" and "fairness/reciprocity."[41] Harris has his doubts, writing, "It seems possible, for instance, that these five foundations of morality are simply facets of a more general concern for harm/care."[42] (Of note, at the time when Harris wrote this, Haidt and Joseph hadn't yet realized that one of their foundations needed to be split into two, creating six in the process, explaining Harris's statement of five foundations instead.)

Both Harris and Haidt are right, though at first it seems impossible. Haidt and Harris seem to be talking about the same topic on two different levels. Haidt is talking about the moral systems that individuals and groups adhere to, and Harris is clear that he is talking about something else that would include *evaluating the moral frameworks themselves*, and thus the people who adhere to them by extension.

The necessary observation supporting Harris is so simple it should hardly bear mentioning:[43] the goal of all moral systems is to enable human (and other sentient) flourishing, whatever its constraints. This is a point Haidt recognizes. In his 2012 book *The Righteous Mind*, Haidt writes about all animal behavior, saying, "Brains evaluate everything in terms of potential threat or benefit to the self, and then adjust behavior to get more of the good stuff and less of the bad."[44] He supports this point further in an endnote claiming it is "a reasonable approximation of the central claim of behaviorism."[45]

Thus, on some metric relevant to human flourishing, we should be able to evaluate moral frameworks on their merits and failures, a point Haidt also grasps on some level.[46] Despite the objection that human flourishing is a notoriously difficult subject to make sense of, Harris asks us to recognize two plain facts about it. First, it, in principle, can be done (and done with scientific means). Second, we are under no burden to feign complete ignorance on the subject of human flourishing, however incomplete our knowledge of it is now or is doomed forever to be.

This, incidentally, is why I insist on using awkward terminology like "framework-moral system" to talk about the values that define moral communities. The frameworks these people are using are, indeed, built of moral values, but those values might be poor choices for *human values*. Harris is attempting to set an objective standard by which moral frameworks are to be judged, even if that renders many of them abjectly immoral.[47]

All of this psychological and philosophical theory is presented here to facilitate the understanding that when people use the word "God" to refer to something to do with morality, all of it is specific to particular moral frameworks. What this implies is that "God" cannot be divorced from morality at the level of moral frameworks. Still, following Harris's insights in *The Moral Landscape*, we can carve a path to divorce those moral frameworks from a better understanding of morality. Particularly, in light of this set of ideas, we face three facts.

First, "God" and morality are probably intrinsically tied together at the level of moral frameworks. Second, religion, and belief in God, offer only one of many possible roads to building moral frameworks, and not only are there secular alternatives, but there is also no choice but for them to exist in every kind of secular community at every level. And third, we are already equipped to perform limited evaluation of those moral frameworks and reject clear failures. We could also note that among the possible ways to build moral frameworks, because of their reliance on faith and adherence to Iron Age (or older) traditions, barbarism, and mythology, religions, and thus belief in God, are likely to be *particularly bad ways* humans go about building moral frameworks that are truly moral.

Theistic Approaches to Morality

We have good reasons to suspect that theistic approaches to morality are, generally, bad ones. The primary reason is faith; a secondary reason is the reliability of where theistic morality originates; and a tertiary reason is a belief in the absolute, unchanging, and universal nature of the moral preferences of an alleged deity.

There are two major problems with faith that lead us to believe that theistic moral frameworks are likely to be bad ones. First, faith is an unreliable method of justifying a belief as it is, in even the most generous definition, simply an extension of trust that the belief is true despite not being able to know that fact. Second, faith is inherently closed to belief revision, which means that any bad moral guesses it has made are very likely to be slow to change. These two issues are significant reasons for us to expect, knowing nothing else, that theistic moral frameworks might be worse than those not beleaguered by faith-based adherence.

The secondary reason is the origins of theistic moral frameworks. It's tempting to argue that the source is what gets claimed to be "divine revelation," which is incidentally indistinguishable from either making things up or certain kinds of mental illness, but it is slightly more nuanced than that. Theistic moral frameworks arise from the moral frameworks adhered to by certain people, usually branded prophets, church fathers, or the like. These people belong to certain moral communities, misidentify their source of morality with a deity, and then, by "revelation" or theological pondering, commit the central ideological error of deciding that their moral attitudes are the uniquely correct ones. Note, of course, that if we had reasons to believe that they arrived at their claims of moral truths via methods that we could deem reliable—something akin to a moral science—we'd have reason to pause and take them somewhat seriously. As it stands, this is not the case, and so we have precious little reason to believe that they possessed the enormous luck and insight to have arrived at the uniquely perfect moral attitudes and precepts from their obviously limited perspectives.

A third reason follows from the first and second: theistic moral frameworks often take on the impressively arrogant baggage of claiming perfection, universality, and timelessness. History, however, could literally be written through the lens of the failures of this exact belief. Because morality is very complicated, because we lack good ways to ascertain legitimate moral truths (to say nothing of absolute, universal, timeless, and perfect moral truths!), and because we've seen theistic moral frameworks left with their pants down so many times so far, we have every reason to believe that a theistic moral framework has less chance of being a good one than one possessing enough humility to recognize that such arrogant bags are better left behind.

Here's a fascinating example of what I mean. It is plausible that much of the hangup the Abrahamic religions have regarding human sexuality—and much of this being extraordinarily damaging to women—boils down to a morally codified set of beliefs based upon a lack of knowledge about genetics. If today one erroneously believes, as was common under the rise of the Abrahamic religions, that paternity is impossible to determine in a child borne by a woman who has had sex with more than one man, then one is likely to adopt a great many framework-moral attitudes that prize virginity in girls and ownership of women in general. (The reader is here encouraged to pause to think of as many abuses of women as possible that might have grown out of this dead-wrong "timeless, universal, and absolutely perfect" set of framework-moral beliefs.) These beliefs are harmful on their own, of course, but what makes them particularly horrific is their stunning resistance to revision by better information. We have good reasons to believe that had these moral attitudes not been given theistic force, they might have given up their damaging grip on the world much earlier than what actually happened, which is not yet.

Note, of course, that none of this is to say that there aren't excellent moral attitudes to be gleaned from religious frameworks. There are, lots of them. Religion, maybe more than any other effort humanity has engaged in, has sought to provide moral understanding, and the world's religions are often very sophisticated proto-psychological systems. Their weaknesses are in lacking a reliable method to sort the good from the bad, a certain reluctance to reject attitudes that are clear moral failures (slavery, among others, stands out), and believing a bit too righteously in themselves. There are certainly worse moral frameworks possible than the world's current major religions have provided us with, but we have very good reasons to believe that we'd do better without notions of a perfect deity clouding our capacity for moral reasoning.

Furthermore, note also that theistic moral systems are antithetical to anything like a science of morality—and moral philosophers who naysay any hope of a science of morality would do well to remember this. A science of morality would have to be built upon two primary supports. First, we'd need some means to evaluate moral frameworks against one another, as discussed previously. Second, a science of morality would require a rejection of the notion that any moral attitude is sacred—that is, exempted from reconsideration and the possibility of being overturned by properly obtained data. Theistic moral frameworks are centrally—and by definition—concerned with making certain moral beliefs sacred. This attitude is a straightforward summary of why we should regard any theistic moral framework with suspicion.

Summary

"God" means something when people say it, and that something is related to their attempts to meet their psychological and social needs. These needs manifest primarily in three ways: attributional, for a sense of control, and regarding sociality. When people talk about their "God," they are talking about how they make sense of ideas that allow them to meet or ignore these needs, and they are telling us that they do not really know how to meet them.

Of particular importance among all of these needs is making sense of morality because it is fundamental to effectively all social and many personal needs to understand what "good" and "bad" mean. Thus, the notion of framework-morality is intrinsic and inseparable from the notion of "God."

Framework-moral attitudes are used to engage in psychosocial valuation (of self and others) in order to make sense of the moral communities, cultures, and broader societies that we live in. Importantly, psychosocial valuation takes place in at least three independent ways, the most subtle of which has been termed "divinity" because of its obvious connection to a sense of moral purity and the obsessive levels with which the religious attend to it. "Divinity," though, is probably best understood as adherence to the moral framework—and the symbolism that is tied to it—that prevails in a particular moral community, nothing more.

Moral frameworks, we must realize, can be judged independently on some yet-to-be-identified metric related to human flourishing, which is the goal of moral systems in general. Figuring out the relevant metrics and applying them will form the foundations of a moral science that will reveal moral relativism to be the staggeringly bad idea that it is.

Finally, we have every reason to believe that theistic systems are likely to house relatively bad moral frameworks. Their methodology (revelation and faith) is not reliable, and, more importantly, their openness to belief revision is insufficient. This problem is a *feature* of theism that follows from the unquestionable—that is, ideological—nature of beliefs about God.

Notes

1. Hood, Hill, and Spilka, *The Psychology of Religion*, p.7

2. *Ibid.*, p. 20.

3. This definition came from Google.

4. Hood, Hill, and Spilka, *The Psychology of Religion*, p. 44

5. Haidt, *The Righteous Mind*, p. 313. In the given quote, Haidt refers to what I termed "intuitions" as "the elephant," drawing upon a rather brilliant metaphor of his that our psyche works rather like an elephant (the intuitions and emotional mind) that does as it wants with a rider (our rational mind) on top exerting only a little control and mostly trying to make a coherent and sensible picture out of what the "elephant" is up to.

6. Hood, Hill, and Spilka, *The Psychology of Religion*, p. 45.

7. Here, Hood, Hill, and Spilka cite M. B. Lupfer, K. F. Brock, and S. J. DePaola, "The Use of Secular and Religious Attributions to Explain Everyday Behavior," *Journal for the Scientific Study of Religion* 31 (1992): pp. 486–503.

8. Here, Hood, Hill, and Spilka cite M. Hewstone, "Attribution Theory and Common-Sense Explanations: An Introductory Overview," in *Attribution Theory:*

Social and Functional Extensions, ed. M. Hewstone (Oxford: Blackwell, 1983), pp. 1–27; and B. Spilka, P. Shaver, and L. A. Kirkpatrick, "A General Attribution Theory for the Psychology of Religion," *Journal of Religion and Health* 22 (1985): pp. 98–104.

9. Hood, Hill, and Spilka, *The Psychology of Religion*, p. 45.

10. To avoid overcomplicating matters, saying that "God" is an attribution is a simplification of the more accurate idea that the powers alleged to the mythological character called God and "His" agency are the referent of the religious attributions that rely upon it.

11. On the claim that fundamentalism, so characterized, qualifies as delusional, note that it satisfies Karl Jaspers' three criteria for that state: falsity of belief, conviction, and incorrigibility. The existence of nonfundamentalists, in fact their majority, proves that the needs can be met in other ways. Incidentally, *quasi-religious* beliefs held with similar tenacity would be grounds for an identical psychopathology.

12. At this point, I feel it is appropriate to raise a quibble with the terminology employed by Hood, Hill, Spilka, and other psychologists of religion who use the terminology "naturalistic attribution" versus "religious attribution." The proper term for religious attributions, as the sentence in which this note is embedded clearly indicates, should be *superstitious* attributions. Not only is it more general and more accurate, it is also the better contrast to "naturalistic," in this case.

13. Because moral attribution is one of the key roles played by the term "God" for most believers, the observation made at the beginning of this chapter that perhaps no word has generated more controversy than the world "God," among other things, is easily understood. To this day, most human beings seem simultaneously completely sure and yet almost completely clueless about morality because we lack a reliable method backed by consensus for determining moral truths (i.e., a science of morality).

14. Hood, Hill, and Spilka, *The Psychology of Religion*, p. 17.

15. *Ibid.*, pp. 17–18.

16. Here, Hood, Hill, and Spilka cite J. P. Gibbs, *A Theory About Control*, (Boulder, CO: Westview Press, 1994).

17. Here, Hood, Hill, and Spilka cite S. A. Vyse, *Believing in Magic: The Psychology of Superstition* (New York: Oxford University Press, 1997).

18. Hood, Hill, and Spilka, *The Psychology of Religion,* p. 18.

19. Here, Hood, Hill, and Spilka cite G. L. Welton, A. G. Adkins, S. L. Ingle, and W. A. Dixon, "God Control: the Fourth Dimension." *Journal of Psychology and Theology* 24 (1996): pp. 13–25.

20. Here, Hood, Hill, and Spilka cite D. G. Myers and E. Diener, "Who Is Happy?" *Psychological Science* 6 (1995): pp. 10–19.

21. Hood, Hill, and Spilka, *The Psychology of Religion,* p. 17.

22. *Ibid.,* p. 18.

23. This is consistent with Hood, Hill, and Spilka, who note, "Self-control can thus be viewed as personality's 'moral muscle,' and therefore in some sense as a master virtue" (*The Psychology of Religion,* p. 18). They go on to note how sin and vice are often seen as failures of self-control, citing particularly research done on the so-called seven deadly sins in traditional Christianity (gluttony, sloth, greed, lust, envy, anger, and pride).

24. Here, Hood, Hill, and Spilka cite M. B. Brewer, "On the Social Origins of Human Nature," in *The Message of Social Psychology,* ed. C. McGarty and S. A. Haslam (Cambridge, MA: Blackwell, 1997), pp. 54–62.

25. Hood, Hill, and Spilka, *The Psychology of Religion,* p. 19.

26. Here, Hood, Hill, and Spilka cite C. J. Lumsden and E. O. Wilson, *Promethean Fire: Reflections on the Origin of Mind* (Cambridge, MA: Harvard University Press, 1983).

27. Hood, Hill, and Spilka, *The Psychology of Religion,* p. 19.

28. As the situation often manifests, all that is clear to both parties who claim to believe in "God" is an assumption that the other believes in essentially the same concept called "God," whether that is true or not. However often this is true—and it may be quite frequently—it also makes a claimed belief in "God" one of the easiest ways to perpetrate frauds of any sort involving bypassing the natural distrust people have regarding strangers. This may form one facet of the problem of sexual abuse that takes place in churches.

29. These are sometimes referred to, not quite correctly, as *dogmas,* although I prefer the term *supertruth.* At any rate, lacking a science of morality, it's a special kind of arrogance or ignorance that allows a person to believe her own moral attitudes are so likely to be correct that they aren't open to rational debate.

30. It strikes me as important to note that I find Haidt's *interpretation* of his moral psychology difficult to agree with, although his work and observations are incredibly interesting, thought-provoking, and impressive.

31. Jonathan Haidt, *The Happiness Hypothesis: Finding Modern Truth in Ancient Wisdom* (New York: Basic Books, 2006), chapter 9, pp. 181–211.

32. *Ibid.*

33. I, for instance, can find nowhere in Haidt's three-dimensional valuation schema for "appearance." Whether it is just to judge on appearance or not, we certainly do, and research bears out that we often will rate attractive people as being more morally good than unattractive ones on that superficial judgment alone. Perhaps he files it under "reputation," but it seems not to fit squarely in that dimension.

34. In this sense, I might suggest that "framework-moral" is a better term than "divinity" for this third dimension of psychosocial valuation.

35. Haidt, *The Happiness Hypothesis*, pp. 140 and 188–189.

36. This rather crude term enjoys rather enormous popularity currently for precisely the reason described—enforcing subtle social hierarchies in overlapping moral communities along the "divinity" axis. The term "cool," among hundreds of others, mostly slang, serve exactly this same function.

37. Evolutionary psychologists such as Steven Pinker might argue that we can pin down satisfactory explanations for our psychosocial valuation schema, but that doesn't change the fact that, from our own perspective, it happens in practice all but invisibly and for reasons that are often entirely inscrutable. See Steven Pinker, *How the Mind Works* (New York: Norton Books, 1997).

38. An excellent summary of moral foundations theory is present in chapters 5–8 of Haidt's *The Righteous Mind*.

39. Haidt, *The Righteous Mind*, pp. 146–148 and 197–205.

40. Sam Harris, *The Moral Landscape: How Science Can Determine Human Values* (New York: Free Press, 2010).

41. Jonathan Haidt, "Moral Psychology and the Misunderstanding of Religion," *Edge.org*, 21 September 2007, http://edge.org/conversation/moral-psychology-and-the-misunderstanding-of-religion. Of note, it is not clear why Haidt chose to represent what he has otherwise called "fairness/cheating" as "fairness/reciprocity" here, but to understand his moral foundations theory reveals it likely to be a

clerical error of some kind since he defines fairness in terms of reciprocity. See *The Righteous Mind*, chapters 7–8 (pp. 150–216) for more detail.

42. Sam Harris, "Response to Jonathan Haidt," republished from *Edge.org* to Sam Harris's blog at samharris.org, 13 September 2007, http://www.samharris.org/index_dev.php/site/full_text/response-to-jonathan-haidt.

43. And it wouldn't bear mentioning if moral philosophers didn't seem to be so bent upon forgetting this simple point about all of their beautiful abstractions.

44. Haidt, *The Righteous Mind*, p. 64.

45. *Ibid.*, p. 387.

46. *Ibid.*, pp. 114–115. Haidt writes, "I'll set aside the question of whether any of these alternative moralities [to "Western," to summarize briefly] are *really* good, true, or justifiable" (emphasis in the original). Even without the context, which is to say that he thinks we should understand what moral frameworks are for before judging them, it is clear that Haidt thinks that they *can* be judged. My contention is that Harris is paving the way for that judgment.

47. As this may be potentially confusing, what I am claiming is that morality is a *constrained system* defined upon the constraints of human psychology, which, however malleable by culture and other influences, are not infinitely malleable. Indeed, as a moral framework defines a moral community, and thus broadly, a culture, my assertion here is that some cultures do better by the constrained system of human psychology (and the experiences of all sentient life) than do others, and we can use the realities of that constrained system to determine which cultures are more successful at meeting the goals of moral systems than others. Note, however, that I'm only arguing that there's some objective standard by which we could compare moral frameworks—which implies only an underlying goal of morality—not that there is necessarily one correct, or even optimal, moral approach that is true in all times and for all people.

CHAPTER 5

"GOD"

The groundwork is all laid, and now we can make sense of the term "God" without relying upon theism. Before doing so, I would like to warn the reader ahead of time that this chapter is abnormally long, comprising nearly a third of the entire length of this book. It is advised to treat the various sections of this chapter as miniature chapters in their own right.

I also wish to impress upon the reader again that the forthcoming analysis rests firmly on two observations: (1) very many perfectly sane people, some very intelligent and some very educated, have believed in, still believe in, and *must mean something by* whatever they call "God," and (2) whatever that something is, theism—the belief that it is a deity that actually exists—does not capture it.

The claim then is that "God" exists, and God doesn't exist. "God" is an idea, an abstraction, that people use to attempt to make sense of the world. The primary application of this abstract idea is to meet various psychological and social needs, to fulfill them by imaginary proxy, or to pretend that those needs do not need to be met.

In broad summary, the psychosocial needs that people use "God" to satisfy or ignore fall into three categories: attribution (making sense of the world and what happens in it), control (overcoming a sense of powerlessness), and sociality (community building and finding context for self and others within that community). God, which does not exist, is a mythological construct representing the combination of ideas that get called "God."

What Does "God" Mean?

In a sentence, "God" is an abstract idea that is used to meet, fill, or ignore a variety of core psychosocial needs experienced by almost all human beings. The primary needs "God" exists to address relate to meaning making, control, and esteem, which manifest in terms of attribution, control, and sociality in various complicated and overlapping ways.

"God," as an abstract idea, is often accepted as an *axiom*, or a presupposition, in the pseudo-philosophical framework called theism. Usually, "God" is understood in theism as being a deity, which is a mythological construct. The purpose of this construct (consciously derived or not) is to stand as a seemingly concrete emblem of the ideas captured by the term "God." We can understand theism, then, as a pseudo-philosophical point of view that makes the mistake of taking a certain kind of mythology seriously on its own terms, and thus we can reject it for the mistake that it is.

Human needs are very complicated, particularly when it comes to understanding complicated elements of reality like the working of the universe, the phenomenon of life, the human mind, experience, culture and society, and, literally, all manner of things. "God" was invented, bit by bit, to provide explanations for everything, meeting our needs for attribution (explanations), giving us a feeling of control over our circumstances, and allowing us to make sense of ourselves and each other in the cultures in which we live. "God" is the ultimate ad hoc concept, filling every gap exactly as it needs to be filled specifically because it needs to be filled.

Still, we must realize that when people say "God," not only do they mean something that refers to things that are real, those things are *very important* to them. They are talking about their core values. They are talking about how they make sense of and see the world—often the only way they know and have ever known to do this. They are talking about how they resist feelings of powerlessness. They are talking about how they understand themselves and the communities they live in. For believers, whatever mythology may lay on top of these very important somethings, these are at the heart of what they mean by the word "God."

For these reasons, when nonbelievers say, "there is no God," which we have every reason to believe is true as they mean it, they are saying something utterly unintelligible to believers. Believers believe there is a God because they *know* there is a "God"—a set of ideas that speak to and help them make sense of their core needs and values. What they don't realize is that they are making a mistake by accepting theism. By accepting theism, they mistake a myth for reality.

Since beliefs in "God" stand to serve the individual psychosocial needs of believers, it is unsurprising that specific beliefs about "God" manifest in ways almost as varied as the believers themselves. The different needs that people have manifest in different ways, sometimes slightly and sometimes significantly, and thus they seem to worship different "Gods." This, really, is the problem with trying to shoehorn mythology onto reality when subjects like psychology are so much better suited to the task.

An Analogy to the Sea

In case it seems strange to suggest that God is a mythological object instead of a philosophical one, it is appropriate to draw an analogy to another mythological object that stood in place of a complicated real-world phenomenon that people, at the relevant time, did not possess the tools to understand in its own terms.

A couple of millennia ago, human beings in the Mediterranean had great need to sail and yet, for all their experientially gained knowledge of sea, sky, and storm, they had precious little knowledge of the underlying influences that give rise to maritime conditions. In fact, they lacked even the kind of information-gathering capacity—weather data from both near and far, particularly—that would produce a truly reliable understanding of wind and wave. Lacking a cogent natural description for the important but apparently temperamental sea, among the other reasons humans engage in such behaviors, the mythological figure called Poseidon was invented to satisfy many of the attributional and control needs lying at the center of practicality in a seafaring culture. (Sociality needs would have come up under cults to Poseidon as well.)

These days, Poseidon is easy to understand as a mythological construction used to account for the various and sometimes unpredictable behaviors of the sea, and thus the fates of sailors and those living upon the coasts. To the persistent question of why the sea behaves in the way it does, Poseidon, or his will, became an answer. Here, then, we see people applying a superstitious attribution due to the want of a natural one, and Poseidon became a mythological construct standing in place of the real machinations of wind and water. As a result, to the persistent concern that the sea would destroy ships and lives, propitiating Poseidon, in all of its magnificent worthlessness, became a method. The stories and "knowledge" about Poseidon grew over time as people used this model and did the best guess-and-check they could, as except in dreams and delusional states, no one actually ever met Poseidon.

Eventually, humankind outgrew Poseidon. By observations, including inaccurate but naturalistic ones, we gradually came to realize the processes that legitimately govern oceanic and atmospheric behavior. This process accelerated tremendously as the scientific methods grew following the Enlightenment, and that acceleration increased as we started to develop technology like satellites to gain more understanding of the relevant dynamic processes. As a result, Poseidon fell away into irrelevance so profound that (nearly) everyone today realizes with pristine clarity that he was always a mythological account utilized to attempt to make sense of some underlying physical reality.

God is no different except in the physical process being mythologized. God is a mythological entity used to account for a wide variety of psychological and social needs. On one level, like Poseidon, people use God to account for their need to understand and feel a sense of control, but these needs are psychological. Like that which happened with Poseidon, by centering our attention on the operative psychosocial needs, together with ways we can fulfill those needs, the need for God evaporates. In that moment we can see with staggering clarity that, for all this time, we've all been wrong about God.

A Metaphor: A Mixer Board

As the topic of making sense of the term "God" without theism is amazingly complex in the details (though simple in premise), I will employ the metaphor of a mixer board to make clear how individual uses of the term "God" manifest from the milieu of possibilities roughly outlined above. To be clear, a mixer board, as I am meaning it, refers to the device employed by audio professionals, sometimes called a soundboard or mixing console. It is an electronic device used to combine, modify, and route various audio signals, and the visual image useful to my metaphor is a large desktop board covered with knobs and sliders that adjust the "volumes" and "timbres" of the different possible reasons a person employs her individual God-concept.

One can imagine a knob on this mixer board for "moral attribution," one for "teleological (purpose) attribution," one for "spiritual attribution," one for "sense of active control," and so on, for all of the categories listed above and perhaps a few more. We can imagine that each knob runs from zero to ten.

Each individual will have unique psychosocial needs that are defined by her individual psychology, her culture, her religious beliefs, and other influences. In order to attempt to best fill those needs, or, at least as often, to pretend they are filled though they are not, each individual will have set the knobs on her "God" mixer board to the levels that seem to best satisfy them, so far as she can tell. When she says "God," the unique "sound" that comes out of the board is what she means by that word, even if it happens to be contextually dependent and variable from time to time and situation to situation.

Maybe, for instance, she will be like the Vatican scientists, who are noteworthy for accepting essentially all of established science and recognizing its immense utility, including over theology, in describing and explaining the physical universe. If so, she undoubtedly has her "phenomenological attribution" (which uses "God" to explain the physical processes of the universe) knob turned close to zero, noting the possible exception of the phenomenon of the universe itself. Perhaps instead, she will be like those Muslims who believe that the Qur'an is a perfectly scientific book, and that knob will be near ten. Instead, maybe she will be like most American mainline Protestants and have that knob set somewhere, to guess, between four and six.[1]

The same would apply to other knobs on the board, one or more for each need, be it a kind of attribution, control, or sociality. Some would be set higher for this person and lower for that, and others would vary in other ways. In every case, the unique expression produced by that combination of notions, all of which exist in service to satisfying various psychosocial needs the person has, would be what that individual means by the term "God."

One thing to understand is that "God" isn't the mixer board. In this analogy, "God" is essentially the overall effect created by the arrangement of knobs on the board. In reality, "God" is the combination of abstract ideas employed in the service of satisfying the underlying psychosocial needs represented by the knobs. Obviously, each individual believer will have a different arrangement of the knobs and thus a different "God." On the other hand, all of these takes on "God" aren't so widely varied because they all serve the same underlying goal, and many are similar because religions are ideologically motivated moral communities that demand a great deal of conformity of belief.

The "Master Volume" Knob—Transcendence

One very important knob on the mixer board is akin to the master volume knob, a single knob that turns everything up or down. It would be easy to mistake devoutness or sincerity for this knob, but it is actually a belief in a kind of *transcendence*. The use of this term here simply entails "going beyond the obviously human," especially in terms of the individual mind grappling with it.

This knob doesn't exactly define "God." Instead, the role it plays is more of a necessary condition to regarding the whole "sound" that comes out of the board as being Deity. In the metaphor, when this knob is turned up high enough, the concept it represents (as the total sound coming out of the board) becomes synonymous with the Divine, and calling it "God" makes sense. Below that threshold, other terms like "idealization" may fit better, although there is no need to split hairs for our purposes. We just want to understand what believers mean when they're talking about "God." Part of what it means is that their "master volume" transcendence knob is turned way up. The role of this knob is to make the beliefs in question *sacred*, which is to say revered and set aside from examination and reconsideration, and thoroughly beyond the human ken.

It may be easiest to understand this knob by one of its common historical applications: the notion of divine right to rule of kings and queens. Besides making the royals feel more important and entitled to their crowns, among other psychosocial functions, we should wonder what the "divine right to rule" implies. What does it mean? Among whatever else, the divine right to rule implies *unquestionability* of nobility. No one alive has the authority to question divine right. And where does this notion of being unquestionable come from? Transcendence of the "human" level of affairs.

It does not matter that this transcendence (of reality) is effectively imaginary.[2] What matters is that with "God" comes a sense of being so far beyond, or transcendent, of the worldly that it cannot be questioned. The matter is believed simply to be outside of the bounds of human influence. When it comes to the notion of "God," it seems that this knob cannot be turned all the way up, not because of some limitation, but because it apparently doesn't have a maximum setting.

To understand, in commenting on human nature, moral psychologist Jonathan Haidt has written, "We humans have a dual nature—we are selfish primates who long to be a part of something larger and nobler than ourselves."[3] He also notes that a good understanding of the term "sacred" is "the ability to endow ideas, objects, and events with infinite value."[4] The term "God," then, can be—and often is—understood as an infinitely larger, infinitely more noble something of which we are a constituent part. This is unsurprising if we understand that "God" is most frequently meant in moral terms, and morals are sets of social constructs, which are abstract ideas, that define moral communities so seamlessly that they seem simply to be "how it is."

"God" is a special case, however, in that being conceived of as a deity, the notion is taken fully beyond anything human and utterly perfect, to boot. By qualifying one's morals and beliefs as *perfect*, reality and any hope of effective communication are left completely behind. In terms of the "master volume" metaphor, then, the effect of this transcendence knob is to make certain aspects of the idea called "God" so loud that contradictory thoughts simply cannot be heard, and it seems to be the case that such an incredible volume is always a possibility.

The term "transcendent" isn't entirely a bad one, then, although "sacred" and "holy" are functionally synonymous. The term "transcendent" fits because the notion of "God" is meant to rest beyond humanity and the universe. A convincing case—not least based upon the fact that "God" is often imagined to be infinite[5]—could be made that "beyond the universe" really means *abstract* like all other timeless, eternal, absolute truths. (These are all timelessly and absolutely true as abstract ideas that follow as a consequence of applying logical methods to various presuppositions.)

This last parenthetical comment merits a brief aside. In the second chapter of my book *Dot, Dot, Dot*,[6] I sought to provide an argument for why we might become confused about timeless, absolute (read: abstract) truths as being real and discoverable. The analogy that I used was the abysmally boring (to adults) children's board game called Candy Land.[7] In that game, cards are shuffled before the game starts, and they are drawn in turns by the players. The entirety of the game is determined by the order of the cards, though, and so it is utterly impossible to win a game of Candy Land by skill. Once the cards are shuffled, the winner is determined, and doing the work of "playing" the game is simply a matter of sifting through an outcome that already "exists" to see what it is. Likewise, in axiomatic systems like those used in mathematics, philosophy, and theology (which includes a "God axiom" of some kind), once the axioms and a logical system are chosen, all of the truths of that axiomatic system are determined as well—whether we will ever or can even know them or not. In that sense, mathematics and philosophy have a real sense of *discovery* to them that is merely an illusion of the fact that timeless abstract truths determined within any axiomatic system are defined in precisely the moment the axioms and logical system are chosen. The hard work is sorting out what they are, and in all that effort it is easy to lose sight of the original presuppositions that were chosen as the scaffolding for the whole system. Most of theology is the never-ending job of twiddling the "God axiom" to overcome the challenges that always eventually reveal it to be merely abstract instead of real.

The core, however, of this master knob, when it comes to understanding what "God" means to those who believe in it, is that the set of ideas called "God" is taken to be timeless, perfect, true, and ultimately *unquestionable*. The glue that holds this preposterous mental architecture together is called "faith," which seems to be the invocation of a number of cognitive biases employed specifically for the purpose of deflecting questions that would challenge belief. Confirmation bias—the bias by which we seek information that confirms what we already believe—is likely to be chief among those defining faith, although other biases, such as *optimism bias* (a bias to believe that if there's a good chance that something bad can happen, you are especially likely to be an exception), play clear roles as well.[8]

"God" being unquestionable is obviously one of the most troublesome aspects of belief and a core one that needs to be addressed. Philosopher Peter Boghossian has offered a wonderful method based upon Socratic dialogue to help break the bonds of the glue of faith by leading people into being willing to question the unquestionable.[9] He calls that method "Street Epistemology" and outlined it in tremendous detail in his book *A Manual for Creating Atheists*.[10] Boghossian's method will receive more attention in chapter 7.

Throughout all that follows, then, bear in mind that core to the definition of "God" that believers take nearly always includes an aspect of being *unquestionable* and beyond human influence. Note further that any ideology or moral community can end up turning up the master volume knob beyond the "unquestionable" threshold, effectively enshrining their core values as their "God," even if they don't call it by that name. This phenomenon is seen in nonbelievers as well as in believers, and it is exactly what we must be on guard for as we continue to break the bonds of faith and progress into a post-theistic world. Being post-theistic does not automatically imply being postreligious or postideological, and those are the real problems that we need to deal with.[11]

Breaking It Down

The rest of this chapter will be dedicated to investigating as many of the knobs on this board as I have been able to identify. Each is a facet of what the term "God" means for some believers, though perhaps not all, and always in varying degrees. Each individual believer will have her own unique expression of what "God" means in terms of the "sound levels" of each knob and, in some cases, what is meant by them (the "timbre" on that channel). This can help us understand why religious beliefs about "God" can manifest in such divergent ways all under one name and yet with such surprising similarities.

Importantly, and central to the thesis of this book, not one of the facets that goes into making up the meanings of the term "God" relies upon theism in any respect whatsoever. In fact, none require dualism (the view that the mental/spiritual constitutes another realm of reality separate from the physical) at all. The goal here is to present a fully natural explanation of the term "God" and to hope that the observation mentioned in the last chapter, that most people prefer natural attributions to religious ones when available, will help us move rapidly and effectively from a world in which theism gets any intellectual or moral quarter. We will see that theism is simply the wrong way to think and talk about "God."

Again, I remind the reader that these categories are hopelessly interconnected, and so pulling them apart as is done here is an artifact of presentation only. I leave it to the reader to synthesize these ideas into a functioning whole that makes sense of the complex web of notions passing by the name "God" and the varied array of psychosocial needs those thoughts are meant to attempt to address.

Since the linear format of a book requires that I present these ideas in some order, I have chosen to order them according to the three major categories (attribution, control, and then sociality) and then by my best guess at their relative importance within that category (and thus likelihood that that particular knob will be turned way up in an individual believer). Of note, however, a sense of control is very high on the importance list, so that it, as a category, appears after all of the attribution modes is not meant to imply that control is less important than all attributional needs. The same applies to sociality as well.

One last note before proceeding is to address a lingering question: should we use the term "God" in this context and say "God" (in scare quotes) exists? No, I don't think we should at all. It seems that bad metaphors help maintain the God delusion, and that shouldn't be encouraged. What is of importance is recognizing that when believers say "God," they mean something quite specific that isn't merely an imaginary friend. It is more accurately a mythologized collection of abstract ideas used to allow them to meet or ignore important psychosocial needs that are very real and very significant.

Moral Attribution

Morality, central as it is to the human experience, is confusing, and anyone who has read moral philosophy knows that our seemingly best thinking on the matter only makes it worse. Religion simplifies morality by providing the heuristic of making it the desire of a deity. Attributing moral salience to "God" makes morality seem real, which makes it more concrete and thus acceptable, and it also makes morality absolute and final, which is to say simpler. These are very attractive notions when it comes to dealing with an inherently complicated subject like morality.

Religious apologists, those who defend religious beliefs professionally or otherwise, often make the case that "God" is the only possible source of moral values. In fact, they often assert that only on theism can we "ground" moral values. What all these apologists are saying is, "'God' is how I give attribution to the existence of morals." Statements like these, often offered in defense of theism, actually make my point for me. If "God" is taken as the foundation for morality, what the word "God" means is an explanation for morality. It is of little use at this point to take the bait and reargue an obvious in an attempt to defeat theism: what philosophers sometimes call the "evidential problem of evil."[12] It is sufficient instead to realize that theism is just a bad attempt to satisfy a need for moral attribution.

For many religious believers, it is simply impossible for them to conceive of "right" and "wrong" without anchoring them against the divine, meaning that they've turned their unquestionability knob way, way up. This has reliably—and unsurprisingly—resulted in the execution of some of the greatest atrocities imaginable. If one's beliefs about right and wrong are in any way awry and yet believed to be perfect and beyond question, we can bet upon horrible results.

Additionally, to have a discussion with almost any religious person whatsoever about the possibility of not believing in God often quickly brings up objections on moral grounds. Some of these are tiresome, like that nonbelievers can't be good people—or can be but cannot make sense of their goodness. Others are apparently terrifying, like that without "God," there is no divine law and thus we would all be raping, stealing, and killing one another on whatever whim we choose. (As we will see, this statement is not actually terrifying at all.)

Notably, the attempts made by some prominent atheists to divorce belief in "God" from morality, however noble, is impossible.[13] This mistake arises from a failure to understand that religion, and thus belief in "God," has (framework) morality as its central occupation.[14] *Religions are moral communities*, and "God" is an idea central to many religions. In fact, moral attribution—the attempt to explain and make sense of morals—is one of the chief purposes for which the abstraction called "God" is invoked. For many, if not most, believers, "God" *is* primarily how they make sense of their sense of right and wrong.

This case should be easy to make. Surveys in the culturally Christian West reveal that many people who have no other discernible connection to religion self-identify as Christians because they want to feel like they are good people.[15] Identifying oneself with a culturally dominant moral community immediately has the result of helping someone identify himself as a moral, thus good, individual. These baffling surveys merely reflect that fact, together with the fact that much of the West has Christianity at the core of its cultural roots, whether anyone likes it or not.

These observations should convince us that whatever is meant by the word "God," it has something important to do with morality. If this is not convincing enough on its face, bear in mind that in the Abrahamic religious traditions, the generally prevailing notion of "God" carries three main qualities: omnipotence (all-powerfulness), omniscience (all-knowingness), and *moral perfection*.[16]

For almost all believers, "God" means first and foremost how they make sense of moral values, including the absolute perfect expression of those. "God" is the idea that allows them to make sense of their morality.

Going further, we need to understand not just *that* but *how* the notion of "God" manifests in the moral context. The obvious answer is probably wrong. "God" is very unlikely to be taken as an idealized symbol of the believer's own moral intuitions. While this approach would explain a great deal of why a believer's "God" always seems to approve of and hate the same things he does, it seems not to be how believers conceive of morality via "God."

At the individual level, instead of being an abstract image of a believer's moral attitudes, "God" is better understood as *an idealized concept of the morals that the believer would exhibit if only she were a better (or perfect) person*. "God" becomes the universalized standard of the moral code that each believer believes she would have if only she were what she deems as morally perfect. It is an impossible standard by its very nature and yet appeals to the individual's moral intuitions in a way that seems utterly profound from within.

Of course, the individual doesn't often manufacture these moral attitudes whole cloth. Notice that her morals are based upon a sense of how she should be *if she were a better person*. We have to make sense of how such an assessment could be made, and much of the input is necessarily cultural, starting with the closest unit of culture, family.

Many do not have the time or resources to carefully work out their own moral values, and even among those who do, most are likely to import a broad swath of them from the culture they find themselves in. We are immersed in our cultural background from the moment we are born, and our very sense of self is built partially in relationship to it.[17] It is fed to us by our parents, our teachers, our older relatives, and literally everyone and everything around us as we grow up learning how best to behave. The prevailing culture we find ourselves born into—particularly as it manifests in our parents and other close authority figures—offers a profound, perhaps unshakable, sense of what it would mean to be a better person, and the less morally reflective someone is, the more powerful this sense is likely to be.

There are serious consequences to using a figure of moral attribution defined in terms of what one would be if only he were morally perfect. Among the consequences of such a conception of "God" are a few rather obvious and glaring ones. These include a tendency for believers toward self-blame, having a sense of God on one's side, an irresolvable (even in principle) debate about moral values, and the inextricability of morality from a belief in "God," each along with all of the attendant problems created by these difficulties. For instance, many are taught, if religious, to believe that they have failed "God" if they sin, where sinning means failure to meet a perfect framework-moral standard (which "God" abstractly represents). It also casts "atheism" as being inherently "against my morals," which goes a long way toward accounting for religious negative attitudes toward nonbelief.

Take a moment to appreciate the exquisite masochism here. "God" is an emblem of how people feel they should think or act if only they were framework-morally perfect, and "sinning" is somehow failing to meet that standard, which is inevitable, if only by mistake. And what have they failed in the process? They have failed their own standard, one they set up literally to be unable to meet! The failure, then, is in establishing the standard they call "God" in the first place and then in blaming themselves for the inevitable.

We all make mistakes—a point that religious evangelists are often quick to point out in an effort to try convince people that they are making sense when they accuse everyone of being sinners. And this is the sinner's lament, a haunting melody of needless self-indictment and guilt sung in oughts, shoulds, and if onlys. That the chords are often sinister, rigid, and composed by institutionalized authority, however well-meaning, only makes the song the sadder.

All that is required to release the grip of this wight is to realize that moral perfection is a scam. We make mistakes, and this does not imply that we break laws of divine importance. To fall short of an idealized take on the moral values held by an imaginary idealized self is not only normal, it is inevitable. And to whatever degree we hold ourselves to a high ethical standard, it is a staggering and harmful error to believe that some personified embodiment of this idealization will hold us morally accountable for the inevitable and that we therefore require its forgiveness.

Another consequence of idealizing morality in this way and calling it "God" is that it is unreasonably easy to reach the conclusion that "God" is on one's side. A belief that "God" is on one's side is one of the most dangerous views a human being can have since it can literally be used to justify *any* atrocity on "moral" grounds.[18] All that is required is for a believer to maintain that her (framework-dependent) moral sense is objectively and universally valid, which is exactly what happens when the unquestionable transcendence knob is turned up to Deity.

Related is that debates about moral values become irresolvable when "God" is brought into them. If two people have even slightly different conceptions about moral values, and both of them believe those to be divine universal truths about the world, then there is no method to settle the disagreement. By the nature of the abstraction called "God" a resolution simply isn't possible. Each person, informed by her religious traditions, family upbringing, cultural attitudes, and a myriad of other influences, holds an idealized conception of moral attitudes that are supertrue, which is to say that they're regarded as truths whether they are true or not, typically placed beyond the reach of reconsideration.[19]

Absent the error of turning an idealized moral sense into a deity, many of the same moral disagreements still arise, but they do so lacking the absolute conviction of assuming divine right. The result is conversation.

Simply recognizing that "God" is an abstract notion, one that happens to include an idealized sense of one's own moral framework, is enough to diffuse the worst part of the tension. The ensuing conversation has open doors to a more conscientious consideration of facts about the world and the conscious beings who experience it and thus how those give our moral attitudes weight.

Many authors have made excellent appeals on these grounds that we must divorce morality from belief in "God," but it may be that such adjurations are in vain. Those who do not believe in "God" can easily conceive of moral values free from religious belief, but for those who believe, moral attribution is often a critical component of the meaning of the term "God." In fact, it is likely to be the central component for most believers, and so, for them, "God" effectively *means* morality. Asking people in this situation to conceive of "God" without the attendant moral component is like asking someone to imagine hydration without water.

To really drive this point home, consider that among evangelical Christians it is a common attitude that without "God's" Law, there is only "man's law." Further, since no one *has* to follow man's law, then if there is no "God," we should expect to see everyone stealing, raping, and killing at a whim. In fact, self-identifying atheist blogger Amanda Marcotte produced a relatively famous statement about this misconception, one that I was initially strongly inclined to agree with. Marcotte wrote,

> Atheists are routinely asked how people will know not to rape and murder without religion telling them not to do it, especially a religion that backs up the orders with threats of hell. Believers, listen to me carefully when I say this: When you use this argument, you terrify atheists. We hear you saying that the only thing standing between you and Ted Bundy is a flimsy belief in a supernatural being made up by pre-literate people trying to figure out where the rain came from. This is not very reassuring if you're trying to argue from a position of moral superiority.[20]

On the surface, Marcotte seems to make a point. Her assessment, though, misses it. The believer who says these things is simply expressing the fact that to him, the word "God" *means* something in which moral values are included integrally, even the most basic and obvious ones. Such believers cannot have morality extricated from belief in "God" because "God" is largely used as a synonym for morality, plus a handful of other abstract notions. Thus, when people make a case that there would be no morals without God, they're really just uttering, from their own perspectives, a kind of tautology: morals exist because morals exist.

As a final note on consequences, Marcotte's statement shows us the threat of misunderstanding "God" by trying to treat it on theistic terms. With a proper understanding of what "God" means, it isn't all that scary to hear believers express such thoughts—they're simply saying "without morals, we wouldn't have morals." By taking "God" under theism, these sorts of statements are properly horrifying, and that fear contributes to more misunderstanding and escalating tensions between those who believe and those who do not. Without common ground, there is very little we can use to resolve those tensions and see one another eye to eye. We cripple ourselves from understanding believers by being wrong about God in taking theism seriously.

Now, there is a fairly good reason that moral values are tied into people's conceptions of "God," and it has to do with the function that morality plays in our societies. Morality, as discussed in the previous chapter, is a tool of psychosocial valuation, meaning that we evaluate ourselves and others along moral lines. As a reminder, psychosocial valuation arises in at least three dimensions, one of which is very abstruse and critically tied to our moral attitudes. Jonathan Haidt calls it "divinity," a term I dislike and that seems to get its name from the sense of goodness that is often conveyed by adhering to "sacred" or "holy" expectations, though this definition seems circular.

Because "divinity" is best understood as being framework-moral, which is to say "doing well by one's cultural expectations" (not unlike the oppressive Hindu dogma called *dharma*), it offers a road paved with good intentions directly to being able to feel moral justification in ideas and actions that are patently harmful (like the abhorrent Hindu caste system). An evangelical Christian who is enculturated with the idea that homosexuality is a sin is behaving in a "divine" way when he attempts to enact legislation that would openly discriminate against gays and lesbians. In a society lacking sufficient countervailing moral attitudes, it would be "divine" to order or participate in their painful and violent deaths, and

I am not merely being hyperbolic here; these things, and worse, happen *routinely* in the world today upon this very justification.

Complicating the matter, "divinity" is also largely invisible, particularly in largely secular societies. The reason "divinity" can be so difficult to see is something like familiarity blindness. We're all enculturated into a great many of our moral attitudes, and it can be very difficult even to conceive that there are other ways to conceptualize "good" and "bad" than in the ways provided by the cultures we are born and grow into.

More importantly, it is very difficult to see "divinity" for what it is: a set of vaguely defined but poignant abstract cultural constructs. For these reasons, it is very easy to misidentify it with the Divine, that is, with "God."[21] Our abstract ideas about moral values and the perceived need to explain what they are and where they come from becomes the backbone of theistic belief for many believers. As a statement of how easily we can fall into that line of confusion, notice that Haidt, a nonbeliever, still felt inclined to call this enormously significant aspect of psychosocial valuation by the term *divinity*.

In fact, in talking about "divinity" in his bestselling book *The Righteous Mind*, Haidt writes the following.

> Our theory, in brief, was that the human mind automatically perceives a kind of vertical dimension of social space, *running from God at the top* down through angels, humans, other animals, monsters, demons, and then the devil, or perfect evil, at the bottom. The list of supernatural beings varies from culture to culture, and you don't find this vertical dimension elaborated in every culture. But you do find the idea that *high = good = pure = God* whereas low = bad = dirty = animal quite widely.[22] (emphasis added)

There is a downside to this, of course. To borrow a term from Isaac Asimov, the "hijacking" of morality by religion lives at the core of religious belief. More likely, moral piracy is a primary *raison d'être* for the organization of cultural values and superstitions into religions. The downside, then, is that to divorce morality from religion is an impossible goal. All that can be achieved on that front is to break the perception that religions possess a monopoly on morality. The necessary observation is that religions lack a reliable method for coming up with a properly good moral framework.

In summary, religious believers frequently use the term "God" in large part to refer to attribution for their framework-moral values. They understand morality in terms of "God," so for them, the word "God" means something like "that which makes morals make sense."

Purpose (Teleological Attribution)

If an explanation for moral values is first among the meanings of "God" for many believers, attributing the purpose of human existence often runs a close second. There is deep existential horror in the idea that our lives are ultimately meaningless; that we are flames that flicker but for a little while in an incomprehensible eternity. Thus, we are meaning makers, and we make meaning of our lives and call it a sense of purpose.

The small things—and most of them are quite small—that we can do with our small hands, often inadequate minds, and our parochial designs may matter, but they seem not to matter *much*, and so we despair. Instead of accepting our humility and doing what we can with dignity, the existential dread tied up in the ghost of meaninglessness deceives us into concocting grand Manichaean dramas in which we cast ourselves in roles that pretend to be in humble personal service to the greatest power in the universe— who loves us and ordered the world specifically for our uses. Delusions of human grandeur become a talisman against all the pitiful frailty they seek to cover up, and we call what allows us to believe in that self-aggrandizing talisman "God."

The topic of purpose by design is called "teleology" by philosophers, and the field as it applies to "God" covers a number of commonly held notions. The term teleology arises from the Greek *telos*, which means "end," "purpose," or "goal," and so the various abstract notions that people hold about the role that "God" plays in making humanity an intended goal of the universe are attempts at teleological attribution. These are attempts to explain why we exist, both in terms of our role in the broader cosmic drama that religions imagine and in terms of the roles that we must play in our own lives.[23] As usual, the process of deifying the abstraction renders it universal and objective for those who believe in it.

In this regard, a hugely significant part of the amalgamated collection of abstractions that define "God" is a belief in a universal, objective, and perfectly noble purpose in life, sometimes believed further to be around which the entire universe was brought into existence and is ordered. The hues of this fantasy vary in intensity according to how fundamentalist and solipsistic an individual believer is, some far more obnoxious and garish than others. All of them seek an imperishable object against which their lives can be given imperishable meaning, even if it's just a comfortable reverie.

Of course, it certainly seems to be the case that for our lives to be really worth living, we need a purpose in life, and what purpose could be better than a universal one of cosmic proportions? Since the notion of purpose is perhaps even more ephemeral than that of moral values, it is no surprise that the abstractions that comprise it get wrapped up in what people call "God," the abstraction that plays the role of a master attribution.

Again we can turn to psychologist Jonathan Haidt for a relevant insight. Haidt's research has indicated that an important component of human flourishing is, indeed, a sense of purpose in living.[24] We seem to be most fulfilled when our lives are filled with challenges that we feel able to meet when we apply our individual skills and talents.[25] And almost everything in the previous sentence can be tied to theological undertones with very little effort. We have our "'God'-given" talents; we are "blessed" to be individuals to whom "God" gave a unique purpose; "God" called us to a purpose, job, or ministry; and "God" will never give us more than we can handle—so despite our challenges, they were tailored to us by "God" to be risen to, providing us with an all-important, even if inscrutable, purpose.

This observation about the importance of having a sense of purpose to human flourishing is corroborated strongly by the researchers who investigate what are called "blue zones." Blue zones are socio-geographical regions named for the fact that demographers chose to use the color blue to indicate regions with the highest average life expectancies. By investigating people who live in blue zones like Okinawa and Ikaria, Greece (dubbed "The Island Where People Forget to Die" in a 2012 *New York Times Magazine* piece[26]), a number of lifestyle factors have been identified that contribute to a long, fulfilling life. Among them, a sense of purpose in life plays a significant role.[27]

But where does this sense of purpose come from? What is the meaning of life? These philosophical-sounding questions rest at the center of much of theology, as theologians pretend to offer an answer in the form of the wide variety of abstractions all called "God." Like so much going by that name, it serves as a proxy for the attribution it pretends to be, a way to take an abstraction and pretend that it explains itself. And thus out of existential dread mismanaged gets poured the foundation for real-world horror, like the vilification and destruction of those who threaten the fragile illusion of purpose by holding heterodox beliefs.

So, as with morality, in a need for a sense of purpose we have a consequential notion that does not appear to admit easy attributional answers, and we have an abstract, idealized "God" to satisfy the resulting disquiet. "God" as a sense of universal purpose is, perhaps, more pitiable than most other aspects of the abstraction that goes by that name. This is because our purposes in life are hardly mysterious or inscrutable; they're just small and local: caring for ourselves and each other, raising our children, doing our jobs well, being good citizens, trying to make a difference for other people present and future, searching for and hopefully obtaining happiness, and helping those we love to do the same.

Somehow purpose becomes a critical part of "God" because we seem unable to accept our smallness, our locality, our relative powerlessness, and our lack of importance outside of the speck that we share for mere eyeblinks of time. All that we have that can matter seems never to be enough for us, and so we have to pretend there's so much more, possibly because we know it will all fall away. We all will die. Humanity will go extinct. We're powerless against it, and we yearn for control. Thus we invent "God," an idea to hide ourselves from this rather pitiable need.

We pretend a great deal in service to this need too. We pretend that the universe was brought into existence for life, by which we mean intelligent life, by which we mean human beings, even if we throw in a nod otherwise (say, to our beloved pets). We pretend this is the purpose—the *telos*—of the universe. We go on to pretend, in consequence, that the human vanity is the fruit of all existence and, particularly, of the tree of life. And we pretend that our duty, in deference to all this pretense, is to honor, worship, glorify, and, in stunning blindness to the irony, humiliate ourselves before the abstract idealization of meaningfulness.

Teleological attribution is endemic to religion. Religions exist largely to satisfy psychosocial needs for people, importantly including attribution, and understanding purpose in everything and ourselves is a major element of that. Recall, in fact, that Hood, Hill, and Spilka, laying out the foundations for their summary of the psychology of religion, referred to the need underlying attribution as *meaning making.*[28]

Though more common with more conservative believers, even those quite liberal with their beliefs are commonly caught empty-handed by the question, "without 'God,' what purpose is there to life?" Put less despondently, we often hear, "'God' gives me hope and meaning." The theme is the same. People are crying out for big-picture meaning, a background narrative into which they can set themselves and thus judge themselves and, at the psychological level, deem themselves decent enough for their small efforts.

Like with so much existential dread, the fear of death is tied into our need for purpose and the abstract "God" we invent to pretend to satisfy it. We tend to feel that death simply cannot be, for the thought can be beyond endurance that, like all other living things, we are yet for a while and then die. Since eventually we all die, it is easy to mislead oneself into believing that no human-centered purpose has any lasting value. Sadly, then, much of our self-importance, and the self-esteem that rides upon it, demands a grand purpose that defeats death, and so obligingly, the "God" we create to avoid grappling with the hard truth is conceived of as the wellspring of eternal life.

Of course, the matter gets sufficiently out of hand with fundamentalists to merit a tangential aside. Creationism, a bag of loudmouthed reactionary rot that began in its present form to respond to the advance in biological understanding known as the theory of evolution, is a prime example of the need for purpose running amok in this way.

However scientifically inept creationists are, they take their theology quite seriously and are aware of the insurmountable problem that biological evolution presents to their beliefs. Thus threatened is their conception of purpose in life, and they are willing to reject one of the most elegant and firmly established scientific explanations of the natural world *en masse* to keep it. The numbers are terrifying, really. Outright creationism hovers around a third in the United States and God-guided "evolution," which is expressly a teleological interpretation of the facts, accounts for a further quarter of the U.S. population.[29] We thus have a good reason to believe that attribution to purpose is what creationists, of either stripe, are seeking to protect because its fulfillment is what they believe gets them to Heaven, allowing them to go on denying death.

To elaborate, in the Christian (and Islamic) religions, "God" created the universe specifically for mankind and further created humans in a separate special act of creation in the image of "God" itself—something of a low-fidelity copy of omniscience (our intellect), omnipotence (our capability to exert mastery over our environment), and moral perfection (that we can be good).[30] Whatever more moderate Christian believers can convince themselves of, creationists know that biological evolution exposes the whole of the Christian narrative as sheer nonsense. Without an act of special creation, the myth is revealed, the redemption is empty, and the core of the purpose of a "Christian life" is shown to be a fraud. Reactionary creationism exists as a flimsy shield that screens their eyes from the sight of the naked emperor.

As a result, religions, perhaps in seeing "God" as their escape from death and purposelessness, often conceive of the purposes of life in terms of "God." To mention one last important example, consider the oft-repeated statement, "the purpose of life is to glorify God," which is sometimes followed with something like, "evil only exists because men glorify themselves."

It seems most likely that what is meant by "glorifying God" is committing to the notions caught up in the word "God" as the perfect standard, both in action and in deed. This includes attributing all good to "God" while apologizing all bad away, a frustratingly duplicitous habit of the faithful if ever there was one. It is unsurprising, then, that "God" is also the core attributive object for the abstract ideal of Goodness.

Saying the purpose of life is to glorify "God" also means putting the notion of what we would be like if we were framework-morally perfect before ourselves in as many regards as possible. What we as individuals want is immaterial (and "evil") against what a framework-morally perfect self would want, or, more to the point, would deny itself. In essence, then, this statement, "the purpose of life is to glorify God," is just an affirmation that the moral and cultural values that we hold are, in some sense, more important than ourselves.

This, then, is where "God" being first an idealization of framework-moral shouldness becomes so deadly. We easily come to believe that the very purpose of the universe and our existence in it is to honor—by which is meant enforce—the framework-moral values we think we should have if only we were worthy of them. Thus, we become Death, the destroyers of worlds.[31]

Believers use the term "God" to talk about their sense of grand purpose in life, attempting to meet a need to feel meaningful and moral, often in a way that carries a sense of universality and permanence.

Psychosocial Contextual Attribution

We need to understand ourselves. Not only do we need to understand ourselves, but we also need to understand ourselves in relation to our society. Indeed, these needs are interrelated. Our sense of self, and the self-esteem that follows from it, is largely defined in terms of how we understand ourselves in the context of the (moral) communities in which we identify ourselves.[32]

Our culture, our community, and our sense of family, actual kin and fictive, all provide the necessary references for who we see ourselves to be, and developing a healthy sense of self-esteem in this regard is a basic human need at the psychological and social levels. Because religion provides an extremely effective framework for succeeding at this goal, "God" plays a significant role in grounding the meaningfulness of the whole affair.

"As a Christian, I . . . " could start a sentence this way to immediately contextualize myself, both for the benefit of those I am speaking to and for myself. And I may finish with, " . . . know I am a forgiven child of God, standing beside all of my brothers and sisters in Christ," which, besides being outside epistemic warrant, calls upon the notion of "God" directly to make sense of who I am, including in relation to those I am speaking to. What makes the sentence meaningful is that "God" clearly means something that has to do with establishing a sense of Christian community.

The speaker of such a sentence uses these ideas to understand himself. He sees himself as a child of "God" who has forgiveness, so he recognizes himself to be imperfect and relatively powerless but cared for and accepted anyway. He stands beside his brothers and sisters, so he is in some important sense equals with them. That relationship is forged "in Christ," and therefore we see that he understands himself somehow in relationship to Christian ideals, many of which are written explicitly in the language of morals and purpose in life. Whatever is meant by "God," and therefore "Christ," it has definite elements of defining psychological and social context for Christians. Analogous statements, changing only unimportant details, could be made for Jews, Muslims, or any other theistic religious believers, including New Age pantheists who see everything as being all One.

As another example of cultural context, consider the Declaration of Independence of the United States, penned by Thomas Jefferson and signed in July of 1776. Its second paragraph famously begins, "We hold these truths to be self-evident, that all men are created equal, that they are endowed by their Creator with certain unalienable Rights, that among these are Life, Liberty, and the pursuit of Happiness."[33] Despite Jefferson's well-known leanings away from the usual takes on Christianity,[34] when outlining what became a core tenet of what the nascient American nation would stand for, he plainly suggested that people are "endowed by their Creator" with fundamental rights. But what "Creator" did he mean? He had cited the "Laws of Nature and Nature's God" instead of the Biblical God just previously to this famous passage.

Rights are moral and legal entitlements, defined as "the fundamental normative rules about what is allowed of people or owed to people, according to some legal system, social convention, or ethical theory."[35] Rights have (framework-dependent) moral components and are secured by a social convention and its legal system, often referred to as a social contract, and so they are a critical part of our cultural context. Whatever Jefferson meant by "Laws of Nature and Nature's God" and "endowed by our Creator," he was seeking to satisfy a need to attribute those laws to something powerful and binding enough that we're in no position to question it—the rights are "unalienable." He must have felt he needed to turn the unquestionability knob up to Deity to securely set attribution for his core tenets of American psychosocial context.

Another aspect of how psychosocial context gets attributed to "God" is in the formation of cultural narratives, these often being expressed in the language and metaphors of the prevailing religion. These religious[36] narratives provide people with a story in which they can understand who they are and their roles in life. Because these stories set the stage for how we understand ourselves, we often understand them in terms of morals—a key element of all community building—and we have every reason to believe that this aspect of psychosocial contextualization is very important to people. Anchoring it in an idea believed to be perfect and real strengthens its effect.

As Jonathan Haidt put it,

> The human mind is a story processor, not a logic processor. Everyone loves a good story; every culture bathes its children in stories.
>
> Among the most important stories we know are stories about ourselves, and these "life narratives" are [psychologist Dan] McAdams's third level of personality.... These narratives are not necessarily *true* stories—they are simplified and selective reconstructions of the past, often connected to an idealized vision of the future. But even though life narratives are to some degree post hoc fabrications, they still influence people's behavior, relationships, and mental health.[37]

He goes on to note that "life narratives are saturated with morality"[38] and that "life narratives provide a bridge between a developing adolescent self and an adult political identity."[39] He then cites sociologist Christian Smith, saying that Smith "agrees with Durkheim that every social order has at its core something sacred, and he shows how stories, particularly 'grand narratives,' identify and reinforce the sacred core of each matrix."[40]

Haidt explains, "We are more likely to mirror and then empathize with others when they have conformed to our moral matrix than when they have violated it."[41] The mechanism by which this is done is intrinsic to the religious approach. Anthropologist Roy Rappaport writes, "To invest social conventions with sanctity is to hide their arbitrariness in a cloak of seeming necessity."[42] This is exactly what religions do, and the sanctity is provided by the contextual story that is the religious narrative. The effect is binding on people, creating a sense of community via parochial altruism. As religious communities are moral communities, religious narratives are likely to provide exactly this environment for people who share in accepting them, and "God" is the master object of attribution that grounds for believers how the whole system works.

A person's humanity is a topic that deserves comment to make this point about "God" as well. Many religious believers make sense of their own humanity in terms of "God." The beliefs seem often to insist that

"God" gave them their humanity or that "God" sets the context for what humanity means. Our humanity, though, has entirely to do with how we treat one another. These, then, are attributional efforts dealing with how people see themselves psychologically and within a social context.

One horrifying consequence of understanding one's humanity in terms of "God" is that understanding the humanity of those with no "God" or a starkly different one is made more difficult. This leads to the worst failures of tribalism and self-righteousness: outsiders are easily dehumanized simply for not believing the same sets of highly implausible notions about the universe.[43] The ability to dehumanize heretics, infidels, and others who stand in some way opposed to orthodox views about the prevailing meaning of "God" has proved itself one of the most damaging and consequential problems with religion, and it is couched squarely in the misattribution of our humanity to "God."

Generally speaking, when people attribute their psychological and social context to "God," they are attempting to create a firm sense of grounding for cultural values and how they see themselves and others in relationship to those. "God" is, in part, the idea to which those values are attributed, and so we can see that part of what "God" means is a sense of psychological and social context.

Abstract Attribution, Especially the Virtues

Truth. Beauty. Justice. Fairness. Liberty. Prosperity. Logic. Goodness. Love. Grace. Forgiveness.

Do these things—these ideas, really—exist?

Each of the items on this list is an abstract idea, and each plays a significant role in human psychology and culture. We have a desire to know what's true whenever possible. We appreciate beauty in the world and in our imaginations. We want the world to be just, for goodness to be rewarded and wrongdoing to be punished. We want to believe in fairness. We want to live in prosperity and contentedness. We know that there are ways by which we can make sense of the world by seeing how some ideas logically follow others. We have an immediate, though often unclear, sense of "the Good" that forms much of the basis for our moral and other evaluations. We certainly feel love and can experience it in many forms. Surely, we hope, our wrongdoings will be forgiven, and we will be accepted in grace, if we submit ourselves humbly and with piety. But do these things exist?

The problem is that it seems at once that they do and that they do not, like is the case with any abstract idea that we can think about with any sense of concreteness.[44] We therefore need some way to understand such abstract notions and give them a sense of reality, and "God" is a commonly used attribution in this regard. Believing that "God" made these things into the world gives them a sense of reality that allows people to ignore that they may simply be mental constructions.

If there is a fear that abstracta are merely mental constructions, it is most likely to be in the fact that they then seem to be somewhat arbitrary. As many or most of our ideals are understood within the constrained systems of human psychology and sociology, however, finding ideals and abstracts arbitrary because they are mental is a kind of throwing out the baby with the bathwater. Still, attributing these ideas to "God" bypasses both this concern and the mental effort that gets applied to dealing with it.

I have been asked more times than I can count, for instance, by genuinely curious and well-meaning individuals how I can make sense of love if I do not believe in "God." Surely these people understand, at least on some level, that there are neurochemical processes involved in experiencing an emotion,[45] and just as surely, this isn't what they mean. They want to know how I can give attribution to the phenomenon of love without "God." In doing so, they reveal to me that when they say "God," part of what they include in that term is the attributional schema by which they make sense of the abstract notion of love.

This particular concept, of course, goes further than mere attribution for the phenomenon of love. We often hear that "God" *is* Love. The very idea of love is given meaning in terms of another idea called "God," and the most obvious reason for this is that if one believes God truly exists, then the sense of love that we all experience is made more real. We face exactly the same situation with the statement that "God" is Good.[46] These are crystal clear illustrations that the term "God" is being employed to make these ideas meaningful and seemingly concrete.

Hope is another abstract tied to emotion that people attribute to "God." It is most likely that hope speaks to people in terms of their underlying fear of powerlessness, which is to say their psychosocial need for control. Hope, in this regard, is something like the opposite of the nagging anxiety that comes with feeling powerless in a situation. In order for this to work, the notion of hope needs some degree of solidity to it, and wrapping it up in "God" and the powers attributed to the Deity are exactly how people can achieve that sense. "God" feels like hope because "God" is the locus of a sense of ultimate control, and people can have hope because their notion of "God" exists as the ultimate controller.

Similarly, there are arguments to Beauty, arguments to Creativity, sometimes rather desperate-sounding appeals to Fairness and Justice, a Natural Law interpretation of Liberty, and gratitude for Prosperity that all place "God" as the relevant object of attribution for these abstract ideals. How can we comprehend the beauty of a glorious sunset or a sonata without "God"? Are we really okay with the facts that sometimes bad things happen to good people and the bad guy gets away with it? A belief that "God" will judge and settle the score often seems to help people deal with these kinds of things. Others wonder where our fundamental liberties come from, if not from "God"? Still others worry that without "God," who will forgive us our trespasses, and from what Grace do our blessings and acceptance flow? Applying "God" to each of these concerns is an attempt to make sense of an abstract ideal that is psychologically important to people.

Among all of these kinds of attributions, perhaps the most fascinating is the abstraction known as logic.[47] Indeed, it is apparently altogether too easy to make a case that logic itself is the "fabric" of the universe, and some rather dubious but sophisticated arguments of this sort have been made. An example of such an argument was made rather famously by cosmologist Max Tegmark, who has identified the fundamental nature of reality as being mathematics.[48] While it seems that such approaches "confuse the map for the terrain,"[49] by which is meant confusing conceptual tools we use to understand reality with reality itself, they provide an attributional framework for why the universe seems to be orderly and why logic seems to succeed at letting us make sense of it.

Abstract ideas are very important to how humans make sense of the world, and the abstract itself begs to be made sense of, to be understood in terms of what it means and in what ways it is real. In fact, entire branches of philosophy exist to attempt to work out exactly what the abstract is. "God" is an easy way to pretend to explain the abstract, not least because "God" is abstract itself, in some ways an extension of the ideal of Goodness. Of key importance, though, is realizing that when people say "God" in these contexts, they mean a sense of understanding for what these important ideas and ideals mean to them.

Phenomenological Attribution

Nature abhors a vacuum, and so does the inquiring mind. Unanswered questions and lingering doubts are, for the wide majority of us, uncomfortable. This discomfort can express itself in healthy ways, like curiosity and the determination to find out, or it can express itself in unhealthy ways, like a feeling of powerlessness and resultant anxiety.

"It may be that people gain a sense of control by making sense out of what is happening and being able to predict what will occur, even if the result is undesirable," Hood, Hill, and Spilka point out as an explanation for our need for an attributional process.[50] The advantages of having a working guess at how things will play out in our futures are obvious enough to require no elaboration, and it seems that human beings have a rather strong need to try to make sense of how and why things happen in the universe we are a part of.

Recall the observation from Hood, Hill, and Spilka that is core to understanding why understanding "God" is critical to going post-theistic:

> the evidence is that most people in most circumstances initially employ naturalistic explanations and attributions, such as references to people, natural events, accidents, or chance.[51] Depending upon a wide variety of situational and personal characteristics, there is a good likelihood of shifting to religious attributions when naturalistic ones do not satisfactorily meet the needs for meaning, control, and esteem.[52][53]

In summary, people seek to understand, and when they cannot understand in a way that is consistent with their prevailing psychosocial needs—many of which are understood in terms of what they mean by "God"—they will turn to religious attributions (to "God") in order to make sense of the world around them. A lot of what people mean by the term "God," then, unsurprisingly is the God of the Gaps that merely serves as stuffing for the holes in their knowledge.

There are obvious big-picture cases where this commonly comes up: the origin of the universe, the origins of life, the phenomenon of consciousness, the phenomenon of society, the phenomena of many positive human emotions, the happenstance of fortuitous coincidence and chance, the phenomena we might collectively call creativity and talent, and so on. Many of these are, in many regards, open questions, and some may never get a thoroughgoing answer. Where we lack knowledge, as is familiar to almost anyone who has admitted lacking belief to anyone who believes, the God of the Gaps is ready to step in and fill the hole. This is applying a religious attribution to fill the hole where a natural one is either found lacking or cannot be accepted for other psychosocial reasons.

Among those listed above, a few particularly noteworthy examples of humanity begging for big answers to hard questions stand out. These include the origins of the universe, the origins of life, consciousness, and the phenomenon of the mental—the apparently nonphysical "universe" in which all of our ideas "exist." Probably for little more reason than that these matters are so mysterious, faith seems to latch onto them and pretend it offers something like a working attributional model to fill them in.

The origins of life are, among these, the least mysterious, though the notion of a certain quality, sometimes referred to as a "spark of life" or "vital force," has been a religious standby offered to explain the distinction between the living and the nonliving. It is very nearly as often attributed to something called "God," in this case conceived in part as the creator (and perhaps sustainer) of life. The attribution runs that "God" is somehow the explanation for the difference between living and nonliving matter.[54]

The origins of the cosmos may lie beyond any epistemic horizon and so be unknowable even in principle, although we do possess the capacity to create fantastic models that we know can and cannot work, given what data we currently or will someday be able to access. Still, under the term "Creator," ultimate origins too are often attributed (hastily and superfluously) to "God." For many, "God" is the object of attribution for the existence of everything.

Consciousness and the mind are, to every appearance, phenomena arising somehow from the activity of nervous systems, at least in animals (including humans), though these present a kind of mystery that many philosophers note may be well beyond our capacity to make sense of—calling it "the hard problem of consciousness" and admitting it may not be tractable. Unsurprisingly, then, the mind and consciousness itself are often attributed to "God," often as directly as possible by asserting that "God" *is* a disembodied mind and *is* consciousness itself, sometimes adding that the human mind somehow interfaces with it (the glaring problems with this line of thought apparently undaunting to those desperate enough to maintain it[55]). "God" is given as the explanation for why we have consciousness and minds, since people don't know.

Of course, the goal in this book is nothing like attempting to give a countervailing explanation for the origins of the universe, life, consciousness, or mind, but instead to illustrate that people, lacking such an explanation, often use the word "God" specifically to refer to a sense that these phenomena are explained. So intense and concrete is this sense that many of the (so-called best) arguments for theism—for the existence of God—are simply arguments that these complicated phenomena *cannot* be explained without appealing to some deity to explain them.[56] Every cosmological argument, every argument to the "fine-tuning of the universe," every appeal to "intelligent design," and many to the unique nature of mental phenomena fall into this category, and they all say the same thing. All these people are saying is that they lack an explanation for these admittedly complex and mysterious phenomena and don't like the resulting feeling of psychological discomfort enough to pretend they have one in a myth they call "God."

When people say "God," then, part of what they mean is a sense that every unanswered question has an answer. Why is there something rather than nothing? "God" wanted it that way. How did life begin? "God" made it. Where does our consciousness come from? "God" gave it to us. Admittedly, these are worse than bad answers; they're nonanswers that frequently stand directly in the way of getting to real answers, but they seem to fill the hole left by the believer's ignorance.[57]

Chance and coincidence play significant roles in people attributing phenomena to a Deity. Due to the fact that there are an awful lot of low-probability events that could happen, it is virtually certain that most people will experience a few of these kinds of things pretty regularly—and that's without even having to account for everyday occurrences that seem meaningful because we're such effective meaning-makers.[58] In fact,

Littlewood's Law, named for Cambridge University mathematics professor John Edenser Littlewood (1885–1977), states that a typical person can expect to experience a one-in-a-million event at a rate of roughly once per month. The chances that someone relatively close to you—or within a church community—will experience such a thing that also contains personal significance, a "miracle," as Littlewood put it, in any given week is a virtual certainty. This result is not intuitive, though, and so such occurrences seem to demand explanation.

Often, lacking a salient reason for why certain fortuitous events have occurred—ranging from being in the right place at the right time to having been uniquely spared a natural disaster and all manners otherwise—people often attribute such occurrences to "God." Indeed, many of "God's" apparently "mysterious ways" and much of its "divine plan" come down to little more than post hoc applications of the special case of the God of the Gaps that might get called the Good Luck God. For our purposes, it's sufficient to recognize that this aspect of the attribution of phenomena is part of what people mean by the term "God."

A particularly ugly problem regarding attributional frameworks including "God" is that it isn't only when we lack natural explanations that we resort to religious ones; it also occurs when the natural explanations before us are too threatening to our deeper psychosocial needs. If the need to maintain one's attributional framework—one that provides a sense of control, purpose, morals, or context—is big enough, it can apparently override accepting facts and lead to their systematic rejection. This fact unquestionably leads to the serious problem of religious denial of science.

The most obvious example[59] of this occurrence is, almost undoubtedly, Christian and Muslim creationism rejecting the biological theory of evolution. In both cases, we confront an impasse between a broader narrative that people need to believe and a plain fact that renders it ridiculous, and so, it seems, the needs often win out and the science is rejected, including by enormous and expensive campaigns. Because of the importance of the religious belief structure, believers like these reduce their feeling of cognitive dissonance by rejecting the less important of the two paradigms in conflict, and in these cases, it is science and thereby the threatening facts it has established. Such is the power of an attributional schema that speaks not only to needs to understand, feel in control, and promote sociality, but that also effectively allows believers to deny the reality of mortality.

For these believers, the need to maintain belief in a "God" that satisfies all of their other psychosocial needs—morality, purpose, psychosocial context and values, and control probably leading among those—is so overwhelming that it conquers the evidenced natural tendency that we have to accept natural explanations for phenomena over religious ones. Creationists, then, aren't necessarily stupid, as unlikely as their beliefs about the origins of the world might be. They're most likely terrified. Unable to cope with the psychological and social pressures of life without an attributional schema called "God" based upon ancient superstitions, they reject knowledge that is justified beyond rational doubt in order to maintain their beliefs.

Creationism, then, provides us a perfect case-study of an instance where other psychosocial needs overpower a natural willingness to accept readily available, widely accepted, and robust natural explanations. It thus provides an interesting window into some strains of the phenomenon of religious fundamentalism. The resistance to belief revision exhibited in fundamentalism seems somehow to be directly dependent on psychological needs (for example, the need for purpose in life, which is tied to needs regarding coping with death, and the need for a sense of control in an uncertain and dangerous world) and social needs (say, the need for a strong, cohesive community in which we can understand and value ourselves) that are more powerful than the need to hold beliefs that are actually true.

Belief in antiscientific nonsense, then, isn't necessarily ignorance. Instead, we can see it as a statement that every educated person who believes in "God" has psychosocial needs that they do not otherwise know how to meet and that at some level are more strongly cherished than holding true beliefs about the world.

And in attribution lies an exquisite trap. People who are raised to see "God" in everything do exactly that. If talking about Christians, we might say that they see the world through Jesus-colored glasses.[60] For them, every attribution that they make has "God" buried somewhere in it, perhaps at the very foundation, and so everything they see through Jesus-colored glasses reinforces the idea that the natural world is full of evidence for "God." In fact, as seen through Jesus-colored glasses, everything is evidence for "God."[61] The attributional schema called "God," then, have to be understood to be self-reinforcing, which makes them difficult to break.

For believers, then, "God" partly means the explanation for all that cannot be satisfactorily explained without threatening the rest of their belief system.

Spiritual Attribution

"Spiritual" is another word that clearly means something—and apparently something important—to many religious people, and almost invariably among them, whatever may be that something, it is typically made sense of in terms of "God." This is also the case for the legions of people who now identify as "spiritual but not religious," many of whom still believe in "God" in some capacity. Thus, the difficulty here is not in making a case that "God" is used as an object of attribution for "spiritual" matters but rather in making sense of what constitutes the "spiritual" in the first place. As with everything else in this book, the effort will be to make sense of the term without appealing to anything dualistic.

The "spiritual" experiences people have arise in what some psychologists would call a *transpersonal* aspect of individual psychology, a term we must unpack considerably. The *Wikipedia* entry elaborates upon transpersonal psychology in this way:

> Issues considered in transpersonal psychology include spiritual self-development, self beyond the ego, peak experiences, mystical experiences, systemic trance, spiritual crises, spiritual evolution, religious conversion, altered states of consciousness, spiritual practices, and other sublime and/or unusually expanded experiences of living.[62]

Though many nonbelievers will immediately experience a rather violent, wrenching twitch in the central joint of the lower limb at many of the words in that description, transpersonal psychology is clearly distinguished from parapsychology (and other nonsense) and is a field that makes substantive contributions to psychology and psychiatry, particularly in situations where one's religious or spiritual beliefs have legitimately led to mental illness. Readers who remain skeptical that spirituality is of legitimate worth to human psychology are also strongly encouraged to carefully and thoughtfully read neuroscientist Sam Harris's *Waking Up*,[63] which attempts to discuss many topics branded "spiritual" without the first hints of the usual kinds of confusions that plague the subject matter.

For the purposes of the goals of this book, however, we need not bother with whether or not nonbelievers accept "spiritual" experiences. Religious believers *do*, and they almost universally tie these experiences, whatever they are, to the concept they call "God." They use this term "God" because they need an attribution that explains these aspects of their experience, be those psychological or sociological,[64] be they rather mundane or profoundly transcendent. Mystical experiences in religion are a central component of what many seek in some context within their religious beliefs and practices.

Some of these experiences in Christianity are often equated with the Holy Spirit or an alleged *sensus divinitatis* (sense of the "divine"—something we can now appreciate with significantly less confusion thanks to Haidt's choice of terminology for the more rarefied aspects of psychosocial valuation). Christians take these ideas very seriously. In fact, they are often taken as *direct experiential proof* of "God's" existence, bearing automatic warrant to hold the beliefs fully rationally.[65]

No doubt a considerable component of this problem is that nearly all of the linguistic architecture in existence for handling the "spiritual" is religious or finds itself within the provinces of pseudo-religious crackpots and quacks. Appreciate that it will be very difficult to get over theism if there are arguments convincing people that the subjective experiences occurring in their minds constitute firsthand evidence for God, and such arguments *do* exist and convince people (confused though they are). Again, the reader is urged to read Sam Harris's *Waking Up*, which presents an excellent treatise on wresting the "spiritual" away from the province of religion and into the realities of the human nervous system and its attendant mind.[66]

The thing is, people have experiences they identify as "spiritual," and religion provides a ready way for people to attempt to make sense of them. Hood, Hill, and Spilka write,

> Survey research has long established that a variety of triggers can elicit mystical experiences. Although *some triggers are consistently reported—prayer; church attendance*; significant life events, such as births and

deaths; and experiences associated with music, sex, and entheogens—one seeks in vain for a common characteristic shared by such diverse triggers.[67] (emphasis added)

Citing work done by Ralph Hood in 1977,[68] they go on to note that,

The fact that both nature and prayer settings *reliably elicit reports of mystical experience in traditionally religious persons* has led some to suggest that prayer should be correlated with the report of mystical experience, particularly if the prayer is contemplative in nature. Hood and his colleagues have documented such a correlation in two spearate studies.[69] . . . This finding is consistent with survey research by Poloma and Gallup,[70] in which meditative prayer was related to experiences of closeness to God. Thus several studies suggest that meditative prayer, as opposed to petitionary or other forms of prayer, relates to both mystical (unity) and numinous (nearness) experiences of God.[71] (emphasis added)

The point, then, must simply be stated: *religious people have "spiritual" experiences in the contexts of their religions, and they need to explain them somehow.* The way that they explain them is usually called "God."

Pause to observe the convenience in making "God" both the substance and the account of human "spiritual" experiences. "Spiritual" experiences that are interpreted religiously are almost always set in a person's own cultural narrative, and in not-unfamiliar narratives in the rest of cases. No native Amazonian that has never heard of Jesus has ever had a spiritual experience or revelation of Jesus, and none ever will.[72] This is unsurprising for a number of reasons. To skip the obvious, our spiritual experiences play out within the architecture of our individual psychologies, and a great deal of the shape of that architecture is formed by the cultures in which we find ourselves.

To understand what people mean by "God" in the sense of the "spiritual," it is helpful to recognize that "spiritual" matters seem to refer to at least three distinct things that have nothing at all to do with otherworldliness. These are a social sense of spiritual goodness (understood in terms of framework-moral values, especially "divinity"), a personal quest for contentedness and fulfillment in life, and the transpersonal, meaning the mystical and self-transcendent.

The social aspect is perhaps the easiest to understand, and it is, indeed, largely already covered by the earlier discussion of moral attribution and its connection to social contextualization. Primarily, once a sense of the sacred is intentionally attached to a sufficiently positive evaluation in the "divinity" dimension, we obtain a framework-moral structure in which the "spiritual" can be sought in terms of "purity," as defined by the framework-morality at play.[73]

The role of framework-moral purity in this regard is extremely easy to see by the almost ubiquitous sense of "spiritual" matters being attended to by adhering to dietary and other behavioral taboos; employing particular rituals to sanctify, invoke, or purify a space, meeting, object, food, or otherwise; and by engaging in symbolic acts of "purification" like baptism, dipping one's fingers in holy water,[74] ritual fasting, and so on. Often these activities are imbued with a sense of "spiritual" meaning in explicitly moral terms, as understood by the prevailing framework-moral system, and they are all elements of symbolic psychological and social contextualizing—trying to be a good person, seeker, adept, or disciple, along with reintegration with the broader community after transgressions.

What is critical to realize is that while religions make this activity overt, nearly all human beings use exactly these kinds of behaviors—many either dietary[75] or related to sexuality—and then use them to judge themselves and others. The religions make it explicit and often highly visible, say via specialized clothing or headgear, allowing us to identify who is and isn't a "holy" man or woman often at a glance. Further, communal behaviors like meals offer obvious clues—we allegedly can know something about how "good" a Jew is by how attentively he keeps kosher. What is critical to understand is that this sense of social goodness is part of what people mean when they crave the "spiritual," and it is part of what they attribute to "God" in order to make sense of it.

The second arena in which the "spiritual" obtains psychological relevance is the application of these particular attitudes to the self. We want to see ourselves as good people, and so the self-reflective aspect of a psychosocial purity ethic becomes relevant to us as well.

Additionally, this category of "spiritual" needs refers to whatever is meant when people say, as they commonly do, "it is good for the soul." And take a moment to appreciate that "good for the soul" is a big deal to people.

An enormously popular series of books, collectively having sold millions upon millions of copies, outlines hundreds of little thoughts, ideas, and activities that constitute "Chicken Soup," that is, comforting nourishment, "for the Soul."[76]

Think about times when you might have said that phrase yourself, even if you know good and well that the "soul" doesn't literally exist and is thus a metaphor for, well, *something* (that happens to be psychological). Ice cream is good for the soul. Kicking back and not working, maybe watching a hilarious comedy in the process, is good for the soul. Getting out in nature is good for the soul. Music is good for the soul. By way of contrast, note that nobody ever says, with the exception of some very enthusiastic[77] accountants, that making out a budget for the next six months is good for the soul.

These soulful activities are, in a sense, centrally concerned with the pursuit of happiness and the release of suffering, if only momentarily. They are, then, attempts to seek contentedness in the moment. Even that very enthusiastic accountants would at times say making out a budget is good for the soul reinforces this point. Their statement is a reflection of the fact that we do derive this sense of fulfillment in life from engaging in challenging and useful tasks in which we have interest and the necessary talents and skills to do well. Positive psychologists call this state of being "flow" and rank it very highly in terms of finding happiness and fulfillment in life.[78]

When people talk about wanting to "be well—mind, body, and spirit," this is part of what they're talking about, along with some of the social aspects of the "spiritual." We can scoff at the quaintness of calling it "spirit" all we want, but we do ourselves no favors to ignore the very real psychological needs being summarized by that term. Further, we do not help people break free of their attachment to religion by denying the "spirit" without honoring clearly what people mean by it. Lacking a better way to understand it, people will continue to attribute it to "God."

A third aspect of "spiritual" is the most mysterious and challenging to address, and Sam Harris's *Waking Up* does an excellent job breaking the attachment of this aspect of "spirituality" to religious language and belief. These transpersonal needs speak to our psychology in a more profound way than momentary escapes into happiness and contentedness, or periods in which we can set aside some of our troubles. These are often referred to as being "mystical" and "transcendent," and they talk about a peculiar and yet altogether positive state of consciousness in which the sense of self becomes entirely irrelevant. This state of self-transcendence is what Harris refers to as the "diamond" in "the dunghill of esoteric religion,"[79] one he hopes with that book to pluck out of superstition and nonsense to the betterment of humanity.

These states of mind are significant enough to the psychology of religion that in their textbook on the topic, Hood, Hill, and Spilka devote two full chapters of fourteen to them (and a third concerning conversion experiences, many of which would fall under this umbrella). We can infer that for many millions of people, "spiritual" experiences and states of mind are a significant part of the psychological milieu that serve as the basis for their desire to believe. Being dismissive of this fact because of the word "spiritual" only gives believers more reasons to assume nonbelievers don't understand something that they do—something very important that they call "God."

Whatever they mean by it, the "spiritual" is something that billions of people legitimately seek, may even need, and the glimmers of these states of consciousness motivate them to religious attributions to "God" in the lack of better ones. My point is that when people say "God," part of what they mean is how they understand and attempt to satisfy these aspects of psychological and social need.

Control

Much in life is broadly predictable, such is the incredible power of statistics, but in the details it is often baffling. We know our atmosphere is turbulent and do reasonably well with making sense of the coming weather, but we can only predict the devastation wrought by tornadoes just minutes in advance—and frighteningly imprecisely. We know that we each will die, and worse, that our loved ones will, though we remain ignorant of both the hours and the causes of these deaths until those draw near, sometimes immediately and unexpectedly. Examples of these kinds abound.

On predicting possibilities within all of life's uncertainty, actuaries make a respectable living, but even their masterpieces are vague and impressionistic. The world is variable, often dangerous, and sometimes calamitous, and human beings have a psychological need for control in uncertain circumstances. The theme is human powerlessness, and it lies at the center of most of our feelings of vulnerability and fear. This need is huge, perhaps utterly central to the human struggle and the very foundation of many of our other needs, and we imagine "God" to pretend we have it satisfied.

Our need for control comes in several flavors, and three of them bear mentioning: self, passive, and active. The need for self-control is best understood in terms of other needs, especially social, so it will not be discussed in this section. The term "passive control" here refers to a sense that there are controls in place in our environment that help reduce the sense of uncertainty and risk that we are confronted with. Take "God's" plan, for instance. In contrast, when the unthinkable happens, we often feel a profound need to act, to do something—anything—to gain control over the situation. And thus, even those with an unshakable belief in "God's" plan petition him frantically with desperate prayers to change it in an emergency. The application of various behaviors, be they superstitious or legitimate, in order to gain a sense of control of our circumstances constitutes what is here called a need for "active control."

Active Control

People often turn to "God" when they have a desperate need to be able to do something about circumstances and yet cannot do anything else. In this sense, belief in "God" is a coping mechanism. Psychologists of religion Hood, Hill, and Spilka devote a significant portion of a chapter of their textbook on the psychology of religion[80] to this topic. Religion, they note, plays a major role in the process of coping, which they say is "at the heart of life,"[81] writing,

> In our view, stress, whether it involves harm/loss, threat, or challenge, reflects a situation in which meaning and control are in jeopardy. We may have difficulty making sense out of a situation, or be unable to master it. Religion is one way these needs are met, and the worldwide prevalence of religion may testify in part to the success of faith in attaining these goals.[82]

They go on to note that one of the mechanisms that people use to attain this sense of control is prayer, utilized as a coping mechanism, devoting several pages to the topic. They write, "Religious activities, especially prayer, are usually regarded as positive coping devices directed toward both solving problems and facilitating personal growth."[83] Particularly, they make note of petitionary prayer, which I view as a method of seeking an active sense of control over a bad situation. They write,

> petitionary prayer is the most common kind of prayer offered, and though it is treated negatively by some religionists, others have repeatedly averred that "petition is the heart of prayer."[84] Capps further terms it "the crux of the psychology of religion."[85] [86]

When someone wails in desperation to "God" for help, soliciting the prayers of anyone willing, he does two things. He reveals his need for control in a situation that he has no control over, and he needs reassurance that he is not alone in hoping beyond hope for help that cannot come. Thus the call for prayers in times like these exhibits a social function in addition to its primary utility, a coping mechanism used to wrest a sense of control over stressors to which he is but a victim.[87] "God," the imagined executor of petitioned prayers, is an abstract notion to which people attribute the power to petition for help when no other option seems within reach.

Of course, religious activities that seek to exert control over the world also include ritual, and it is well-known that religious people often engage in rituals in attempts to ensure some kind of outcome or another. The easiest and most immediate examples come from ancient religious festivals, laden with ritual, used to ensure a good harvest, a safe voyage, or some other desirable circumstance, and these can be quite elaborate. Others, including the requests for forgiveness, which Catholics will readily identify as being quite ritualistic in nature, seek to bring control over one's wrongdoing nature (according to the prevailing framework-moral system that the besought believer feels he has failed).[88] Again, "God" is seen as the symbolic object that varnishes such activities with a sense of efficacy beyond their social utility.

Because life is uncertain, we have a need to feel in control of life, and when we lose that sense of control, we often feel the need to act. When people say "God," they are often referring to an object of attribution that makes it feel realistic that, when utterly powerless to affect a situation, it is still possible to do something that will bring about a change for the better. Belief in "God" allows them to believe in other behaviors and mechanisms that give them control over various circumstances over which they have no control, and so part of what they mean by "God" is their sense of being able to achieve some active control over just about any situation. In other words, a belief in "God" gives a sense of potency to an inexpensive coping mechanism.

Passive Control

The notion that there is a higher power in place that makes life in this world go smoothly, or at least smoothly enough, is a significant aspect of what people mean by the term "God." This belief may take the form of "God's" plan, the sense that "God" will never give someone more than she can handle, or, in a weaker sense, that everything happens for a reason that only "God" knows. These are, generally speaking, belief structures that allow believers to feel that the processes of the world themselves are under the control of a competent, caring power. In the case of belief in a personal "God," that competent and caring power is, notably, concerned with the individual believer himself, in addition to whatever higher purposes for which "God" may need to use him.

As Hood, Hill, and Spilka note, "Simply put, being able to comprehend tragedy—to make it meaningful—probably constitutes the core of successful coping and adjustment. For most people, religion performs this role quite well, especially in times of personal crisis."[89] They note many forms of control constructs that occur passively, including using meaning and knowledge as a sense of control, interpretive control, predictive control, vicarious control, among several others.[90] I need not get so detailed to convey the idea that when people say the term "God," a significant part of what they mean is that the world, for whatever reasons, isn't really outside of what they feel that they can handle.

A particularly brilliant example of a sense of passive control being caught up in the term "God" happens, quite embarrassingly, to be the current national motto of the world's greatest superpower: "In God We Trust"—or so citizens of the United States are branded as believing. And to be sure, hundreds of millions of Americans *do* believe this and trust wholly in "God." But what does this mean?

The national motto of the United States since 1956 means, "In pretending to know that things will work out, we trust." This is explicitly a statement of relying upon the notion of "God" as a source of passive control over an uncertain and sometimes dangerous world. The "we" referred to in the motto trust things will work out—that the nation and its citizens will prosper, that calamity will never befall the United States in ways it cannot handle, and that the American culture and way of life are secure. This trust, which Americans actually owe primarily to ourselves, each other, and our friends in other nations, is placed instead in "God," an abstract notion symbolizing a sense of control over our circumstances.

An enormous amount of religious language and symbolism is dedicated to this idea of a caring parent figure, or other custodian, in the form of "God."[91] "God" is repeatedly said to be a shepherd, a steward, a Good Lord, a benevolent King of Kings, a Loving Father, and a "God" who cares. Christians sometimes talk about the "armor of Christ." All of these are themes of protection against the hazards of the world and the wiles of outsiders. The need for a sense of control in life is huge, and religion serves it up (metaphorically) in heaps, and it does so by offering an all-powerful mythological figure as the control construct.

This need is a particularly pernicious one as well if we wish to help people leave their religious beliefs. If "God" means a sense of control, and thus safety, finding other clear, comprehensible, and, above all, honest ways for people to meet the need for feeling secure is instrumental in helping them break free of the prison of their faith.

More on this will be discussed near the end of the book, but the case, at least, isn't hopeless. It is outstandingly unlikely that secure, functioning, healthy governments, like the ones in nations such as Sweden, preside over mostly nonbelieving societies by mere coincidence. Many, though surely not all, of people's needs for control can be satisfied sufficiently by society when states work to make that happen,[92] and when people know these needs will be met, it appears they reduce their reliance on belief in "God" and stop pretending those needs are met in other ways.

When people say "God," part of what they mean is an assurance that everything will work out, that the world isn't as terrifying as it can be, and that overriding everything, there is some sense of control in the world that keeps them safe.

Community Building and Grounding a Moral Framework

We live in communities, and communities are defined in terms of having something in common, most often moral frameworks or other sets of values. For religious communities, including ones that are culturally religious, "God" is something that many members in a community can lock onto as something they have in common. Of course, primarily what is meant by "God" in this sense is an attributional framework, as we have discussed already, particularly where it comes to moral and cultural values, but a sense of "God" as what binds their communities is part of what people often mean by that term.

An excellent way that we can understand this point is that most people seem to know what the term "God" means, even if loosely, *and expect others to know it too*. If people assume that most people mean roughly the same thing by the term "God," they are assuming that they have that in common with other people. In fact, there's an innate sense of strangeness and rejection when people are confronted with a different "God," one symbolizing a different culture. Together, these notions indicate that the term "God" is being used, in part, to make sense of the moral communities involved and to bind the people in them together.

Churches (within Christianity) are an excellent example of this phenomenon in action. The communities that develop within churches, often upon lines related to morality and purpose in life, are often close-knit and genuinely beneficial in many respects for their members. They also frequently explicitly understand their relationship to one another, at least on some level and perhaps first, in terms of "God." Week after week they come together and get reminded of what "God" means to them, engaging in a number of community-building activities in the process.[93]

Some of the community-building activities at churches include gathering together, listening to a common message together, singing together, participating together in rituals (of various levels of solemnity), eating together, working together on various projects (which are often charitable in nature), and directly turning to face one another in greetings explicitly designed to share messages of concern and peace. Even nonbelievers crave this community building and sometimes act upon it in a similar way, though they do not call the sense of community by the term "God." The recently established Sunday Assembly constitutes one example, and most Universalist churches ride the line directly in between.[94]

Rituals and group-cohesive behaviors of similar kinds are core to a sense of community, and many of these that religious people take part in seem to directly call for a reminder to "God." One great example is the prayer request, or its extroverted cousin, the public prayer event. We have already discussed how prayer constitutes a coping mechanism related to the need for control, but prayer that is in some way a show of faith—be it by a request to help in a desperate need (control) or by praying in groups or in front of one another—also exhibits community-building functions. Such activities are, in a significant way, visible reminders that the people involved are "on our teams," almost in a literal sense.

When prayers are done in groups, for instance, the shared sense of communication binds the people involved, as with any ritual.[95] The short, visible sacrifice of one's time is a clear indication that the people involved are all dedicated beyond themselves to a united cause.[96] All ritual, particularly when it involves a show of investment, has this community-building effect, so long as the object of the ritual isn't considered overtly silly by too many of the membership. We are, after all, symbolic, probably at least as much as we are social.

Some of this same effect happens also via public prayer requests, which many nonbelievers find a bit despicable for coming off as being false help. When someone is calling to their friends to reach out to a mythological figure for help in a desperate situation, however, part of what they are doing is building community. They're looking to see who cares and who is proving themselves in a similar moral community, and all of the people involved are likely to end up with increased prosocial feelings toward one another. Additionally, there is another binding effect with the prayer request that is captured by what is known as the *Benjamin Franklin effect*.

Benjamin Franklin was well known as a diplomat, and one of the strategies he realized now bears his name, though it took until the second half of the twentieth century to understand how it works.[97] Franklin was known to ask antagonistic characters to do him a favor, usually something fairly small but important (a famous episode involved being loaned a book). In the vast majority of cases, the result was that an enemy would become an ally, clearly having created a sense of a new and positive social bond.

The prayer request satisfies all of these factors: it is a favor that is small and within the power of anyone to do; it is invested with the sense of being important; and it conveys a sense of cost to the person praying (if nothing else, some time and, if I may, an admission of belief in something so ridiculous that it seems a bit embarrassing[98]). Though it's rarely going to be the entirety of what's going on in the prayer request situation, evoking the Benjamin Franklin effect is a possible outcome, one that might be particularly strong if part of it involves admitting that there is some shared sense of "God," or values in this case, at play.[99] Obviously, in the case of a prayer request, the idea that serves as a mechanism to make this particular magic spell "work" is belief in "God."

For people in religious communities, "God" is what brings them together when nothing else seems to, and the language is often familial. Religious believers often conceive of themselves as children of "God," and see themselves as a community of fictive brothers and sisters,[100] frequently referring to the (male) clergy overseeing them in overtly paternal language.

Much of what is being captured by this sense of community, and even family, is a recognition that these people have something significant in common, and however disparate their views on any number of topics, professions, hobbies, and whatever else, they do: many of their values. Most of these values are framework-moral in nature, and by being united in a single idea, they are able to effect a mechanism that bypasses much of the distrust many people naturally extend to strangers. Though this can be abused—and often is—it is more often advantageous and thus meets many of the social needs of the individuals involved.

The reasons are at the very roots of being human. As Hood, Hill, and Spilka note,

> The *need to belong* is a powerful human drive.[101] A truly fundamental
> principle is that we humans cannot live without others. We are conceived
> and born in relationship and interdependence, and connections and

interactions with others are indispensable throughout our entire lives. . . . We may thus view religious faith as strengthening group bonds, welfare, and positive social evaluation. In addition, religion appears to eventuate in heightened reproductive and genetic potential. Obviously, religious affiliation opens important social channels for interpersonal approval and integration into society on many levels.[102] (emphasis in original)

Note that although Hood, Hill, and Spilka view *religious faith* as beneficial in a number of psychosocial ways, faith is utterly bankrupt as a way to justify the claims held in it.[103] That faith is an all-but-worthless way to justify beliefs, then, is immaterial to the fact that it gives believers a mechanism upon which they can maintain beliefs that allow them to meet many psychological and social needs, including the need to build a community around a sense of shared values. Faith, specifically faith in "God," is the tool that enables believers to feel that these values are well justified when, in fact, they often are not.

Part of what "God" means for believers, then, is the sense of community that arises from a shared sense of moral and cultural values, typically understood via sect-specific framework-moral systems.

Social Context and Hierarchy (Including Attachment/Parental Issues)

This section attempts to address a small handful of interrelated topics, one of which is a sense of one's own social context, and the others are related to the way that context manifests via some sort of social hierarchy. These social hierarchies appear to be nearly ubiquitous, and the metrics that define them are caught up in the complicated psychosocial valuation schemes that we use to make such judgments.

We extract the meanings that we give to ourselves from our communities, including our roles in them. This sense of meaning is primarily concerned with our deep-seated needs for esteem, and these needs are largely understood in evaluation against one another and against the moral and cultural values that we hold. This is the major thrust of social identity theory—that belonging to identifiable groups gives a sense of social identity, social context, belongingness in the social world, pride, and self-esteem. Since religions are often centrally concerned with attempting to tie the human to the universal, almost always in moral terms, they are almost perfectly adapted to the task of amplifying a sense of social identity.

Indeed, religious worldviews, many of them firmly centered upon "God," provide ways to understand ourselves. They set narratives about the universe, about life, and about the human societies that we find ourselves in, and these stories enable us to make sense of ourselves and each other. They also serve as the backdrop for how we understand the framework-moral systems we misidentify with morality, and it is in these terms that we understand ourselves in many of the most important ways.

The religious sense of context can be understood metaphorically as something like an anchor that helps people position themselves in what could be viewed as societal or cultural seas. These seas are often churning with complex currents of varying cultural narratives. Navigating these social waters can be difficult, and gaining some sense of control over the shifting cultural attitudes around us can be useful. Many religious people take their religions and "God" as their anchor that holds them fixed in a region of the cultural sea that they feel they understand. "Know thyself," for instance, is considered extraordinarily timeless advice, and people use the idea of "God" to set the context so that they can follow it.

What it means to accept "God" as one's psychosocial anchor is, usually, to adopt a particular moral framework along with particular thoughts on the purpose and value of life as being a largely immovable core of one's sense of self. This behavior itself is not entirely peculiar to religious people—all of us do it—but by attaching it to the idea of "God," which is often understood as being both perfect and immutable, there are certain advantages and disadvantages that immediately come into play.

Among the advantages of anchoring on a perfect, eternal "God" is simplifying the process of ethical reasoning by essentially eliminating the ongoing requirement to assess and modify one's own ethics. Belief in "God" allows one to cast anchor into a thought-harbor[104] where things seem steady, calm, and unchanging, protected from the buffeting waves of shifting cultural circumstances. Riding the open seas of cultural valuation takes continual effort that is greatly reduced by parking one's ship in some harbor or another.

Of course, one of the greatest disadvantages of anchoring oneself in such a thought-harbor is that the ethical seas we find ourselves in aren't shifting arbitrarily. The evidence points to a clear arc of moral progress, and the current seems, once normalized for some noise and for the relatively trivial, to flow along this arc. Anchoring oneself in a harbor, say one set up in the middle of the Iron Age, causes one frequently to be out of step with this trend, often preventing necessary movement. Many of the ethical attitudes of yesteryear have been revealed clearly, and in some cases unequivocally, to have been abject moral failures. Examples are copious enough and well-cited enough not to require mentioning.[105]

We live in a changing cultural environment, and it seems that people often want (or need) some kind of an anchor within that environment in order to feel socially and emotionally secure. The reasons, most likely, are related to their needs for esteem and control over powerlessness—consider, for instance, how beliefs in eternity affect fears of death. Nonbelievers, generally speaking, appear to be more comfortable sailing these changing seas, and they seem also to be more at ease with the realization that their legacies are every bit as human and finite as the rest of their experiences.

This point is important because it indicates that being nonreligious appears to be a much bigger challenge than being religious when it comes to security and social context, especially since once the spell is broken, it isn't often easy to go back to believing nonsense. Believers are likely to sense these facts, and part of their tightly knit defenses of their faiths may rest upon them. This sense of security, then, constitutes another advantage of hitching one's sense of psychosocial context to an idea like a perfect, eternal "God," even if the advantage is based entirely in a comforting illusion.

Importantly, however one handles the cultural seas, all communities, including nations and cultures, appear to develop social hierarchies. "God" often allows people to make sense of these social hierarchies and thus understand their own places in them. "God" goes at the top of any theistic framework-moral hierarchy, and from that vantage point serves as a social standard to which all are subject.

Perhaps most overtly of all human religious systems, the Hindu religion, with its elaborate caste system and doctrines of dharma, karma, and reincarnation, has used the idea of divine order upon the world to understand and enforce a social hierarchy. For those unfamiliar, under Hindu doctrine, everyone has a particular dharma, which can be roughly understood as one's purpose for being, that dictates how one should behave. One's dharma is strongly influenced by one's caste, age, gender, position in the family, and so on, and one's purpose in life is to live out one's dharma as perfectly as possible.

Deviations from one's dharma accrue karma, something like the "wages of sin" in the Abrahamic traditions, and karma can translate into worldly misfortunes in this life or future lives (under the doctrine of reincarnation). The whole system of dharma is built around the idea, to put it casually, of knowing your role and sucking it up. This system is a hierarchical moral community every bit as much as it is a religion.

Though not nearly as extreme, rigid, or codified, all cultures, societies, and communities develop such hierarchies naturally based upon the methods we use to perform psychosocial evaluation. The Hindu system is profoundly concerned with the "divinity" dimension, as karma is something like a measurement of how not-"divine" one's behavior is. In the Abrahamic religions, the analogous preoccupation is with sin, which is deviation from "divine law." As we discussed, this actually means behaving framework-immorally (even if that means behaving in a way that is legitimately moral—a central theme in our favorite dramas), and it translates into steps in the negative direction in the "divinity" dimension of how we evaluate ourselves and others.

The other facets of psychosocial valuation also come into play in erecting community and cultural hierarchies, these being closeness of kin and reputation. Obviously, within any moral community, those who are close of kin are elevated for each of us, as are those of high reputation. Unsurprisingly, we see "God" cast in the role of the loving Father and the Most-High King of the Universe. The specific ways that these manifest should be sufficiently obvious to need little elaboration, and so now the goal is to understand that when believers say "God," part of what they mean is that this system makes sense and is, in some ways, beyond challenge.

As noted, much of the language involved in talking about "God" in this way is caught up in the paternalistic notion of "God" as the "loving Father." One reason for this fact may be that the family is typically one's first community, one that serves as a model for much of the rest of the way we understand our social context.

A significant way we make sense of the family model and our own roles in it is known as *attachment theory*, which has its roots in our relationships with our parental figures. Much has been made of the suggestion that as we grow up and realize that our parents are not infallible, omniscient, or omnipotent, we rely, particularly when at need, upon a mythologized sense of such a parent figure that we call "God." Note, here, the Catholic language of "God" as "the Father" and the Church as "the Mother." Hood, Hill, and Spilka make a note of this fact, writing,

> it has been suggested that attachment theory has relevance for understanding conceptualizations of God, religious behaviors such as prayer and glossolalia (speaking in tongues), and links between religious experience and romantic love.[106] Subsequent research has confirmed the utility of attachment theory for understanding religion. . . . For example, as children moved from early to middle childhood, their distance from parents decreased as perceived closeness to God increased, just as attachment theory would predict.[107] . . . Dickie et al.[108] also found evidence that seems to support attachment theory predictions; they concluded that "God becomes the 'perfect attachment substitute'" as children become more independent of parents.[109]

Depending upon the relationship that we had with our parents, particularly meaning what psychologists call our attachment style, the research bears out complicated ways in which we use religious beliefs to understand ourselves. A significant study conducted by Lee Kirkpatrick and Phil Shaver in 1990[110] bore the following results, as Hood, Hill, and Spilka summarize,

> Attachment did indeed serve as a predictor of religiousness, but in a somewhat complicated way. There was a tendency for those from avoidant parent-child attachment relationships to report higher levels of adult religiousness, and also for persons with secure attachments to report lower levels of religiousness, but only for respondents whose mothers were relatively nonreligious. The attachment classification apparently had a more direct relationship with reported sudden conversion experiences: Anxious/ambivalent respondents were much more likely to report such conversions at some time in their lives (44%) than were respondents

from other attachment groups (fewer than 10%). Home religiosity did not affect this relationship.[111]

Combining these observations, particularly noting that "God" serves as "the perfect attachment substitute," as Dickie et al. put it, we have good reasons to believe that part of what many believers mean by the term "God" has a great deal to do with being an attachment substitute for the parental figures in their early lives. Forensic psychiatrist J. Anderson Thomson, Jr., agrees, writing in a chapter about attachment theory and beliefs in "God,"

> An omniscient and omnipotent sky parent might, if beseeched often and with great intensity, not only protect us and our loved ones, but also find community in like-minded people, shield us from the fear of death, assure our salvation, and provide an afterlife that more than compensates for all of our human suffering. This is religion's promise. Our parents cannot take care of us forever, but Yahweh can.[112]

He goes on in the next paragraph to mention,

> Religions give us supernormal "parents," magnificent attachment figures the likes of which we never experience in everyday life, and never can. When we are distressed, we turn to a god that hears our prayers, grants our wishes, protects our loved ones, and reassures us of rewards no matter how adverse our troubles.[113]

Soon thereafter, he states it plainly: "This need for attachment contributes both to the ease of accepting religion and the difficulty of rejecting it. Quite simply, we want to believe in something loving and eternal."[114]

"God" as an attachment figure would be the aspect of the mythological figure, then, that is often likened (pejoratively) to being an "imaginary friend," specifically one that is thought of in parental terms. This seems to be a common understanding of the term "God" and is likely to be significant in terms of understanding one's psychosocial context in terms of one's sense of esteem. Incidentally, the Christian notion of a "relationship with Christ," with Christ meaning the "Son of 'God,'" could be understood as an even more complex and thorough sense in this dimension—that of having a brotherly relationship, which could be taken as closer and more personal in many ways than that of an (obviously distant) parent figure.[115] Jesus, as portrayed in the Christian tradition, in fact, is almost perfectly created as a kind of attachment figure as an intermediary to "God."[116]

Hood, Hill, and Spilka do note that there are some noteworthy critics to attachment theory in general as well as to a possible Western bias,[117] but as the goal of this book is simply to provide an overview for what people may mean by the word "God" without appealing to theism to make sense of it, these challenges are not significant to the present work.

Our psychosocial context is critical to our esteem needs and a part of how we establish our sociality needs, and believers may be able to form some sense of meeting these needs in the abstract notion they call "God."

Belief in Belief

Philosopher Daniel Dennett has noted very articulately, many people's religious beliefs seem to be maintained on a belief in belief, by which he means a belief that it is virtuous to believe.[118] Furthermore, religious beliefs often involve believing in "God." Thus, in part, "God" for many believers represents the notion that belief itself is a virtue.

This, then, is where we encounter the notion of the "virtue of faith," which when properly understood is difficult to see as a virtue at all. To phrase it according to the heuristic offered in philosopher Peter Boghossian's *A Manual for Creating Atheists*, the "virtue of faith" can be taken as meaning, "the virtue of pretending to know things that one does not know."[119] It is ridiculous to, as Boghossian clarifies, "extend belief beyond the warrant of evidence supporting that belief,"[120] and it is ridiculous to consider this behavior a virtue. Yet almost like a motto, at least in contemporary American culture, we hear that "it's just good to believe in something."

Of course, it isn't "just good" to believe in "something." Neither is it good to stick by one's beliefs because they are one's beliefs. One can be completely convinced of a belief that is completely wrong, and, in fact, most of us are wrong about something much of the time. In most cases, it's obviously not good to believe things that are explicitly false, and it's only good to believe in something one thinks might be true (but doesn't know is true)—moral intuitions being by far the most important example in this category—to the same degree as one can actually be justified in that belief. All excess confidence in a belief is an impediment to conversation and compromise, which are necessities when it comes to matters people know something, but not enough, about. It simply is not a virtue to be too invested in one's beliefs to refuse to revise them in light of the evidence. Further, it's not a virtue to believe for the sake of having an opinion. Honest doubt and frank ignorance are vastly superior to pretending to know or believing for the sake of believing, so far as intellectual virtues go.

The function belief "in something"—often in "God," in one guise or another—plays for people is probably woven into all of the categories of psychosocial needs listed above. Faith, in many regards, is the glue that holds the entire religious framework together (but only because genuine evidence doesn't), and faith means unwarranted confidence in a belief. Since the framework is how people satisfy, pretend to satisfy, or ignore many of their psychosocial needs, they must believe in belief itself to make the whole thing work. "God" is both the source of their belief and the object of it. The false virtue of believing in belief, however, remains part of what some people mean when they use the word "God" in making "God" out to be something worth believing in for its own sake.

Special Topic: Death, or Rather, Its Denial
A special topic when it comes to dealing with what the term "God" means to people is death, or, more accurately, *denying* death.[121] Religion is often centrally occupied with denying death, in fact finding itself so occupied with it that it even denies that it denies death.[122]

Religious language often reveals both the denial of death and the denial of the denial of death, phrasing matters more triumphantly, as in "defeating" or "overcoming" death, or saying that death is an illusion such "that whoever believes in him shall not perish but have eternal life."[123] As death is a reality, and as we have no legitimate reasons to believe that any kind of life or consciousness survives beyond it (and many good reasons to believe it doesn't), this use of language is actually a kind of puffery used to meet and ignore the psychosocial needs surrounding death and dying. Many people want—and here I do not think *need* is truly the word—to deny their own mortality in service to real psychosocial needs (most notably control and purpose). "God," presumed to be eternal and "[made] of the spirit," is the mechanism by which they are capable of believing this feat is possible, and a large part of what believers mean when they say "God" is the elaborate mechanism of beliefs that lets them deny death.

Note, of course, that it isn't necessary to believe in "God" to deny death. The notions of reincarnation employed in Hinduism and many schools of Buddhism could operate perfectly well on their own, without the influence of any deity, though they do require a dualistic notion that something like a soul is separable from the body.[124]

Death is a terrifying affair. Hood, Hill, and Spilka are not softer in their analysis of death and religion, writing, "We humans do not take kindly to death. . . . its immediate reality is terrifying to virtually all of us."[125] They note the seriousness further in foreboding terms, ending pitifully,

> We lament those who die, and dread the fact that we too, in time, will confront the end of our own existence. Many of us, however, refuse to come to terms with death. We repress, deny, shun, and withdraw where possible from reminders of death, and above all, we fight to delay death. If there is a basic purpose to medicine, it is to reduce mortality and increase longevity. And finally when we die, the customary North American way of death includes embalming, which Aries[126] interprets as a "refusal to accept death." In other words, we wish to keep our bodies unchanged. Furthermore, our faiths inform us that we do not simply die; we move to another realm—heaven, hell, limbo, purgatory, or life with God. Finally, there is resurrection: We return to everlasting life. In sum, we never die; our destiny is immortality. Religion guarantees it.[127]

They go on, tying religion and the denial of death tightly,

> Theologian Paul Tillich[128] championed such an inference [that our destiny is immortal] by claiming that "the anxiety of fate and death is the most basic, most universal, and inescapable." Reasoning further, the noted anthropologist Bronislaw Malinowski[129] maintained that "Death, which of all human events is the most upsetting and disorganizing to man's calculations, is perhaps the main source of religious belief." In one study of clergy, only 2% felt that concern about death was not a factor in religious activity.[130] [131]

Continuing, they drive the point home,

Religion has historically been our culture's dominant means of coping with the inevitability of our own demise. Religion makes death meaningful. Death is a mystery that we must unravel. It belies meaning and demands explanation. We have questions and religion offers us the desired answers. Taken at face value, death implies a simple, final termination. Understandably, we do not easily accept the prospect of ultimate extinction; it is not just that we want to live on indefinitely, but that we desire certainty that this will occur. Religion provides assurance that this will occur.... Institutionalized faith, as we have seen, plays many roles in life, but the issue of death lies at its core.[132]

Recent research by Corey Cook, Florette Cohen, and Sheldon Solomon in terror management theory[133] bears this out in another way. It seems that part of the distrust and dislike believers often have for those lacking belief is connected to feelings of mortality. Specifically, there is some connection in believers between thoughts of those lacking belief in God and experiencing feelings of mortality and existential dread. In the abstract to their paper, they write,

Terror management theory posits that the uniquely human awareness of death gives rise to potentially paralyzing terror that is assuaged by embracing cultural worldviews that provide a sense that one is a valuable participant in a meaningful universe. We propose that pervasive and pronounced anti-atheist prejudices stem, in part, from the existential threat posed by conflicting worldview beliefs. Two studies were conducted to establish that existential concerns contribute to anti-atheist sentiments.... These studies provide the first empirical link between existential concerns and anti-atheist prejudices.[134]

There is simply no avoiding the obvious conclusion. When many people use the word "God," some of what they mean by it is their sense of assurance that their own death and the deaths of their loved ones are either not real or not final. In other words, for many, maybe most, religious believers, "God" means "I and those I love will not die." It is likely that whatever other aspects of the term "God" are manifest, this particular thought lurks in the background, either just beneath the surface or close enough to be felt.

The intent of this book, and particularly this section, is not to develop the complicated and intense interrelationship between religion, "God," and death, but rather to impress upon the reader that a core part of what "God" means to those who believe in it—perhaps the most important core, possibly outstripping even needs for morality, purpose, social structure, and control—is the fantasy of denying death.

The reasons are at the bottom, it seems, both of what it means to be alive and what it means to be human, with so much of our psychology so intimately dependent upon our social environment. We *must* recognize that for many believers, the assurance of eternal life, which is the denial of death, lives at the core of what they mean when they say "God." This recognition should lead us to treat the matter differently, hopefully better.

There's a second and deeper matter involved here as well. If death is one of the hard facts of living a human life, the ultimate extinction of human-kind (and all of our endeavors) is a harder fact still. This fact directly challenges any sense of ultimate purpose that we can possibly hold because, as the first chapter of the Old Testament book of Ecclesiastes proclaims, "everything is vanity"[135] (also translated as, "everything is meaningless").

This woeful statement is true in the sense that within some number of years—hopefully relatively large by our standards—humanity *will* meet its final end, and the machinations of the universe will grind everything we've ever done to dust. This observation, which eventually haunts many of us, provides a poignant sense of existential dread. Perhaps because of the preoccupation on eternity, it seems frequently missed that this dread may best be characterized by an outright lack of perspective on the (admittedly local but still significant) importance our lives have to the people with whom we're interconnected.[136] Local purposes are as meaningful as human purposes get, and it's nothing but a damned shame to disparage the positive impacts we can have on others and ourselves in pursuit of a desperate fantasy to persist forever.

Many religions go beyond preoccupation with individual death—and its denial—and deal also with eschatology, that part of theology made up to handle the final destruction of humankind. In many of these fantasies, often termed "Final Judgment," the idea of "God" plays the role of judge of every human being that has ever lived, determining a final fate that allegedly settles the score by awarding paradise, punishment, or destruction.[137] To believe the author of Ecclesiastes, which I recommend against, the ultimate destruction of humanity renders all human efforts vanities.[138] The psychological avoidance of existential dread by this poisonous mechanism accounts for some of what is meant by the term "God."

A Word about Satan
"Satan," or "the Enemy," is a strange idea. It, like "God," is an idea, but Satan is something of an anti-God, an embodiment of Evil, Corruption, Chaos, and Decay (capitalized to emphasize their status as ideas here). These stand in opposition to Good, Sanctity, Order, and Purity, respectively. While the idea of devils, including a great Tempter, Liar, Deceiver, Enemy, or Evil, isn't unique to Christianity and Islam, in these two religions Satan is set against God in a battle for the souls of humanity.

Thus, like "God," Satan is a mythological entity. Satan, though, is a myth that probably was not invented to explain anything more mystifying than the fact that no God exists. Satan, as an idea, exists because no amount of theological mental gymnastics has or ever can satisfactorily surmount the Problem of Evil—that things that are genuinely bad seem to happen (as it turns out, in a way that appears indistinguishable from utter indifference).

If "God" is the grounds for one's moral framework, Satan can be conceived of as the embodiment of the temptation to violate the rules. Typically, of course, the role of Satan is to lure someone into doing self-serving and (framework) immoral things,[139] to let one's self-control lapse, and to coax one to fall into "sin."[140] Satan, by these virtues, of course, makes the religious propagandizing easier, and not just as an explanation for that which doesn't really fit with the concept of "God." Key among Satan's believed attributes is that the figure is used to convince people that the world is "spiritually" dangerous, offering countless tricky ways to pull them from the correct way to live and into corruption and "sin."

If "God" is the way in which someone makes sense of purpose in life, Satan can be cast as the lure into idleness, away from right purposes, to bad purposes, or to shallow, self-serving purposes. In this sense, Satan is an idea that represents corruption upon the purpose of life, leading the person into a squandered existence that focuses on all the wrong things and thusly becomes meaningless.

People use "God" to make sense of the phenomena of the world, and where reality contradicts those beliefs, Satan provides an attributional object that explains away the discrepancy. Satan, to some biblical creationists, after all, is allegedly responsible for putting the dinosaur bones in the ground to trick people into rejecting the ludicrous story of Noah's Ark and thus the biblical narrative.

If "God" grounds someone's sense of "divinity," Satan is taken as the temptation that leads her away from it and into corruption, degradation, and pollution. If "God" is what is Good and Noble and Beautiful about the world, Satan is used to account for the opposites. If "God" lets someone believe in Justice, Satan can account for unfairness and injustice.

When "God" means someone's sense of control in life, then Satan represents chaos, which ultimately means powerlessness and fear. Calamity—when not caused by "God" as a punishment—can be attributed to the influences of Satan, and this seems to be the case surprisingly often with certain biblical literalists where diseases and other infirmaries are concerned. The Gospels of the New Testament devote a considerable amount of space to this very theme, in fact.

It goes on like this. If "God" holds our communities together, Satan tears them apart, defeating human efforts to live and work together fruitfully and peacefully. If "God" means Life, then Satan means Destruction and Death. If "God" means Love; then Satan means Cruelty and Hate, and particularly Torture.

These, though, are all still ideas, just as "God" is an idea. These are all psychosocial constructs, expressed at the level of cultural mythology, and they all serve the same purpose that "God" does: to help human beings meet or ignore certain among their psychosocial needs that they do not know how else to meet. The notion of Satan accounts for the obvious failures that are left by God's lack of existence, and the whole set of mythological narratives are built around helping people make sense of their world when they don't know as much as they need in order to do better.

As an aside, Satan's origins on the religious mythological stage, as part of the Abrahamic tradition, are telling when it comes to exposing theism as a kind of mythology. Satan, sometimes called Lucifer, referred to the planet

Venus as it appeared in the morning sky. Satan was the Lightbringer, who brought humans the fruit from the Tree of Knowledge, and in the morning sky, Venus, the Morning Star, shines just ahead of the rising of the Sun (a celestial object symbolic in almost every conceivable way of "God") and does so brightly enough to cast weak shadows. The myth painted Satan as having stolen the fire of the gods (or Light of God—Knowledge and Wisdom) from Heaven in order to deliver it to humankind, but the myths sought to explain the brightness and position of the planet Venus. The key thing to take from this is "the myth."

Satan, then, helps us understand the mythological nature of theism, and thus it helps us realize that going post-theistic makes sense in exactly the same way as the activities related to oceanic navigation are best engaged in with post-Poseidic models of the sea.

On God and Delusion

In 2006, biologist Richard Dawkins published a book that neatly juxtaposed the words "God" and "delusion" without a hint of fluff about his point. *The God Delusion* was, in many respects and for many people, a complete game changer, and it would be difficult to deny that the title had something to do with this fact. One fiercely debated question since its publication concerns whether belief in God constitutes a kind of delusion.

It certainly looks like it. A delusion is defined to be a "belief held with strong conviction despite superior evidence to the contrary." The psychiatric criteria that identify a belief as delusional, tracing back to psychiatrist Karl Jaspers' book *General Psychopathology*, published in 1913, are "certainty, incorrigibility, and impossibility or falsity of content."[141]

The only thing like evidence for God is that a lot of people talk about it. All of the evidence we possess, other than that cultural fact, makes the case that if there is actually a God, the way that God behaves is utterly indistinguishable from there being no God at all, including the so-called revealed "wisdom" we allegedly have received in the form of holy scriptures. Religious belief, however, (1) is nearly always based upon the *certainty* of faith—this sometimes being taken as a doctrine of what faith means[142]—(2) rarely changes in the face of contravening evidence (*incorrigibility*), and (3) is *false in content* (and often patently ridiculous in this regard). That is, the superior evidence is to the contrary yet beliefs in God are held in a delusional way, with strong conviction, and so the delusion shoe seems to fit pretty snugly.

Religious belief, however, is not typically delusional belief. One somewhat unsatisfactory reason that delusion doesn't quite describe religious beliefs is that there is some relationship between them and social norms. Believing in God, lamentably, is still quite normal, and so belief isn't, itself, an indication of mental illness so much as simply being mistaken.

The main reason that delusion isn't quite the right idea to describe religious belief, and that *mistaken* is a better term, is that while God does not exist, "God" does. It is the acceptance of theism (usually with attendant certainty, denial of death, and other issues in their own rights) that is the actual issue. That is, religious believers aren't so much deluded; it's more that they are confused about the meaning of the term "God." It isn't exactly a delusion to believe in something real, even if one goes on to misunderstand its nature via a mythological construct made to that purpose.

The distinction is subtle but consequential. Branding religious belief delusional tars billions of genuinely sane people with a pejoratively understood disorder (down to its original linguistic roots, *de-* implying a pejorative reading of *ludere*, which means "to play," the combination meaning "to mock"). For religious belief, we need to appreciate that *belief is secondary to the application of the beliefs*. Religious believers believe in order to meet certain needs, and the beliefs follow the needs. What they end up believing is a mythological rendering of a collection of abstract ideas that help them meet or ignore some of their needs.

People who believe in God do so because they don't know how else to meet certain psychological and social needs. By labeling these people as delusional, we miss the opportunity to address the actual issues in play. Probably more importantly, we also lose the nuance necessary to identify the legitimate delusions that arise from mistaking the mythological for the real. Of note, though, some of the beliefs that spring from this confusion are genuinely delusional. That said, religious beliefs tend not to, but can be, delusional and they are likely to serve as the source of genuine delusions that are unlikely to be recognized as such. It is delusional, for instance, to believe that prayers will heal someone or that a deity will protect one's home in a natural disaster. This is a problem that deserves serious attention.

Still, "the God delusion," as a phrase (to be distinguished from the book), falls very near the mark, but the classification is neither satisfactory nor accurate. Theism isn't quite a delusion; it's an attempt to make sense of the world mythologically. It is possible, however, that with a robust understanding of the meaning of the term "God" without invoking theism at all, continued belief in God could become considered genuinely delusional.

Atheism in a New Light

We now should pause and consider "atheism" in this new light, which I will combine with a short summary of what has just been covered.

Consider the 2014 study conducted by psychologist William Gervais titled "Everything Is Permitted? People Intuitively Judge Immorality as Representative of Atheists."[143] Gervais was able to conclude that there exists "a prevalent intuition that belief in God serves a necessary function in inhibiting immoral conduct," which "may help explain persistent negative perceptions of atheists." This is consistent with the point that because "God" largely means the object of moral attribution for many believers, lacking belief in God gets tangled up with a perception of inherent immorality.

I'd suggest it goes further. When nonbelievers want to insist that they are atheists, on some level, many theistic believers will hear a rejection of many of their core values. Further, they will hear a rejection of the grounding for how they understand themselves, other people, their culture, the broader world, and the contextual interrelationships between each of those facets of their experience.[144] If people want to push "atheism," in the form of "atheism movements" and an "atheist community," they must do so in recognition of these facts. A better approach than what happens now is advocated.

When we realize that when people say "God" that they mean some combination of concepts developed and employed to meet a variety of their core psychosocial needs, it becomes very odd to describe oneself as an "atheist." When someone describes herself as an atheist, she unintentionally takes on a lot of baggage, some of which is outright nonsense in light of the fact that there's a conflation between the ideas summarized in the word "God" and the notion of a deity called by that word. This will prove to be a perennial problem for atheism.

If atheism continues to become more and more identifiable as a "thing," as a kind of worldview and a philosophy, it become easier for the religious to conceptualize it in terms they reject. On those terms, as something like a competing religion (a set of moral communities, to be precise), they will find it easy to dig in their heels in their beliefs. Not believing is not another kind of believing, and we should shun anything—like positive atheism—that gives people the excuse to get that fact wrong.

An excellent way to avoid all of these issues is simply to move beyond atheism and to go post-theistic, as discussed earlier in the book, and a proper understanding of what "God" means can help that goal. What such a change entails is a shift in thinking that positions us as disinterested in theism because it talks about its central object in entirely the wrong way. The rest of this book is dedicated to outlining some preliminary suggestions about how to shift to a post-theistic world that is no longer concerned with theism or atheism.

Notes

1. Obviously, exceptions exist, and some staggeringly mainline Protestants in the United States may have their "phenomenological attribution" knob set all the way up to ten. Many hardline Biblical creationists could be one example, and we have good reasons to believe that there are rather a lot of them.

2. More accurately, it is understood in terms of a framework-moral taboo against questioning or revising the beliefs.

3. Haidt, *The Righteous Mind*, p. 255.

4. *Ibid.*, p. 193.

5. My book *Dot, Dot, Dot: Infinity Plus God Equals Folly* is largely a sustained case that to call "God" infinite is to admit that "God" is an abstract idea, not a real entity.

6. Lindsay, *Dot, Dot, Dot*, chapter 2.

7. See *ibid.*, pp. 34–37.

8. I wrote about this on my own blog, posting about a discussion between Tim McGrew and Peter Boghossian on the meaning of faith. In the discussion, McGrew offered the example of a skydiver trusting his parachute on a skydive

as an analogy to how faith operates like trust (separately from hope, following a challenge Boghossian has posed). He analogized that faith in "God" is like the trust that lets skydivers overcome the slight odds against their lives and jump anyway, though optimism bias is often in play in these situations in exactly the way McGrew described as "faith." Optimism bias seems to be part of what is meant by phrases like, "I have faith that God is in control" as well—forces beyond the individual are at work to enable him to always end up on the right side of bad statistics. See James A. Lindsay, "Going Skydiving with Tim McGrew," *God Doesn't; We Do*, blog, 25 May 2014, http://goddoesnt.blogspot.com/2014/05/going-skydiving-with-tim-mcgrew.html.

9. For more, see Peter Boghossian, "How Socratic Pedagogy Works," *Informal Logic: Teaching Supplement* 23, no. 2 (2003): pp. 17–25; and Peter Boghossian, "The Socratic Method (Or, Having a Right to Get Stoned)," *Teaching Philosophy* 25, no. 4 (December 2002): pp. 345–359.

10. Boghossian, *A Manual For Creating Atheists*.

11. Of note, religions are particularly bad forms of ideologies because of their ties to (1) a sense of perfect goodness beyond capacity to question and (2) ancient scriptures filled with barbarism and astounding levels of tribal hate. In this sense, then, quasi-religious developments that have broken themselves from either or both of these features are extremely likely to be far more benign, if still entirely unreasonable and troublesome, than their ancient religious counterparts.

12. This is a philosophical argument that boils down to "evil exists, and that's evidence against an all-good, all-able God." It has been reargued again and again, apparently with little point, since the days of Epicurus and his famous trilemma, dated roughly to the fourth century BCE.

13. Do not despair at this impossibility of divorcing morality from religion. The goal isn't actually to divorce the two concepts; it's to help people realize that theism doesn't provide warrant to the belief that one's moral attitudes are the solitary correct moral values for everyone everywhere and in all times. In other words, the goal of "divorcing religion and morality" is to help believers understand that certainty about their moral intuitions is an error, encouraging understanding, conversation, and compromise across moral communities with different framework-moral systems.

14. Some would argue—and I mention the point later—that the denial of death is the central occupation of religion, but I disagree on this point. Of course, it varies from one believer, or one tradition, to the next, but defining a moral code

and giving it a sense of veracity is probably more substantial an occupation of religious belief in practice. Of course, the drive to gain illusory control over human powerlessness ranks pretty high up there too, and it is very likely to be unproductive to split hairs arguing over which aspect is bigger than which for any given set of believers.

15. The Richard Dawkins Foundation for Science and Reason conducted an Ipsos MORI poll to this effect, "Religious and Social Attitudes of UK Christians in 2011," 14 February 2012, https://www.ipsos-mori.com/researchpublications/ researcharchive/2921/Religious-and-Social-Attitudes-of-UK-Christians-in-2011. aspx.

16. Note that it requires very little imagination to see how omnipotence and omniscience are tied to fulfilling needs for control along with some of the other kinds of attribution.

17. Brené Brown, "The Power of Vunlerability," *TED Talk*, video, June 2010.

18. That it is possible to rationalize atrocities in moral language and with moral conviction is essentially all the proof that anyone needs that moral frameworks *can be* evaluated, if only we can determine how to do it

19. The best that can be achieved when two faith-based moral attitudes clash is conversation and compromise, which we increasingly see works best when religious beliefs are relegated to the private sphere without state endorsement, that is, under secularism. When religious moral beliefs are taken to be universally applicable—the *one true faith*—a serious impasse results because conversation and compromise become far harder, if not impossible.

20. Amanda Marcotte, "10 Myths Many Religious People Hold About Atheists, Debunked," *AlterNET*, 13 September 2011, http://www.alternet. org/story/152395/10_myths_many_religious_people_hold_about_atheists,_ debunked?page=entire.

21. A leap to belief in an all-knowing moral judge, while also politically useful, is not at all surprising given that we use such evaluations to define and maintain our communities. If there are morals, which means a sense of right and wrong, then there is a sense of judgment and enforcement of those adjudications. Once people have mistaken their sense of framework-morality for being grounded in a deity, ascribing to that deity the role of Supreme Judge is a natural and utterly unsurprising step. If the lawgiver and judge is a perfect entity positioned entirely outside of the human realm, then all the better—moral adjuration becomes a

matter as simple as claiming to know what the Supreme Being wants us to do and the punishments for our failures to do it and then acting upon those.

22. Haidt, *The Righteous Mind*, p. 121.

23. It should be noted that the moral attribution that makes up the abstraction people call "God" is also related to this sense of a broad, cosmic drama in the form of the perennial and epic battle between Good and Evil, with "God" conceptualized as the forces of Good and Love, which are believed to be eventually triumphant, of course.

24. Haidt, *The Happiness Hypothesis*, pp. 217–219.

25. Haidt, and other researchers working in related fields, call this state of being *flow* and connect it at a profound level to finding happiness and fulfillment in life. See *ibid.*, pp. 94–98.

26. Dan Buettner, "The Island Where People Forget to Die," *New York Times Magazine*, 24 October 2012, http://www.nytimes.com/2012/10/28/magazine/the-island-where-people-forget-to-die.html?pagewanted=all&_r=0.

27. Dan Buettner, *The Blue Zones: Lessons for Living Longer from the People Who've Lived the Longest* (Washington, DC: National Geographic Society, 2008), p. 87.

28. Hood, Hill, and Spilka, *The Psychology of Religion*, p. 13.

29. "Public's Views on Human Evolution," Pew Research Center, 30 December 2013, http://www.pewforum.org/2013/12/30/publics-views-on-human-evolution/.

30. This story reaches perhaps its most desperate in the Christian mythological narrative, in which humanity was created in perfection, failed of its own uncouthness, and required a vicarious blood redemption not just of a human but of "God"-made flesh.

31. This, of course, paraphrases Robert Oppenheimer's very famous utterance ("Now I am become Death, the destroyer of worlds") regarding the first test of a nuclear bomb, quoting from the 1944 Vivekananda-Isherwood translation of the Gita (chapter XI, verse 32), according to *WikiQuotes*, accessed at http://en.wikiquote.org/wiki/Bhagavad_Gita.

32. This follows from Brown, "The Power of Vulnerability."

33. Declaration of Independence, http://www.archives.gov/exhibits/charters/declaration_transcript.html.

34. See *The Jefferson Bible*, for instance. It makes it impossible to believe that Jefferson was a *theistic* Christian.

35. Quoted from "Rights," *Wikipedia*, http://en.wikipedia.org/wiki/Rights.

36. Cultural narratives need not be religious, of course. They are often nationalistic, political, or otherwise symbolic to a moral community in question and almost every bit as mythological in those cases.

37. Haidt, *Righteous Mind*, p. 328.

38. *Ibid.*

39. *Ibid.*, p. 329.

40. *Ibid.* p. 330.

41. *Ibid.*, p. 274.

42. Roy Rappaport, "The Sacred in Human Evolution," *Annual Review of Ecology and Systematics* 2 (1971): pp. 23–44, p. 36.

43. Arguably, the same thing happens with all moral ideologies. That moral communities establish parochial altruism (in-group prosociality and out-group distrust and hostility) has already been discussed, and this process can run amok when the beliefs become ideological, which is to say unquestionable, in nature.

44. Immediately, abstracta like numbers, geometrical figures, and other mathematical objects jump to mind, among many other topics in the philosophical discipline of *ontology*, which concerns itself with what existence really means. "God" does as well. It is my opinion that this field of human inquiry is largely a waste of time.

45. Or, as the case may be with love, a variety of emotions bundled together.

46. The point about "God" being Good clearly carries a double meaning. One of these refers to God's alleged nature as a perfectly benevolent, or at least morally perfect, entity. The other calls to "God" being identical with the ideal form, in the Platonic sense, of Goodness. These two ideas are typically conflated to an especially annoying circumstance that all good things that happen are credited to God whereas no bad things ever are—which makes perfect sense in light of the assumption that "God" simply means "that which is good" or "that which makes goodness make sense in the first place" in the mind of the believer.

47. It is well-known that the Christian Gospel of John begins with an appeal that God's Word *is* the *Logos*, the idea from which we derive the term "logic."

48. Max Tegmark, *Our Mathematical Universe: My Quest for the Ultimate Nature of Reality* (New York: Knopf, 2012).

49. I use this phrase repeatedly throughout my book *Dot, Dot, Dot*.

50. Hood, Hill, and Spilka, *The Psychology of Religion*, p. 17.

51. Here, Hood, Hill, and Spilka cite M. B. Lupfer, K. F. Brock, and S. J. DePaola, "The Use of Secular and Religious Attributions to Explain Everyday Behavior," *Journal for the Scientific Study of Religion* 31 (1992): pp. 486–503.

52. Here, Hood, Hill, and Spilka cite M. Hewstone, "Attribution Theory and Common-Sense Explanations: An Introductory Overview," in *Attribution Theory: Social and Functional Extensions*, ed. M. Hewstone (Oxford: Blackwell, 1983), pp. 1–27; and B. Spilka, P. Shaver, and L. A. Kirkpatrick, "A General Attribution Theory for the Psychology of Religion," *Journal of Religion and Health* 22 (1985): pp. 98–104.

53. Hood, Hill, and Spilka, *The Psychology of Religion*, p. 45.

54. Pressing a believer for *how* "God" is responsible for life is almost sure to reveal exactly the problem Sean Carroll, in his debate with William Lane Craig in 2014, at the Greer-Heard Forum in New Orleans, referred to as theology failing to constitute a mature field of study. *That* "God" is responsible for life is wholly unsatisfactory as an answer because it does nothing to address *how* that might work. One can often detect a religious attribution in process when some mystery is being invoked to answer a question with a *that* answer that lacks a clear *how*.

55. These problems have been outlined thoroughly in other places, but only a moment's reflection on debilitating brain diseases like Alzheimer's disease or certain kinds of brain tumors, or of certain kinds of traumatic brain injuries, completely embarrasses such attempts to shoehorn dualism onto the human brain.

56. One simply marvels at the intellectual arrogance required to suggest that no explanation other than a deity is possible to account for some phenomenon. It comes down to "nobody knows this (perhaps because it cannot be known), therefore I know it."

57. As noted in a previous note, that these religious attributions are nonanswers is revealed simply by pressing one further question in each case: "how?" The invariable answer has to be some variation of "I don't know" or "'God' knows and can," and/or some attempt at a natural explanation with "God" shoved unnecessarily into the mechanism, as with "God-guided" evolution. These are all red flags that a religious attribution is being applied.

58. As mentioned before, this is covered by the observation known as Littlewood's Law, which indicates that rare events happen frequently.

59. That it is the most obvious example does not imply that it is the most consequential. The wars some people of faith wage upon medical science and, of course, other people, are often far more serious, even if they're not necessarily as obvious an instance of this phenomenon.

60. From my own blog, Lindsay, "Jesus-Colored Glasses," *God Doesn't; We Do*, blog, 18 January 2014, http://goddoesnt.blogspot.com/2014/01/jesus-colored-glasses.html.

61. It is beyond value to note that if everything is evidence for "God," then really, nothing constitutes evidence for "God" because there is absolutely no way to tell the difference between that which would support belief in "God" and that which wouldn't. Therefore, the idea of "evidence for God," as it is usually understood by religious believers, is effectively meaningless.

62. Quoted from "Transpersonal Psychology," *Wikipedia*, http://en.wikipedia.org/wiki/Transpersonal_psychology.

63. Sam Harris, *Waking Up: A Guide to Spirituality Without Religion* (New York: Simon & Schuster, 2014). Note particularly the poignant line, "In subjective terms, each of us is identical to the principle that brings value to the universe. Experiencing this directly—not merely thinking about it—is the true beginning of spiritual life" (p. 206).

64. Recall that Haidt referred to his third dimension of psychosocial (moral) valuation as *"divinity,"* a term with overtly "spiritual" overtones. That suggests that there is a strong sense of being a "spiritually healthy" person tied up in regarding oneself as a *framework-morally good person*, which is measured mainly, if not purely, in terms of our perceptions of our social bonds and standing within them.

65. Evangelical Christian theologian William Lane Craig refers to the "self-authenticating witness of the Holy Spirit" as an "intrinsic defeater-defeater," meaning that it is direct experiential proof of the existence of God that overrides any argument to the contrary. It's good, in my view, that he has a clear and unquestionable experience of a vibrant and important dimension to psychosocial valuation that might get called "divinity." See William Lane Craig, "The Witness of the Spirit as an Intrinsic Defeater-Defeater," *Reasonable Faith with William Lane Craig*, Q&A, 23 November 2009, http://www.reasonablefaith.org/the-witness-of-the-spirit-as-an-intrinsic-defeater-defeater.

66. Harris, *Waking Up*, particularly the introduction.

67. Hood, Hill, and Spilka, *The Psychology of Religion*, p. 365.

68. R.W. Hood, Jr., "Eliciting Mystical States of Consciousnes with Semi-structured Nature Experiences," *Journal for the Scientific Study of Religion 16* (1977): pp. 155–163.

69. Here, Hood, Hill, and Spilka cite two studies, (1) R. W. Hood, Jr., R. J. Morris, and P. J. Watson, "Religious Orientation and Prayer Experience," *Psychological Reports* 60 (1987): pp. 1201–1202; and (2) R. W. Hood, Jr., R. J. Morris, and P. J. Watson, "Prayer Experience and Religious Orientation," *Review of Religious Research* 31 (1989): pp. 39–45.

70. Here, Hood, Hill, and Spilka cite M. M. Poloma and G. H. Gallup, Jr., *Varieties of Prayer: A Survey Report* (Philadelphia: Trinity Press International, 1991).

71. Hood, Hill, and Spilka, *The Psychology of Religion*, p. 367.

72. Thanks to philosopher Jonathan MS Pearce for these observations and some of the phrasing. See Jonathan MS Pearce, "Religious Revelations Never Disagree with You," *A Tippling Philosopher*, blog, Skeptic Ink, 21 April 2015, http://www.skepticink.com/tippling/2015/04/21/why-religious-revelations-never-disagree-with-you/.

73. In *The Righteous Mind*, Haidt points out something important regarding purity. He wrote, "I could see the dark side of this ethic [an ethic of "divinity"] too: once you allow visceral feelings of disgust to guide your conception of what God wants, then minorities who trigger even a hint of disgust in the majority (such as homosexuals or obese people) can be ostracized and treated cruelly. The ethic of divinity is sometimes incompatible with compassion, egalitarianism, and basic human rights." He goes on to note, particularly where "purity" is concerned, that "the ethic of divinity lets us give voice to inchoate feelings of elevation and degradation—our sense of 'higher' and 'lower.' It gives us a way to condemn crass consumerism and *mindless or trivialized sexuality*" (emphasis added). Religious purity culture (regarding sexuality) is undoubtedly one of the most damaging harms of many religious beliefs, and Haidt notes that it arises directly out of an ethic of divinity, in this context being attached to "God."

74. The irony here is too sweet to ignore. Don't put your fingers in holy water to purify yourself. There's poop in it. (See Michael Shields, "Holy Water in Austria Unsafe to Drink," *Reuters*, 18 September 2013, http://www.reuters.com/article/2013/09/18/us-austria-water-idUSBRE98H0AG20130918.

75. Note the existence of *orthorexia*, an increasingly common eating disorder in which its sufferers torture themselves over a perceived need to eat only "clean" foods, as defined, more often than not, by outright bullshit.

76. *Chicken Soup for the Soul* is a series of inspirational books by Jack Canfield and Mark Victor Hansen published from within their own publishing house.

77. Given the common rejection of the term "spiritual" by nonbelievers, it is worth noting that the etymology of the term "enthusiasm" reads, "from Greek *enthousiasmos*, from *enthous* 'possessed by a god, inspired' (based on *theos* 'god')," according to Google.

78. Haidt, *The Happiness Hypothesis*, pp. 94–98. Note that even if positive psychology turns out to be a bogus field, as some critics insist, the research indicating that this psychological state they've called "flow" is somehow integral to human flourishing should prove valid regardless.

79. Harris, *Waking Up*, p. 10. His exact wording is, "my goal is to pluck the diamond from the dunghill of esoteric religion."

80. See Hood, Hill, and Spilka, *The Psychology of Religion*, all of chapter 13.

81. *Ibid.*, p. 460.

82. *Ibid.*, pp. 461–462.

83. *Ibid.*, p. 465.

84. Here, Hood, Hill, and Spilka cite D. Capps, "The Psychology of Petitionary Prayer." *Theology Today* 39 (1982): p. 130.

85. Here, Hood, Hill, and Spilka cite the same as the above, p. 131.

86. Hood, Hill, and Spilka, *The Psychology of Religion*, p. 468.

87. *Ibid.*, pp. 465–468.

88. Fascinatingly, it seems that the method of asking for forgiveness for one's sins is a successful way of resetting someone to a commitment to one's framework-moral attitudes. The mechanism seems to be that once someone believes himself bad enough, he will be more willing to give into that and act that way, but by receiving forgiveness, he is able to reset himself to a perceived net-positive state of moral purity and will work to maintain it. See Dan Ariely, "RSA Animate— The Truth About Dishonesty," *YouTube*, video, 14 September 2012, https://www.youtube.com/watch?v=XBmJay_qdNc.

89. Hood, Hill, and Spilka, *The Psychology of Religion*, p. 462.

90. *Ibid.*, pp. 463–475.

91. This reliance on parental imagery for the mythological character of "God" is almost certainly rooted in the fact that people also use "God" as an object of attachment, which will be discussed later.

92. Incidentally, what we are seeing in cases like Sweden and Japan is that when people have good reasons to put their trust in functioning societal systems, many will put their trust there instead of in a mythological construct. This is little more, then, than the tendency to accept natural attributions over religious ones when those are available. Ironically, because of the social aspects of what people mean by the term "God," when they call upon "God" for control, they're calling essentially on the same thing: people. This happens even when they don't really trust their neighbors, communities, and governments. Relying upon "God" instead narrows the focus to the moral community that they feel they can most easily trust, and it is plausible that the effect would be greater when calling upon larger, more organized social structures (like healthy, strong, functioning governments, which exist for exactly that purpose).

93. Thomson discusses the community-building role of church (or other religious) group activities at length, indicating that many of the activities and rituals that they engage in serve precisely this purpose. The predictable result is that many people tie what they mean by "God" directly to the community of the church. See Thomson, *Why We Believe in God(s)*, pp. 79–102.

94. Such movements are explicitly committed to helping people meet the needs many religious believers turn to belief in a deity to pretend to meet. They may play a significant role in a post-theistic society.

95. Anderson, *Why We Believe in God(s)*, pp. 82–102.

96. *Ibid.*, pp. 80–81 on "costly signaling." He writes, "Hard-to-fake, honest, costly signals of commitments are part of our relationships. Religions use these quite nicely. . . . How do I judge your commitment to the faith and to me as a brother in the faith? I watch your hard-to-fake, costly participation in the rituals of our faith."

97. It is now understood that the Benjamin Franklin effect works by creating a sense of cognitive dissonance with a particularly prosocial path of easing being the easiest and most likely to be taken. It makes no sense to do a favor for someone that we do not like, particularly for someone to whom we are hostile, but it seems

almost outrageously rude to refuse it, especially if the favor is relatively trivial. In many cases, the favor is done, and the doer is left with a sense of dissonance on the juxtaposed ideas "I helped her" and "I don't like her." The easiest resolution to this conundrum and thus easiest path to dissonance reduction is to revise the latter belief to "I must like her more than I thought," and thus prosociality is encouraged.

98. I base this observation on my personal experience and upon countless observations of people insisting that it is "hard to be a Christian" and "hard to admit/show your beliefs." While many Christians do firmly believe without the slightest traces of doubt, I think it is likely for some untold many that there is a real sense that somehow this all may be silly. Those people incur the greatest sense of cost in performing this favor, aside from very hostile antagonists who may have to swallow considerable personal insult, and are likely, paradoxically, to be the most drawn together by this effect.

99. Revealing one's values to strangers certainly invokes a certain kind of vulnerability that may make the prayer request seem a little bigger a favor in some or many cases than others. For example, if a Catholic man who strongly does not see eye to eye with a Muslim woman sees a prayer request for a dying family member made by the woman and fulfills it, he has to overcome a kind of hesitation following from the recognition that his religious beliefs, and thus what he is petitioning, are not perfectly in line with hers and then decide to do it anyway.

100. Thomson insists that building a system of fictive kin is one of the primary functions of religion. Haidt's research on moral communities corroborates this view.

101. Here, Hood, Hill, and Spilka cite R. F. Baumeister and M. R. Leary, "The Need to Belong: Desire for Interpersonal Attachments as a Fundamental Human Motivation," *Psychological Bulletin* 117 (1995): pp. 497–529.

102. Hood, Hill, and Spilka, *The Psychology of Religion*, pp. 18–19.

103. See, for example, Boghossian, *A Manual for Creating Atheists*, chapter 2.

104. See my chapter: James A. Lindsay, "Only Humans Can Solve the Problems of the World," in *Christianity Is Not Great: How Faith Fails*, ed. John W. Loftus, (Amherst, NY: Prometheus Books, 2014), pp. 445–461, where I discuss this at somewhat greater length.

105. One need only cite religious resistance to any clear progress along the moral arc (say the abolition of slavery, improvement of human rights, improvement of women's rights, improvement of minority rights, and so on and so forth) to get a

strong sense of how anchored ships in our moral seas slow down progress overall. One also should note that once a religion becomes sufficiently secularized to have lost its absolute authority over the communities in which it exists, the religions themselves get dragged along behind the rest, riding the same current along the same moral arc while making it unnecessarily hard to proceed. John W. Loftus has written and taught upon the theme of the slow but steady liberalization of Christianity, for instance, a theme Mark Twain was also famous for pointing out with a considerably harsher pen.

106. Here, Hood, Hill, and Spilka cite four studies by psychologist of religion Lee Kirkpatrick, one with Phil Shaver: (1) L. A. Kirkpatrick, "An Attachment-Theory Approach to the Psychology of Religion," *International Journal for the Psychology of Religion* 2 (1992): pp. 3–28; (2) L. A. Kirkpatrick, "The Role of Attachment in Religious Belief and Behavior," *Advances in Personal Relationships* 5 (1994): pp. 239–265; (3) L. A. Kirkpatrick, "A Longitudinal Study of Changes in Religious Belief and Behavior as a Function of Individual Differences in Attachment Style," *Journal for the Scientific Study of Religion* 36 (1997): pp. 207–217; and (4) L. A. Kirkpatrick and P. R. Shaver, "An Attachment-Theoretical Approach to Romantic Love and Religious Belief," *Personality and Social Psychology Bulletin* 18 (1992): pp. 266–275.

107. Here, Hood, Hill, and Spilka are referring to research they cite by A. K. Eshleman, J. R. Dickie, D. M. Merasco, A. Shepard, and M. Johnson, "Mother God, Father God: Children's Perceptions of God's Distance," *International Journal for the Psychology of Religion* 9 (1999): pp. 139–146.

108. Here, Hood, Hill, and Spilka cite J. R. Dickie, A. K. Eshleman, D. M. Merasco, A. Shepard, M. Vander Wilt, and M. Johnson, "Parent-Child Relationships and Children's Images of God," *Journal for the Scientific Study of Religion* 36 (1997): pp. 25–43, quote from p. 42.

109. Hood, Hill, and Spilka, *The Psychology of Religion*, pp. 101–102.

110. Here, Hood, Hill, and Spilka cite L. A. Kirkpatrick and P. R. Shaver, "Attachment Theory and Religion: Childhood Attachments, Religious Beliefs, and Conversion," *Journal for the Scientific Study of Religion* 29 (1990): pp. 315–334.

111. Hood, Hill, and Spilka, *The Psychology of Religion*, p. 102.

112. Thomson, *Why We Believe in God(s)*, pp. 45–46.

113. *Ibid.*, p. 46.

114. *Ibid.*

115. Jesus as "'God' made flesh" can also be seen as a character that symbolizes to Christians that the notion of moral perfection that they attribute to "God" is possible in a human being (obvious theological difficulties here ignored because they're pointless).

116. The extreme proliferation of saints in the Catholic tradition indicates something of a fascination with intermediaries to "God" that can be taken as attachment figures, but Jesus, "Son of God," remains nearly perfect in this role.

117. Hood, Hill, and Spilka, *The Psychology of Religion*, p. 101.

118. Dennett introduces this concept in his book *Breaking the Spell: Religion as a Natural Phenomenon*, (New York: Viking Adult, 2006), and discussed it at length in his talk at the 2007 meeting of the Atheist Alliance International (AAI), "Good Reasons for 'Believing' in God—Dan Dennett, AAI," *YouTube*, video, 11 November 2009, https://www.youtube.com/watch?v=BvJZQwy9dvE.

119. Boghossian, *A Manual for Creating Atheists*, p. 24.

120. *Ibid.*, pp. 23–25. As faith extends the perceived justification for one's belief beyond the warrant of the evidence supporting that belief, it is appropriate to see this as a kind of pretending to know things that the believer doesn't know. When viewed in the plain light, it is patently ridiculous to find such behavior virtuous.

121. Lest any reader find this claim contentious, please continue a few paragraphs to see evidence of ample support for it in the literature.

122. That religions deny that they deny death is most obviously manifest in the fact that many of them are death-centered cults (cult organizations that are centrally concerned with death, either of people or of particular religious figureheads) that claim to exist purely to affirm life.

123. John 3:16.

124. This, among other possibilities, is one reason that many without belief are simply incorrect at assuming that it is impossible to believe in spirits or the supernatural if one is an atheist. There are supernatural possibilities other than God or gods that do not depend upon deities to "make sense." Thus, lacking belief in *gods* does not imply philosophical metaphysical naturalism. Of course, it is my own opinion that there is no legitimate reason to talk about the supernatural at all. It, like theism, is mythology that sometimes gets taken too seriously by philosophers. It strikes me as plain that anything that is relevant to the natural world is *natural*, not *supernatural*, whether it might best be described as *extranormal* or *paranormal* or not. In that sense, there is no reason to bother discussing or

defending metaphysical naturalism. In fact, that term doesn't really even need to exist because it is the only real game in town.

125. Hood, Hill, and Spilka, *The Psychology of Religion*, p. 184.

126. Here, Hood, Hill, and Spilka cite P. Aries, *Western Attitudes Toward Death from the Middle Ages to the Present* (Baltimore: Johns Hopkins University Press, 1974), quote from p. 99.

127. Hood, Hill, and Spilka, *The Psychology of Religion*, p. 184.

128. Here, Hood, Hill, and Spilka cite P. Tillich, *The Courage to Be* (New Haven, CT: Yale University Press, 1952), quote from p. 40.

129. Here, Hood, Hill, and Spilka cite B. Malinowski, "The Role of Magic and Religion," in *A Reader in Contemporary Religion*, ed. W. A. Lessa and E. Z. Vogt (New York: Harper & Row, 1965), pp. 63–72, quote from p. 71.

130. Here, Hood, Hill, and Spilka cite B. Spilka, J. D. Spangler, M. P. Rea, and C. B. Nelson, "Religion and Death: The Clerical Perspective," *Journal of Religion and Health* 20 (1981): pp. 299–306.

131. Hood, Hill, and Spilka, *The Psychology of Religion*, p. 184.

132. *Ibid.*

133. Terror management theory is a model in social psychology that attempts to explain the conflict between the desire to live and the inevitability of death. As the first sentence in Cook et al. indicates, it is centrally concerned with examining the ways in which human beings use cultural constructs to define meaning and purpose in life, thus mitigating the terror associated with death. Obviously, religious beliefs about immortality or the illusory nature of death would be key examples. The reader should note that terror management theory has received a fair amount of criticism, especially in the vein of being overreaching in the centrality of death to human social psychology (this centrality possibly stemming from the seminal piece of the model, Ernest Becker's 1973 book *The Denial of Death* [New York: Free Press], which may exhibit an overreliance on Freudian ideas drawn from Otto Rank's work). As with many other points raised, for my purposes of establishing that the word "God" is somehow related to the idea of denying death, any failures of terror management theory as a social psychological model are irrelevant.

134. Corey L. Cook, Florette Cohen, and Sheldon Solomon, "What If They're Right About the Afterlife? Evidence of the Role of Existential Threat on Anti-Atheist

Prejudice," *Social Psychological and Personality Science*, 27 April 2015, http://spp. sagepub.com/content/early/2015/04/27/1948550615584200.abstract.

135. Ecclesiastes 1:2.

136. That our sense of personal meaning is defined in terms of our social environment is very probably the foundation for the best ethical argument against suicide, God or no God. The argument proceeds upon the fact that the personal meaning of those connected to our lives are partly defined in terms of ourselves, and in many cases, it is a wantonly selfish act that violates their rights in that regard to end our own lives except under very particular circumstances. It is thus also the foundation of a compassionate and sensible discussion and subsequent decisions about the right to die (and death with dignity), the right to choose euthanasia in certain terminal circumstances and thus the ability to maintain human dignity and some modicum of comfort in our final days or hours. Many religious attitudes are directly antagonistic to such a debate and an unconscionable source of unnecessary human suffering, and because they are religious, they are given unfair precedence in the ongoing debate about what should be a straightforward ethical discussion.

137. Inserting ideas of infinite reward and suffering into these judgments technically prevents anything like "settling the score" because no amount of finite good or wrong can be justifiably compensated by being given infinite reward or punishment, or even missing one or the other in the event that only one is believed in. In fact, infinity completely breaks a moral calculus. See my own blog post on this: James A. Lindsay, "How Infinity Breaks a Moral Calculus," *God Doesn't; We Do*, blog, *Web*, 9 September 2014, http://goddoesnt.blogspot.com/2014/09/how-infinity-breaks-a-moral-calculus.html.

138. While I don't go in much for offense, a properly offensive notion is that the work, friendship, and love I have done to help those around me and those to come after me is a vanity because in some untold number of millions of years, or longer, humanity won't exist. Religious beliefs centered upon the denial of death have no quarter to steal the meaning contained in my life and the relationships in it.

139. Obviously, some of these behaviors will genuinely be immoral. The addition of "framework" here, in context, refers more to the idea that Satan serves as a lure to sin (break the framework-moral code), though any even remotely workable framework-moral system will contain elements of a genuine moral system (like not murdering, not stealing, and so forth).

140. Recall that "sin" means little more than deviation from an extant moral framework.

141. Wording obtained from "Delusion," *Wikipedia*, http://en.wikipedia.org/wiki/Delusion, where it cites Karl Jaspers, *General Psychopathology*, vol. 1 (Baltimore: Johns Hopkins University Press, 1997).

142. Consider, for instance, the Catholic dogma of complete assent to one's faith.

143. William M. Gervais, "Everything Is Permitted? People Intuitively Judge Immorality as Representative of Atheists," *PLoS ONE* 9, no. 4 (9 April 2014), e92302. doi:10.1371/journal.pone.0092302.

144. Corroborating this claim, recent research by Corey Cook et al. found that "atheists were perceived to pose significantly greater threats to values, and elicit greater moral disgust, than other groups also perceived to pose values-related threats (gay men, Muslims)." See Corey L. Cook, Catherine A. Cottrell, and Gregory D. Webster, "No Good Without God: Antiatheist Prejudice as a Function of Threats to Morals and Values," *Psychology of Religion and Spirituality* 7, no. 3 (August 2014).

CHAPTER 6

OKAY, NOW WHAT?

When I first told Peter Boghossian about the concept for the first half of the book, his immediate response was, "Okay, suppose by fiat that you're right. Now what? That's the most important thing."[1] The rest of this book is dedicated to addressing that question, and this chapter is its introduction.

Before getting to that, I need to bring back to mind the purpose of this book. This book is a debate opener. It's presented here to start a much-needed conversation. It is a call for us to go post-theistic and (hopefully) a clear expression of why doing so makes sense. It is not, however, a manifesto about how this can be achieved in the pragmatic minutiae, even if it hopes to provide some overall guiding mechanisms and useful suggestions. The following material is quite general, and necessarily so. It would be foolish to attempt to develop and demand an actual plan of the exact things we should do, and so it is not that. I am providing a new way of thinking about an ages-old problem, a framework, and some generalized mechanisms for others to take on and develop more detailed plans. This book is a signpost at a crossroads and little more.

The "what now" is straightforward: a number of things have to change, and first among them is a lot of minds. An enormous number of people consequentially accept ancient mythology that no longer has either scientific or philosophical legs to stand upon, and they accept it on faith. Faith, though, is its own kind of poison, the sort that allows human beings to pretend that they are absolutely right about something they absolutely do not or cannot know, and it has its tendrils extending into all ideological commitment. Religion, then, is simply the least confusing example of a particularly bad brand of thinking. Uprooting faith, then, is an absolutely critical endeavor whether I am right or not.

We also have to change gears and stop arguing about the claims of theism. Those ideas are dead, and their terms are obsolete and mythological. The fight that remains is cultural, not academic or philosophical. We need to help people abandon faith, mythology, and superstition and to do everything we can to help them come to terms with the psychological and social needs that keep them clinging to ancient stories—as lone sources of ethical guidance, as coping mechanisms, as personal or cultural contextual narratives, and as a means of making sense of a confusing and difficult world. Part of this means giving up on bad approaches, like those that are branded "atheism." Making this change requires a powerful shift in perspective to a *post-theistic* mindset, and, if I am right, the time to make that change has already passed. We need to catch up.

Of course, a number of additional challenges face us as well because uprooting faith and realizing theism is dead simply will not happen universally or all at once. Theism has died at the level of ideas, but few—even among those lacking belief—truly realize this simple fact. That leaves us with a lot to do.

Therefore, we must, at the least, maintain a strong vanguard against religious and all other ideological domination in our societies, a goal usually called *secularism*. Furthermore, we have to recognize that religion and belief in God *meet needs for people*, and thus we absolutely must start diligent and serious work into figuring out how to help people meet those needs in a better way. In the process, we should aim to avoid succumbing to ham-handed attempts or atheistic ideological approaches that are as bad (or worse) than the religions they attempt to unseat. The data seem uncontroversial; where societies are very successful at providing opportunities and security, reliance on religious belief drops.[2] Put another way, *if people can have their needs met without religion, they often will*.

Making these goals possible will require devising means by which we can service them at various levels. It is an easy thing to say that we need to have better education on a variety of topics, and I quite agree with this point, but such a statement is useless without clear indications both of the sort of education that is necessary and the means by which it can meet people. These are very hard problems, and I can but offer some meager suggestions on them here.

Perhaps most challenging, and maybe most pressing, is that these ideas, attitudes, and efforts have to spread around the globe. It is not enough that the educated, mostly secular West adopt these ideas. They must go where they are least likely to be accepted, and time is not on our side in this need. This challenge is, I think, well beyond the scope of this book (and this author), but it is an extraordinarily worthy one that deserves a great deal of attention and collaborative effort.

Since I was challenged to think of this topic in terms of imagining that I am right, I think I should go further and consider what happens if our society, Western society or some significant group within it, were to go properly post-theistic; what then? That case is the long-range goal of this book, and by taking a moment to recognize it, we should find it easier to realize.

Our long-term effort is to create a society that fully sees religion and belief in deities only in the rearview mirror. It has rightly been said that religion and its attendant superstitions belong to the infancy of our species,[3] and the effort now is to grow up and leave it there. In order to accomplish such a feat, we must set up and put in place certain protections in our culture that do not prohibit religious faith but that render it largely unnecessary and unattractively obsolete. Such a goal must be met by engaging in near-term efforts in uprooting faith in individuals, maintaining and expanding the insulation between faith and state, establishing educational systems that help people learn to value and embrace informed skepticism, and finding satisfactory ways to meet people's most challenging psychological and social needs. None of these are easy.

With these main challenges that await us drafted, we must consider how to approach them. The easy answer to how we should proceed is vague but critical: *with authenticity and honesty, with a mind to do good to the best of our abilities while readily admitting our epistemic limitations.* The last thing we are after is launching another morally charged ideology, and it's through honesty and humility that we avoid that error.

The remainder of this book is dedicated to the goal of outlining, hopefully for the first time in a single place, a first draft of what to do now that we understand that we've all been wrong about God and that theism has been the wrong way to think about that complicated idea all along. The goal is to cease with theism and atheism and leave belief in God behind entirely, to go post-theistic, and we need to do it now. There's just no good reason to willfully persist in pretending that the word "God" means something other than what it does, and seeing it as a psychosocial construct can take us post-theistic almost at once.

Notes

1. Personal communication, summer 2014.

2. Frederick Solt, Philip Habel, and J. Tobin Grant, "Economic Inequality, Relative Power, and Religiosity," *Social Science Quarterly* 92, no. 2 (June 2011): pp. 447–465, http://onlinelibrary.wiley.com/doi/10.1111/j.1540-6237.2011.00777.x/abstract.

3. This wording, of course, paraphrases from the late, great Christopher Hitchens.

CHAPTER 7

UPROOTING FAITH

For the purposes of the ensuing discussion, the term *faith* will be defined rather broadly as *that which extends confidence in a belief beyond the warrant provided to it by reliable ways of claiming knowledge.*[1]

Before discussing the myriad ways that this plain-language definition gets dragged fruitlessly into philosophical weeds—about what knowledge means, about what constitutes valid ways of knowing, about what constitutes *evidence*, and so on—let us pause to consider in general just how obvious it is that uprooting faith is a goal of incomparable value and importance.

Few things, in fact, could be more obvious than that whenever possible, we should only be as confident in a belief as we have good reasons to be. Plainly, it is almost incredible that nearly all of us sometimes lose sight of the importance of this sort of intellectual honesty. So it is, though, that literally billions of us hold it as a virtue to believe the indefensible for reasons that, however psychologically satisfying, are anything but good ones. Accepting what is true, however, does not require us to exaggerate the confidence in any of our beliefs beyond what we can reliably claim to know. Helping ourselves to become skilled at pulling out faith-based thinking by the roots, then, is one of the most critical values we can cultivate—all of us, whether we believe in deities or not.

Because so many people take so much on faith, we don't even need to imagine the alternative to uprooting faith. We already live with it and have done so for centuries. The historical record of the needless abuses of unjustified certainty hardly need another reiteration here, though it is worth noticing that religion has proved itself a nearly perfect tool for making a morally driven and horrific force out of failing to have the slightest idea about what one is talking about. Because unjustified beliefs held by ideologically motivated moral communities possess the full potential for evils that only moral righteousness can provide, we must cultivate a virtue of doubt, not of certainty, and uproot faith.

Philosophical Weeds

Unfortunately, the working definition of faith here, *that which extends confidence in a belief beyond the warrant provided to it by reliable ways of claiming knowledge,* lands itself in the exact kinds of philosophical weeds that perpetuate theism and that cause academic philosophy to stagnate. Let's clear that up.

Certainly, the questions of what constitutes knowledge and how we can know it when we see it, which are addressed by a philosophical endeavor known as *epistemology*, are important ones, *but they are not important here.* Tenets of religious faith often have an obliging habit of looking nothing at all like things people can be justified in claiming to know to be truths, and some are unknowable by their very definitions.[2] Furthermore, many of the ways that religious believers claim to know that their beliefs are true are readily understood as being completely unreliable, such as *tradition, authority,* and *revelation.*[3] Others appear indistinguishable from certain cognitive biases like confirmation bias[4] and optimism bias.[5]

Just as certainly, questions related to how we can best justify beliefs, especially when it comes to what constitutes valid evidence supporting them, are interesting and worth pursuing,[6] but again, they are not important here. Not only do many religious tenets lack anything even resembling evidence, but they are also talking about the wrong thing. "God" is a mythological construct to give a sense of reality to a complex set of ideas that people use to meet their psychological and social needs, and given this understanding, there's no compelling reason to consider a deity at all. The philosophy of religion as an entire academic subdiscipline seems to have come into existence, in fact, specifically to equivocate upon this matter, and for that reason at least it should really be seen for the waste of time that it is.[7]

Furthermore, the predictable commentary from the peanut gallery that colloquial uses of the term faith mean something different from the definition given here, something more akin to trust, are equally irrelevant. That we make contracts "in good faith" and have "faith" in those people we trust has next to nothing to do with religious faith. The distinction isn't even subtle. For me to say that I have faith in my friend to do a favor for me is wholly different from saying that I have faith in God to deliver me from troubles on the simple observation that I do not require faith of any kind to believe my friend exists. Having faith in God means both trusting the deity on its alleged promises and pretending to know it actually exists in the first place.[8]

All of that said, there is no need to wade into these bogs of academic arcana or ordinary pedantry in order to see the plain sense in minimizing all sources by which we express more confidence than we are warranted by reliable methods. In other words, we require no sophisticated—or Sophisticated™—argumentation to conclude that, indeed, uprooting faith is of paramount importance, particularly if the concept called "God" has absolutely nothing to do with any of the brands of theism so widely believed.

Is It Wrong to Uproot Someone's Faith?

Generally speaking, no, it is not wrong to uproot someone's faith. To the contrary, if done in ways that respect the individual's autonomy and dignity, helping someone to pull out their own faith by the roots does them an enormous favor. Every article of faith abandoned is one fewer unjustified premise that is believed for bad reasons, and it is thus one fewer opportunity to mislead oneself. There may be special cases, of course, but those are exceptions, not rules.[9] For the vast majority of people, helping them to uproot their faith does them at least two major favors. First, it treats them as an intelligent adult capable of engaging in serious and critical thought. Second, it helps them be less wrong.

If "God" is truly a word that means something that is not accurately accounted for by the mythology we call theism, even if my arguments about what that might be go amiss, then beliefs about God are *always wrong* because they fail even to talk about the correct thing. A stopped clock, they say, is right twice a day, but a correctly functioning clock set to the wrong time is never right.

That said, "by any means necessary" is not a good way to approach uprooting faith. One obvious example of a means that has been tried and that has failed is to do so by forcing it, by the fiat of state decree. Such efforts are doomed to failure for good reasons, not least that they often attempt to replace faith with faith (going from faith in religion to faith in some crackpot state ideology). Even if some such attempt succeeded in avoiding this apparently certain pitfall, attempting to force people out of faith does nothing to help anyone improve the way in which they form beliefs, which is what uprooting faith-based thinking really comes down to. Faith must be left, not stamped out, and people need to learn to leave it by learning to reject certain bad ways of thinking.

Uprooting faith means helping people learn to develop and rely upon more effective ways of coming to knowledge—including the moral attitudes and communities that religion often serves as a shortcut method to developing. Fostering this kind of change, in the long run, is very likely to benefit both individuals and the societies they inhabit. ·

Is Uprooting Faith Possible?

Emphatically, yes. People lose their faiths every day. I lost my faith. Many of my friends and family members have lost their faiths. Many public figures have lost their faiths. Many readers of this book, perhaps even you, have lost their faith as well. There are compelling stories about religious figures losing their faiths, such as former evangelical ministers Dan Barker, now co-president of the Freedom From Religion Foundation, and John W. Loftus, now a prolific author of many books hoping to help people abandon their faith, especially in Christianity.[10]

Stories of lost faith are not uncommon. In fact, they're very common.[11] Millions of people worldwide have lost their faiths and in so doing taken a major step away from believing unjustified assertions. It happens all the time, and these stories are profound sources of hope. Faith can be abandoned, and anyone can do it given the right circumstances.

Not only can faith be abandoned, and not only do we see it being abandoned, we see it in exactly the kinds of situations where we might worry it is least likely to happen. Philosopher Peter Boghossian wrote a book, *A Manual for Creating Atheists*, detailing an effective method that will be discussed shortly. His method is based upon intervention work with prison inmates, and the literature he cites supporting that belief revision is possible via the right methods is substantial. Boghossian writes,

> If we look at the vast body of literature about how people change their beliefs, especially the literature with prison inmates, we *know* that there are effective interventions. We know that it's possible to change the beliefs and behavior of people who don't want their beliefs and behavior changed. We can use identical tools to apply those to dislodging faith.[12]

The questions, then, aren't about whether or not faith can be uprooted; it's about how we should go about doing it, and, particularly, how do we do it within faiths that are currently growing?[13] Sure, there are almost certainly some people who are, for whatever reasons, so locked into or dependent upon their faiths that they will not be willing to revise the beliefs held in them, but that says nothing about the vast majority. As psychologists of religion Ralph Hood, Peter Hill, and Bernard Spilka clearly indicated, "The evidence is that most people in most circumstances initially employ naturalistic explanations and attributions . . . [although] there is a good likelihood of shifting to religious attributions when naturalistic ones do not satisfactorily meet the needs for meaning, control and esteem."[14] Conversely to this observation, in many cases helping people find the space to question the faith holding their religious attributions in place may require little more than finding ways to satisfactorily meet their key psychosocial needs and then asking simple, honest questions.[15]

If correct, what this suggests is that we can help people uproot their own faith by helping them to meet their psychosocial needs and then providing opportunities to question the beliefs they maintain in faith. The former of these matters is complicated and will be likely to depend upon social, political, and economic changes of the right kinds, and some of these will be discussed in later chapters. The latter is the project of the rest of this chapter.

Three Fantastic Tools for Uprooting Faith

Almost all of the most effective tools for uprooting faith rely upon a single core: honesty.[16] Honesty about what we can claim to know automatically *introduces doubt*, and doubt is the antithesis of faith.[17] Methods that will cause a person to doubt his faith are the only real way to uproot it. It is helpful to think of faith rather like a seal put around a belief to prevent doubt from getting in. The relevant question then, is how we might go about helping to introduce doubt in those who have sealed themselves from it (often even while they grapple with it). Fortunately, there are a few fantastic tools geared exactly to this purpose, and here I will discuss three of the best.

Peter Boghossian's Street Epistemology

The first of the three best tools I know of for uprooting faith is philosopher Peter Boghossian's Socratic questioning method that he calls *Street Epistemology* (SE), which he describes in detail and with thorough examples in his book *A Manual for Creating Atheists*.[18]

The core of Boghossian's SE approach is engaging in personal conversations, often one-on-one and quite casual, and simply asking a lot of the right kinds of questions. The goal of SE is to introduce doubt and open-mindedness (which Boghossian calls "doxastic openness," a willingness to revise one's beliefs). Critical to its success is modeling that behavior—you should be willing to change your mind on what you think before you try to change someone else's mind. The questions must be friendly and honest, based in genuine curiosity, while leaving the interviewee to have to explain *how he knows what he claims to know* in his own words and in his own time. A successful "intervention," as Boghossian calls them, will introduce doubt and thus move someone away from unjustified overconfidence in a belief, even if only a little at a time.

Boghossian's method works best by questioning the method by which someone claims to know something as well. For example, if someone were to reply that they "know" God loves him because the Bible instructs it, asking questions that may introduce doubt in the Bible's final authority can be helpful, such as, "Do you think it's possible that the Bible got this fact wrong, given that it seems to have misidentified bats as a kind of bird in Leviticus[19]?" The goal, then, of Boghossian's approach is undermining the process of belief justification, and when it is achieved, it forces people to go through the process of justifying their beliefs differently. This opens space for the person to revise his beliefs if suitable justifications cannot be found.

This method of questioning introduces doubt. In fact, religious apologists very frequently use a method similar Boghossian's—with one crucial difference—to win converts, and they seem to have had considerable success with it. These religious propagandists ask questions to introduce doubt, sometimes sincerely and sometimes with smarmy intention,[20] and then manipulate it. As we have seen, people prefer natural attributions until they are left uncomfortable for wanting one, and evangelists often exploit this feeling of vulnerability to shoehorn God into the conversation. The difference with SE is that Boghossian's method doesn't suggest answers but is instead centered upon *embracing doubt* when we don't actually know something.

That is, Boghossian's SE employs Socratic questioning specifically to induce doubt *for the purpose of fostering intellectual honesty*. His goal with SE is to help people recognize and accept the honest limitations of what they can know and to shape their beliefs accordingly. Core to the process is that a successful SE intervention requires the person with a new doubt to attempt to justify his belief differently.

Apologists and evangelists are not doing the same thing. They are using questions to create doubt (and sometimes fear) in order to manufacture vulnerability and then using their brand of theism to capitalize upon it to bring converts to their religious views. SE uses doubt to cause people to find better justifications for their beliefs or abandon them if they cannot; evangelism uses doubt (and fear) to construct a space into which they place beliefs that may or may not be justified.

Now, Boghossian notes a particular difficulty with his SE method; it frequently requires repeated interventions to help people become more comfortable with doubt and to expand their lines of questioning.[21] Often people will take their doubts back to their religious communities and have the kinds of answers that they want to hear given to them, and often they will rationalize similar answers for themselves as they seek new justifications for their beliefs—which we must remember they hold for important psychosocial reasons.

Two particular difficulties worth mentioning are the well-known "backfire effect," whereby butting up against a strongly held belief can cause the believer to dig in his heels and strengthen the belief, and post hoc rationalization, which psychologist Jonathan Haidt has explored in-depth.[22] Boghossian deals with the backfire effect obliquely in his *Manual for Creating Atheists*, discussing it under the terminology "doxastic entrenchment," wherein an overly aggressive approach may cause someone to entrench themselves further into their current beliefs.[23] Post hoc rationalization may explain why: we often have a tendency to work backward *toward* our previous beliefs when they possess moral relevance. In Haidt's view, we make our moral judgments very quickly, before thinking about them, and then use the cognitive process of moral reasoning to construct reasons (often incorrect) about why we arrived at the judgments we did. These bear mentioning because anyone attempting to help free people from the grip of faith with SE will undoubtedly come across them in their efforts.

Boghossian's SE process will gradually weed out unfounded beliefs but not warranted ones.[24] The process aims to get people to value intellectual honesty and to abandon faith as the unreliable method for claiming justification for beliefs that it is. As a feature of SE, any articles of religious faith that are legitimately true will be left intact. As it stands, though, it is a highly effective method for uprooting faith entirely.

John W. Loftus's Outsider Test for Faith

A second fantastic tool for uprooting faith is John W. Loftus's *Outsider Test for Faith* (OTF), which he has explained and defended in detail in a book of the same name.[25] It, like Boghossian's SE, should successfully help us confirm any faith that happens to be true, and yet it also is a highly effective tool for uprooting faith instead.

Loftus's approach to dealing with faith arises in its core from examining the religious diversity in the world, which he calls the "religious diversity thesis," along with the fact that the most common way for people to arrive at their faith-based beliefs is via cultural influence, which he calls the "religious dependency thesis." Particularly, one tends to be automatically highly skeptical of faith-based positions that compete with those of the culture or subculture one is raised in and yet the prevailing religion of one's parents and culture is by far the best predictor of one's own religious faith.

Facing these facts should lead an honest inquirer to wonder what her faith looks like *from the outside* as a test to see if it is worth believing or not.

His OTF proceeds by asking a person taking the test to attempt to weigh those factors in mind in order to attempt to step outside her own religion and evaluate it from the outside, from a position of *informed skepticism*. A person taking the OTF correctly would evaluate her own faith as though it were one from a different religious culture than her own, for example, a Christian could take the test by imagining that she is a Muslim—or, better, someone lacking religious faith entirely—and evaluating Christianity for the first time from that perspective. Loftus's contention is that any faith that has a hope of being legitimately true must be able to pass this test (and hence that the religious diversity that persists in the world is a strong argument against any religion being true). True things possess the virtue of being true regardless of who is evaluating them.

Loftus's OTF is a fantastic tool for cutting across many of the biases that come part and parcel with faith. Most Christians are able to see plainly that Islam and Hinduism are desperately unlikely to be true, and most Muslims and Hindus feel the same way about Christianity.[26] When one is not caught in perceived need of the beliefs, and particularly in the moral communities formed around those beliefs, the absurdities gain a salience that is difficult to overstate. Three in one? Really? I don't think so.

The primary difficulty with the OTF is that to get someone to take the test legitimately, he has to be able to think outside of his faith—an object to which he gives full assent. This is often not possible and sometimes results in religious apologists claiming that Christianity has passed the OTF (it hasn't).[27] Openness to consider that one's own faith might be wrong is a requirement before the OTF can be taken properly, and this makes the OTF a wonderful accompaniment to Boghossian's SE.

Taken together, the OTF and SE present a formidable pair of tools for uprooting faith at the level of personal interactions. Applying SE— asking honest questions that should induce doubt and willingness to revise beliefs—can create the perfect environment in which to suggest that the OTF is an excellent tool for testing faith in an intellectually honest way. Evaluating one's faith as if one didn't already believe it seems corrosive to belief in a way that, perhaps, few other things can be. We can think of SE as a method of introducing doubt and the OTF as an intellectually honest way of exploring doubt. They make an excellent pair.

As a general note, the effectiveness of these two methods isn't limited to religious faith. It should apply to any *supertruth* (a proposition regarded as true whether it is or not, usually an assumption of some ideology). This would include religious, political, doctrinal, ideological, and other types of beliefs, and the faith maintaining any false supertruth should be able to be uprooted by this approach—introduce enough doubt to wonder and then explore that doubt as if one didn't already accept the supertruth. That's the goal; that's why they work; and that's why they're legitimate! The point of both of these tools is to help someone think more clearly and to abandon unwarranted beliefs, not just to reason better but also to reexamine her assumptions with intellectual integrity.

Faith, understood as belief without sufficient evidence (or, as the *Oxford English Dictionary* gives as its second definition, "belief based upon spiritual apprehension instead of proof"), cannot survive this process. While this method will not necessarily lead us to truths—other tools are likely to be needed for that difficult endeavor—it will lead us away from false beliefs maintained for bad reasons.

The lingering questions of relevance, then, are when and how to apply these two tools. By their nature, these tools are best suited to application in rather limited settings, often in one-on-one communication with some degree of rapport already present between the individuals. This is particularly true of Boghossian's SE. The OTF has the advantage of being effective in larger groups, say being explained with an invitation to try it during or after a talk, especially one that is broadcast over the Internet. Both have the advantage of being very accessible in a classroom environment as well, particularly one that facilitates a lot of open discussion. As to the question of when, the answer is now. We can and should be applying such techniques now.

Laugh a Little
A third fantastic way to uproot faith is via *satire*, which is a form of mockery that is easily ethically justified in that it is not intended to belittle or intentionally harm the majority of its targets. Certainly, one can be

satirical of a particular public figure or his work, but the broader audience for whom that satire is intended is not on the receiving end of mockery.

Mockery and satire have to be carefully distinguished, then, because satire is a type of mockery that is generally to be encouraged (and thus, reciprocally, we have a justified expectation of its acceptance by those being satirized and the broader community), while outright mockery of individuals or groups of people (to be distinguished from sets of ideas those people hold) with the intent to belittle them specifically is to be discouraged.[28] The line between these two forms of criticism isn't exactly fine, but it isn't always completely glaring either. And it would be a significant and largely misguided effort to attempt to catalog here that which constitutes satire from that which constitutes mockery.

The benefit of satire in uprooting faith is in helping people see the laughable for what it is. A great many articles of faith are, when seen in the right light, absolutely ridiculous—in the literal sense. A skilled humorist can often shed the right light on these beliefs to expose at least a glimmer of this fact, and, once that is done, a central taboo of faith is broken, and faith is weakened. The sacred, rather by definition, is never funny exactly because "sacred" means little more than always being considered with only the utmost seriousness. Humor cuts through the vain pomposity of faith deftly and, if the joke is good enough, permanently.

The power of effective satire is to take the puff out of the sails of faith and expose it as a false virtue that people will want to avoid. It does so by breaking the powerful taboo on profaning the allegedly sacred (this being a point understood in moral terms[29]). Once sacredness falls away, the belief in question can more easily be reconsidered and, in many cases, revised. The ideological, including the religious, we must note, are anything but unaware of this fact. Indeed, they sometimes go to great lengths, some murderous, in order to protect their core beliefs from "blasphemous" satire.[30] Few testaments to its effectiveness could be more telling.

An obvious example of this phenomenon in action is the cultural impact of successful comedians. Entertainers like Richard Pryor and Chris Rock have done enormous damage to racism by mocking it and people who are racists. The comedian George Carlin destroyed a significant number of taboos concerning religion and politics by making them into jokes, often obscene ones. Almost anywhere we turn in the comedy world, we find clever individuals doing tremendously effective work at getting people to laugh at what they believe they shouldn't laugh at. That laughter fosters, and often directly engenders, belief revision as a result.

This, of course, isn't to say that we should take comedians necessarily at all of their jokes—often humor lies in slightly mischaracterizing, exaggerating, or misplacing the context of certain ideas, and those weaknesses do not lose relevance just because the joke is funny. The same critical thinking tools we should always strive to apply to new (and old) information still matter, but so does allowing humor to expose that not only are the beliefs themselves often funny, but so too is the pretense with which they are regarded. Shattering the pretense of seriousness surrounding certain beliefs is of incredible value where it comes to helping people uproot the faith that uses it as a shield. And this is the point and the reason that satire is such a fantastic tool for uprooting faith. It serves to remove taboos and it allows ideas to be pulled down to the level where they can receive any criticisms that they deserve. This levels the playing field in the marketplace of ideas and renders any worldview fair game by bringing it down off its self-erected pedestals. As a result, cultural acceptability pervades in seeing something being freely criticized, and attitudes can change even by mere exposure to such freedom.[31]

Nonreligious Faith
Religious faith is by far the most obvious example of the employment of faith to maintain a belief because it lacks no temerity in using the term and trumpeting this special form of intellectual arrogance as some kind of virtue. We all maintain beliefs for bad reasons sometimes, though, and, particularly when those beliefs get wrapped up in our values and become sacralized—by which we can mean being assigned effectively infinite value—we exhibit identical resistance to belief revision as the faithful. The problem is the same: we maintain a degree of confidence in those ideas exceeding the warrant supporting them.

By definition, every ideology does this, and it can be a problem as big as or bigger than religious faith, depending on the particulars of the ideology, the related moral framework, and the willingness of the ideologues adhered to it to engage in reprehensible means to achieve their ends. The idea of God (or Hell), at least, scares a lot of people out of engaging in a lot of bad behavior[32] (though with its own attendant and serious problems[33]—please see this and the preceding note as they are very important to addressing this topic properly). Still, if it inflates the confidence in a belief above its legitimate warrant, it is faith, religious or not. Sociopolitical activist movements are particularly rife with this phenomenon, and the faith employed in those cases is often very consequential and harder to detect and dislodge than religious faith.

All faith possesses the power for great and needless harm, and all faith is unjustifiable because it mishandles information we pretend constitutes knowledge when it doesn't. It simply has no room in the process of determining what is true and, thus, what is most likely to produce good results for people impacted by human beliefs, which is all of us. All faith has to go.

Uprooting faith, particularly religious faith, is possible, beneficial, and important. Whatever is worth knowing is worth knowing for good reasons. If faith is the method by which people maintain belief in God, and everybody is wrong about God, then quite clearly, faith is a problem that needs to be pulled out by its roots.

Notes

1. This definition paraphrases Peter Boghossian and is best attributed to him. See his *Manual for Creating Atheists*, pp. 23–24.

2. God, itself, is sometimes defined as "the unknowable" or "that which is beyond knowing," as are many of the "mysteries" of faith like the Christian Trinity or the details of the Catholic transubstantiation.

3. Biologist Richard Dawkins has been noted for saying that these three factors are acceptable bases for claiming to know something in religion, at least part of the time. Note that where revealed religions are concerned, traditions and authority are themselves based upon revelations, and that, whatever metaphysical "reality" may be, revelation remains utterly indistinguishable from making things up. This is an argument I explored at length in my own *God Doesn't; We Do*, see pp. 195–201.

4. Confirmation bias is the tendency to interpret new information in a way that confirms existing beliefs. When the Bible (Hebrews 11:1) discusses faith as

"the assurance of things hoped for, the conviction of things not seen," it sets the stage perfectly for believers to fall into the trap of confirmation bias. This definition lends itself neatly to a predisposition to interpret new information in light of the certainty of conviction that those things hoped for are being provided by God.

5. See, for example, my own blog post, "Going Skydiving with Tim McGrew," *God Doesn't; We Do*, blog, 25 May 2014, http://goddoesnt.blogspot.com/2014/05/going-skydiving-with-tim-mcgrew.html.

6. See my own lengthy discussion on this point, "A Problem with Evidence," *God Doesn't; We Do*, blog, *Web*, 2 June 2014, http://goddoesnt.blogspot.com/2014/06/a-problem-with-evidence.html.

7. John W. Loftus has written a number of excellent pieces on this topic on his blog, *Debunking Christianity*. A couple of noteworthy examples include: (1) "I'm Calling for an End to the Philosophy of Religion Discipline in Secular Universities," 24 July 2014, http://debunkingchristianity.blogspot.com/2014/07/im-calling-for-end-to-philosophy-of.html and (2) "More on Ending the Philosophy of Religion Discipline in Secular Universities," 28 July 2014, http://debunkingchristianity.blogspot.com/2014/07/more-on-ending-philosophy-of-religion.html.

8. It's rather stunning that those who would spin faith as "trust" fail to recognize this gaping hole in their alleged epistemic foundation for believing in God. The usual case is that these people trust God in faith to do something and then use anything that can be stretched to fit the bill as evidence that God exists and, presumably, did it, ignoring all other possible explanations or, more often, insisting that those are how God came through. It would be farcical enough to be worthy of an absurdist comedy to concoct any recipe more perfect for mistaking confirmation bias for evidence than mislabeling faith in God as a kind of trust.

9. It's tiring to note that callously trying to pry away the faith of someone who is rapidly approaching death is almost as pointless and reprehensible as attempting to squeeze a deathbed conversion out of them.

10. See, for two noteworthy examples, Dan Barker, *Godless: How an Evangelical Preacher Became One of America's Leading Atheists*, (Berkeley, CA: Ulysses Press, 2009), and John W. Loftus, *Why I Became an Atheist: A Former Preacher Rejects Christianity* (Amherst, NY: Prometheus Books, 2008).

11. Daniel Dennett remarks on this trend in his article "Why yhe Future of Religion Is Bleak," *Wall Street Journal*, 26 April 2015, http://www.wsj.com/articles/why-the-future-of-religion-is-bleak-1430104785, writing, "Religion has been

waning in influence for several centuries, especially in Europe and North America. There have been a few brief and local revivals, but in recent years the pace of decline has accelerated. Today one of the largest categories of religious affiliation in the world—with more than a billion people—is no religion at all, the 'Nones.' One out of six Americans is already a None; by 2050, the figure will be one out of four, according to a new Pew Research Center study. Churches are being closed by the hundreds, deconsecrated and rehabilitated as housing, offices, restaurants and the like, or just abandoned." The Pew Research Center study he mentions may be this one: http://www.pewforum.org/2015/04/02/religious-projections-2010-2050/, which indicates that, while Dennett's claims are accurate for Europe and North America, Islam is expected to experience a meteoric rise globally in the same time period—unless something drastic occurs to change that sobering fact. At any rate, Dennett's observation suffices to show that there are many, many stories of lost faith.

12. Peter Boghossian, personal communication, 8 January 2015.

13. Boghossian gave a talk in June 2015 at the *Imagine No Religion 5* conference in Vancouver, British Columbia, that specifically was targeted at using his methods and related ones to deradicalize extremist Islam.

14. Hood, Hill, and Spilka, *The Psychology of Religion*, p. 45.

15. Note also socioeconomic needs, since as people become more secure, their belief in God tends to diminish as well. See, for instance, Frederic Solt, Philip Habel, and J. Tobin Grant, "Economic Inequality, Relative Power, and Religiosity," *Social Science Quarterly* 92, no. 2 (June 2011): pp. 447–465.

16. Boghossian tends to prefer the term *authenticity*, and in the present context, I consider these terms essentially interchangeable.

17. Crafty religious apologists will try to warp this point to their own advantage by arguing that faith requires doubt because it's putting belief (which they often equivocate as confidence) in something you cannot or do not know to be true, but faith, sometimes *by definition*, requires full assent, which is to say, as the Catholics put it in the *Catechism of Trent*, that which "the faithful cannot doubt." The relevant section of the Catechism can be read here: http://www.cin.org/users/james/ebooks/master/trent/tcreed00.htm, accessed 16 May 2015. These apologists are playing a game with words to hide the fact that the degree of belief in the proposition is 100 percent *even while they know that cannot be justified*, and so the apologists undercut their own case with this embarrassing bit of verbal chicanery.

18. Boghossian addresses common criticisms to the use of the Socratic method in Peter Boghossian, "Socratic Pedagogy, Race, and Power: From People to Propositions," *Education Policy Analysis Archives*, 10, no. 3 (January 2002): pp. 1–9; and Peter Boghossian, "Socratic Pedagogy: Perplexity, Humiliation, Shame and a Broken Egg," *Educational Philosophy and Theory* 44, no. 7 (2011): pp. 701–720.

19. Leviticus 11:13–19.

20. "Would you consider yourself to be a good person? I'd like to ask you a few questions about that. What do you call someone who tells a lie? Have you ever told a lie? . . . " Smarmy intention.

21. Boghossian, *A Manual for Creating Atheists*, pp. 78–79.

22. See Jonathan Haidt, "The Emotional Dog and Its Rational Tail: A Social Intuitionist Approach to Moral Judgment," *Psychological Review* 108, no. 4 (2001): pp. 814–834.

23. Boghossian, *A Manual for Creating Atheists*, pp. 42–62.

24. And thus the immense and angry backlash against Boghossian from evangelical Christians is telling in and of itself.

25. Note: while the OTF gets book-length treatment in Loftus's book *The Outsider Test for Faith*, it was first discussed by Loftus in his book *Why I Became an Atheist* as a part of the thought process that helped him abandon his Christian faith—even as a trained evangelical Christian apologist!

26. Given that Hinduism is monistic, things are a little more complicated than this, but certainly very few Christians would accept that Jesus is an avatar of any Hindu deity, and so in that sense, Hindus would still see Christianity as false as it is presented, even if only because of narrowness.

27. For the curious, examples—and rebuttals to those examples—aren't hard to find if one simply queries "Christianity passes the Outsider Test for Faith" in a search engine. None of them are worth citing directly.

28. There is a generally accepted exception to this rule for public figures, although even in that case, satire and outright mockery are typically pretty easily distinguishable.

29. Recall that preserving sacredness (sanctity, in their language) is one of the dimensions of Jonathan Haidt and Craig Joseph's moral foundations theory, which in this case posits that, whatever a moral reaction may be, say at the level of the brain or psychology, sacredness should often manifest as a moral feeling at that

level. The reaction felt when someone challenges or disrespects an idea held as sacred will in those cases be handled as a (framework) moral object.

30. This includes crafting blasphemy laws to render such satire as illegal speech—laws which all who wish for a post-theistic world should be eager to help dismantle.

31. There is a well-documented psychological process known as the *mere exposure effect* that makes people more comfortable, and thus accepting, of ideas and circumstances with which they have some familiarity. Mere exposure to satirical "blasphemy," then, is potentially very corrosive to faith, and so its production should be encouraged. Thanks to Jonathan MS Pearce for some of the observations and phrasing in this paragraph.

32. See, for instance, Azim Shariff and Ara Norenzayan, "Mean Gods Make Good People: Different Views of God Predict Cheating Behavior," *International Journal for the Psychology of Religion* 21 (2011): pp. 85–96, in which they found that only belief in a vengeful God had any impact on cheating behavior of undergraduate students. Of course, it must be noted, it scares a lot of people *into* stunningly bad behavior too, so perhaps this isn't much consolation (see the next note). Indeed, if a vengeful God's real psychological role is to scare people into behaving according to the believed dictates of that God, the more appropriate title would read *mean gods really do motivate people to act upon their beliefs*.

33. The statement made here is not meant in any way to diminish the facts that (1) religion possesses at least two unique features that render its abuses disproportionate in many cases—(a) a (bogus) claim to the absolute authority of a perfect deity, and (b) an incredible capacity for creating a sense of fictive kinship bonded into a single ideologically motivated moral community—or (2) that religion is at least indirectly and in many cases directly responsible for many of the worst horrors mankind has succeeded in unleashing upon itself. In fairness, state (and other political) ideologies can do and have done their fair share of incredibly heinous things. The crucial point, though, is that all of these sorts of incredible failures of humanity depend upon faith, in the general sense—the undue inflation of the confidence we give to a belief, typically to a point of being beyond the bounds of doubt or question. See previous note.

CHAPTER 8

SECULARISM

It is a bad idea that some claims to truth or knowledge regarding our societies are privileged to a weaker standard of justification than others. Secularism is the rejection of that bad idea.

Secularism is therefore a rejection of the notion that sincerity of conviction is sufficient to cover any of the ground toward a belief's verification. It is a demand that all beliefs about society and culture are held to and measured against a common standard that is as objective as it is possible to be. Secularism is the rejection of faith as a political force.

Indeed, it's not so much that we need another argument for secularism as it is the case that there is literally no legitimate alternative. Theocracy is mythocracy, and the rest of the defense of secularism is obvious: no mythology deserves to be favored by functional modern governments. If we care at all about basing our social and political institutions upon actual guesses about the real world—never mind good guesses—secularism is the only option we have.

Suppose we decide that we do need, or at least want, an additional argument in favor of secularism.[1] The nearest relevant thing follows directly from the observation that religions are moral communities. As we have not yet successfully produced something that could deserve to be called a science of morality—an approach to morality based upon the kind of epistemic firmness that only the scientific methods have produced so far in human history—we can easily see the nearest thing to a necessary defense of secularism. We need secularism specifically because we lack sufficient reasons to accept that any particular moral community is correct in its guesses about how to maximize the Good. Furthermore, least qualified of all attempts are those centrally informed by mythology, wishful thinking, and the kind of lunacy people call "revealed wisdom." All other arguments for secularism, really, are superfluous at this point.[2]

Since we lack a successful moral science at present, where it comes to making guesses about how to achieve the Good for humanity and other sentient life, we need an ongoing discussion between our moral communities.[3] Secularism means conversation. Sectarianism wedded to the state, or even the belief that it should be wedded to the state, means pretending the most important ongoing conversation humanity engages in is over—and many would have us believe that it was settled once and for all in the Iron Age or earlier by people too ignorant to realize that the ownership of human beings might not be a great thing for their welfare.

Of course, secularism is also the unique vanguard that keeps sectarianism from eating itself, along with the rest of us. If history has been clear on one lesson, it is that anywhere sectarianism is able to secure power and privilege, it will abuse them, be the sect church or state. Secularism is the only known shield from this utterly predictable consequence of giving lots of power to people who pretend that they're right for reasons no better than "just because."

It is, of course, possible in theory that sectarian solutions could succeed, if only they were done right. There's nothing in principle to stop a religion or political ideology that *actually is correct* from being a successful basis for managing sociopolitical affairs. Of course, were an ideology actually correct, it wouldn't need to be maintained as an ideology, but more pressingly, because of a few uncomfortable facts (for religious people), this has never worked and probably never will.

The first big catch working against a theocratic utopian dream is achieving a broad-reaching social and political understanding that is correct. The second is, if such a thing were obtainable, being able to know it. Sociopolitical concerns in large societies are complicated things. At a bare minimum, a fully developed and robust *science* of morality and another of politics would be requirements to overcoming these problems, and, far from having anything of the sorts, we're still mired arguing about whether or not such sciences can even exist *in principle*.

Thus, it is the case that every arrangement of sectarian power we've ever seen in the world has proven inherently unstable. The core of this instability is the failure of faith as a method to justify beliefs. Without a serious and mature methodology to justifying beliefs, no one outside of a given moral community has any good reasons to accept the claims of those within it.

This fact follows from a recognition that there are really only two functional possibilities that inform how we organize societies, and neither requires faith. First, as we have with some scientific matters, we could have sufficiently good reasons for claiming we know certain sociopolitical truths (including moral ones). In this case faith is irrelevant. Second, we might lack sufficient information to make so bold a claim, in which case the only functional possibility is to maintain an ongoing dialogue between disputing factions, all of which are open to compromise and revision of their beliefs. In this case, faith must be rejected because it is a clear impediment to the foundations of that discussion.

Outside of these inherently secular possibilities, we find ourselves in the baleful position of lacking sufficient information to claim to know what we're talking about and yet pretending we possess it anyway. We call this position faith. When relying upon faith, we have no legitimate way to know which sect or faction, if any, even holds a good assessment of the data available to us, let alone a correct one. Worse, as faith blocks compromise and belief revision[4] by its insistence on certainty, the results of the eventual impasses that will arise are predictable: recalcitrant squabbling at best, balkanizing in the middle, and violence at worst. That some of the faithful are eager to revise their beliefs and compromise on many sociopolitical topics is irrelevant to this point because that eagerness exists in exact proportion to the degree that those people have adopted secularism as a core societal virtue.

For some, it may be tempting to think that even yet there is an eye to this needle through which a theocracy could usher us into heaven on earth—a case where there is no dispute on the dogmas at hand—but we have no reason to believe that this is possible at all. Uniformity of opinion seems to require either a reliable and thorough method to knowledge[5] or the brazenly unacceptable: complete and utter totalitarianism. Here we find the Catholic Inquisition, Stalin, Mao, jihadist Islam, and many others on perfectly level footing, and by examining the ground upon which they made or make their stands, we see little reason to wonder why they were such larger-than-life failures. Similarly, it's no surprise at all that fundamentalist interpretations of religion and many political theories are so frequently infused so thoroughly with totalitarianism.

Differences in the interpretation of any religion or political theory, or the relevant texts, manifestos, and treatises defining them, will evolve as reliably as differences in opinion and temperament among individuals, which is to say everywhere and effectively continuously. Anyone who can read a scripture or political treatise can cleave to his interpretation of it,[6] and with a little charisma he can turn it into a rival, heterodox sect. The only good way to resolve such differences is via the use of some reliable means at prying the truth from the universe. Obtaining reliable claims upon the truth, however, requires specialized tools that simply do not yet exist at the level of society and culture. Lacking such a means, compromise is the only good option, and once compromises are deemed a threat to orthodoxy, force is all that's left.

Religious people, though, can be committed secularists in the way that is most important: keeping religious privilege away from the state. Religious people who embrace secular ideals should be encouraged in doing so. Differences of belief on particular matters are a distant second in importance to a commitment to secularism. This is why a reformation of Islam is of such critical importance and why evangelical Christianity represents the vast majority of the reason anyone pays attention to America's religiosity problem at all; these groups are desperately short on secularism. Thus, no matter how valuable and important it is that we move to a fully post-theistic society as quickly as we may, a more immediate and crucial goal in the meantime—one that may well be a necessary stepping stone on the way to post-theism—is establishing secular states and embracing secularism as a modern political *virtue*.

And it is fair to consider secularism as a virtue because it is inherently the combination of epistemic humility, the willingness to admit that one might be wrong, and personal confidence. When a religious person embraces secular ideals for her society, she is saying that, while she may be fully convinced of the truth of certain precepts of her religion (that's faith), she's at least humble enough to admit that other opinions hold enough merit to warrant space, discussion, and compromise.

Religions are moral communities, typically ideologically motivated ones, and embracing secularism is the act of breaking free of the most potent poison that religion has to offer, totalitarian absolutism. If there are going to be religious people in the world—and for some time yet there will be—we need as many of them free of this poison as possible, and that is to say that we need as many of them committed to secular ideals as can be. Their role in society is important, even if they are in no way prepared to let it or themselves go post-theistic, and they are to be embraced, encouraged, and helped at every turn. In fact, it may be the case that such *reformers*, meaning those who secularize their religions and resist fundamentalism, are absolutely essential elements in helping to free us from the grip of the worst that religion has to offer.[7]

The role of the secularly religious will be to do what they can to showcase their religions at their best while encouraging others to do the same—critically, from the inside. Those of us who do not believe, even if we would like to help them free themselves from their religions, should do everything we can to support and facilitate the secularization of religion.[8]

As a last word on the need for secularism and the need to encourage it, we should note the chief difficulty with secularization is the one we cannot lose sight of: again, *religions are moral communities*, hence *morality and religion cannot be separated*. That means that secularism inherently faces the challenge of asking people bound together on a belief that they have the uniquely correct take on morality to revise that belief in favor of tolerating moral plurality, at the least. We must help religious people see that other moral communities exist, and that people in those communities can also be morally good individuals. Since possessing an absolute conviction on having a unique corner upon the truth is a cornerstone of many religious beliefs, achieving this goal will require incredible finesse and patience.

It cannot be overstated, however, how important it is that we work, using tools like Peter Boghossian's Street Epistemology,[9] John W. Loftus's Outsider Test for Faith, satire, and others, to change the particular belief that any specific religion has a unique and absolute finger on moral truth. The necessity and difficulty of changing this belief is perhaps the best light possible in which to see the abject failure of faith and the need for embracing secularism as a sociopolitical virtue.

Notes

1. For some rather good ones written at book length, consider David Eller's *Atheism Advanced: Further Thoughts of a Freethinker* (Austin, TX: American Atheists Press, 2008); Ronald A. Lindsay's (no relation) *The Necessity of Secularism: Why God Can't Tell Us What to Do*, (Durham, NC: Pitchstone Publishing, 2014); and Russell Blackford's *Freedom of Religion and the Secular State*, (Hoboken, NJ: Wiley-Blackwell, 2012).

2. This statement is not meant to trivialize the recent spate of strong books arguing for and defending secularism—those books are excellent and, in a way, needed. Like with the matter of theism, the *conceptual* argument regarding secularism is too straightforward to require elaboration, but the *practical* arguments designed to change cultures that haven't been able to figure out this rather astounding fact are important to creating shifts and movements that successfully spread and reinforce secularism as a core political ideal. This work is not intended to argue that case and leaves it to those others. For more information, see the previous note.

3. This, in a sentence, is the primary theme of Jonathan Haidt's book *The Righteous Mind* and the purpose to which it was written. Readers are strongly encouraged to read it.

4. Some might argue here that many of the faithful are eager to revise beliefs and compromise on any number of sociopolitical concerns, and this is certainly true on *some* beliefs for most believers, but always, when there is faith, there is at least one belief that resists revision and that admits no compromise. This is likely to be the case *by definition*.

5. It isn't clear that such a state of acceptance of *reliable* methods is even possible. There are, after all, still people out there who are flat-earthers, who reject the overwhelmingly confirmed fact that the Earth is an oblate spheroid.

6. Which is a significant reason that it was considered a capital crime to print or possess a Bible in any vernacular language of Europe up until the Protestant Reformation changed that.

7. The comparison between much of Christianity, which has largely been secularized, to much of Islam, which has not, is too obvious to require direct

mention. Reformers in Islam are almost certainly completely critical to helping those billions of Muslims, not to mention the rest of us, get out from under the oppression and terror of fundamentalist Islam, which remains one of the most significant threats to humanity, and most of all to Muslims. Until Islam is reformed and secularized, people anywhere near its thumb have little to no chance of going post-theistic without also going post-alive. Given modern weaponry, this threat is essentially global, and it is nontrivial. Islamic reformers, since Islam is a collection of very strict, very tight-knit moral communities, are an essential ingredient in changing Islam—or at least the minds of enough Muslims to make a difference— in a way that can best mitigate this threat.

8. Those prone to pedantry will, no doubt, want to make a fuss that the "secularization of religion" is technically an oxymoron, but the meaning intended is that the religions themselves should increasingly bring secular ideals on board, and religious people should (eagerly) adhere to them, promote them, and spread them instead of seeing them as a threat to their beliefs and the psychosocial needs underlying those.

9. Moral beliefs, like all beliefs, have a backbone of justification that is every bit as open to being questioned as any other. Street Epistemology targets the belief-formation and belief-justification processes and forces them to be reevaluated. A difficulty with moral attitudes is that their content is often taken to be "just how it is" and expressed in deeply emotionally resonant terms, requiring more patience and skill than beliefs about various facts.

CHAPTER 9

UNTHINKING ATHEISM

Atheism, as it stands, doesn't make sense because theism doesn't make sense. Sure, those of us without belief in a God are in some boring and technical sense "atheists," but there's not any reason to make atheism into a thing based upon that de facto state of affairs. Further, the use of the word atheist is probably best to get away from. "Nonbeliever" is enough, if we need some term, although a simple statement of "no, I don't believe that" when presented with any unsupported belief is better still.

As many of these topics have been covered before, this chapter will be kept brief, though its inclusion is important as a summary of specific changes we'd do well to make as we transition from the theism-versus-atheism paradigm to a post-theistic world. Atheism is big business now, and it carries a significant and growing voice in our public discussions.

We have atheism as political advocacy (as in American Atheists); we have atheism as social advocacy; we have atheism all over the Internet. Phrases that begin with "as an atheist, I . . ." increasingly possess some kind of meaning, and many self-identifying atheists seem increasingly interested in learning how to be better at being an atheist. Some such people are very likely to have purchased this book for exactly that purpose, in fact. Here, I want to explain better uses of human talent and potential than developing another set of moral communities committed to some ideological cause, particularly one as inherently misguided as what we call atheism.

It is telling that when I contemplate the phrase "the usual trappings of atheism," the first thought that comes to mind every single time is *squabbling*.[1] Atheists squabble. They squabble with believers; they squabble with each other; and they squabble about things that just don't need to be squabbled about.

Of course, not everything "atheists" do is a waste of time. An example well worth keeping alive is the sort of legal advocacy for maintaining secularism in the United States provided by the Freedom From Religion Foundation. Their work is an example of an excellent use of time and energy because keeping a firmly drawn line between church and state in any government, particularly one that is explicitly secular in its foundational documents and ethos, is the only path that makes sense since we want our societies to be governed by conversation and collaboration instead of uncompromising ideology and privileged mythology.

Furthermore, organizations that encourage people to feel safe and accepted as they transition from religious belief to having lost it are very worthwhile uses of our time and energies,[2] so long as we're conscious not to let them become moral communities that might themselves run amok. Of special note in this regard is the effort known as the Clergy Project. This worthy endeavor helps facilitate the transition for members of the clergy who have lost their faiths and yet who are trapped by the fact that being a faith leader is both their profession and the centerpiece of their social identity. Such efforts, of course, do not need to be as well organized as the Clergy Project, and any sorts of support groups for those losing faith can be of great value—again noting the care needed to prevent the birth of problematic moral communities within those spheres.

As mentioned before, working to uproot faith and help people learn and want to revise their beliefs cannot be overstated in its worth. This should constitute an active area of research and effort, because every person who learns to overcome faith-based thinking is helped while helping the rest of us as well. The call here is to use fair and honest techniques and to be authentic about it. Of particular need is more work in the vein of what Peter Boghossian has done in finding ways to help people adopt a stance of willingness to change their minds and not to believe more than evidence warrants.[3]

In that, being forthright and open about a lack of religious belief is also of great worth.[4] This, though, is a place where it is critical we constantly check ourselves against condescension and unnecessary confrontation. The goal is to have open, honest conversations that move people away from myth and toward more fruitful and solidly grounded topics, and achieving that is an art that often requires swallowing a lot of pride and frustration.

Figuring out which activities are good and bad uses of our time is important, and of all the things listed here, it is probably the most straightforward once we're honest about what the term "God" means. Anything that treats theism on its own terms, except in particular one-on-one conversations meant to help people uproot their faith, is probably a waste of time. That which sees "God" in the light of psychosocial needs that people have and do not know how else to meet is likely to be fruitful.

That means recognizing that the philosophical fight is over, and the social effort is best not engaged in as a fight except where legal matters are concerned. The social and cultural changes that need to come about as we go post-theistic are not best waged between competing moral communities but rather by people who reject the notion that a moral community is the right tool by which to assert a social truth. Lacking a firm science of morality, the best we can hope for is conversation that is informed by what facts we have, those largely ones that mean to inform us about the future welfare of human beings.

Religious Science Denial and Religious Supremacy
There's still much to be done where it comes to dealing with religious science denial and attempts at cultural religious supremacy—and that's to speak only about secular nations like the United States.[5] On the one hand, we need to maintain a strict divide between church and state, as indicated previously. On another, we should do what work we can to advocate for public trust and familiarization with science.

If the public trusts science as a means of getting to know facts about the world, then we can all benefit from the fact that scientists will continue to be motivated to do good science. Public distrust of science is an unnecessary impediment to doing the best we can. Where it comes to cultural change, fostering trust is more important than increasing familiarization (or even interest) in science. Not everyone needs to know a lot of science. People just need to know generally how and why it works, and thus why the results of scientific inquiry can be trusted. Never is this more true than when good science (like biological evolution, for instance) returns facts that run contrary to extant beliefs that meet deep psychosocial needs for people.

While it may be of some continued use to engage in criticisms of science denialism in service to these goals—as we can be quite sure the properly motivated will continue to produce it—it seems more productive to encourage educational campaigns that help foster public trust in science. These should focus on how and why the scientific methods successfully help people determine facts about the world together and the obvious and copious benefits employing those methods has wrought for humanity.

No More Philosophy of Antireligion

On the other hand, engaging in criticisms of religious apologetics and religious philosophy is of limited utility. The core reasons people hold religious beliefs have little or nothing to do with the weight of philosophical arguments for those beliefs; those arguments are utilized after the fact to secure beliefs that are already held for other reasons and are little more than the age-old attempt to lawyer sense into nonsense. Still, having good repositories of rebuttals to stock religious arguments, perhaps ones that grow at the hands of qualified enthusiasts, would be of some use as a reference or for people who are engaging in efforts such as taking the Outsider Test for Faith[6] in an earnest way.[7]

In a similar vein, then, those lacking belief who take arguing about religion and God as a kind of hobby should curtail that behavior, insofar as it is arguing. There are vastly better ways to have discussions than to argue if the goal is to change someone's mind. We're better served by working to gain the needed skills to treat people with sufficient dignity to hear them out, to ask genuine questions (that might help them undermine their faith-based beliefs), and to treat them like adults than we are to argue with them. There's little room for argument here, and there's little need. The intellectual argument over theism is over.

Refocus the Social Movement

Sadly, antitheistic philosophy of this kind is something of the cream of what it means to promote "atheism," and that should tell us a lot about what "atheism" is doing for us. It's time to move on from that kind of thing, and it is also time to move on from much of what passes for "promoting atheism" in the social sphere, a wildly popular endeavor at present. Frankly, much of what gets called the "atheism movement" has to die. It should have died years ago, at least.

Why? Because there's a category mistake involved in turning atheism into an identifiable kind of thing, say a philosophy or a worldview. In light of that observation, it's an even bigger mistake to turn atheism into a contentious social and political movement. Again, such a "movement" is simply a loose confederation of disparate and highly motivated moral communities that hold roughly in common little more than a desire to see religion and belief in God diminish.[8] Realizing that such a thing is what passes for a "movement," to say nothing of the fact that it's inherently misguided over a category error, is all it takes to understand why an "atheism movement" is an ill-advised way to promote a post-theistic society.

Ditching Atheism

We shouldn't even keep doing atheism. We should ditch it. We should move on from it at the conceptual level, be settled in not believing what doesn't have justification, and do what we can to help free other people from the confusion of faith. Some strategic advantages to this course of action include (1) being better able to focus on what matters, (2) not confusing a lack of a thing for a thing that needs to be (or even can be) done right, (3) not creating a quasi-religious monster out of a lack of belief, (4) allowing us to be more straightforward and honest, (5) allowing us to avoid the challenges associated with being branded "atheists," and (6) allowing us to begin to practice behaving in a manner befitting the waning period of religious influence in our world.

Notes

1. Astute readers will realize that this parallels religious squabbling along denominational lines, and the reason is the same: both are examples of moral communities, and the squabbling is primarily had along moral (and political, which are related) lines with its ultimate root being a lack of requisite moral knowledge to resolve the differences.

2. Though it will be discussed more later, efforts like a Recovering from Religion Hotline constitute a great example. See Valerie Tarico, "Controversial Recovering from Religion Hotline a Hot Commodity," *Valerie Tarico*, blog, 30 April 2015, http://valerietarico.com/2015/04/30/controversial-recovering-from-religion-hotline-a-hot-commodity/.

3. See, again, Boghossian, *A Manual for Creating Atheists.*

4. Readers are again encouraged to check out the Openly Secular project, openlysecular.org.

5. The case is obviously much more poignant and pressing in Muslim countries, but those represent a unique sort of problem because most of them neither have secular governments already in place nor have gone through a proper religious reformation, which is probably the first necessary step to changing the situation there.

6. See Loftus, *The Outsider Test for Faith.*

7. Though they can get overly into the importance of the philosophy of religion, the Secular Web, presided over and maintained by Jeffrey Jay Lowder, infidels.org, is an excellent example of such a resource.

8. It is probably the case that all social movements form around moral communities that, if they aren't ideologically driven to their activism, teeter very near the brink.

CHAPTER 10

FILLING THE RELIGION GAP

Achieving a post-theistic society may require filling the religion gap. The *religion gap* is the space between (1) where our societies and culture presently are in terms of naturally helping people satisfy the various psychological and social needs for which they turn to religion and belief in God and (2) where those need to be for most people to be able to meet their needs successfully *without* turning to religion or belief in God. Here, I'd like to impress upon the reader that these last two chapters are intended to start a conversation and thus will be vague. My goal is more to illustrate what kinds of things may need attention than it is to describe specific societal prescriptions.

The recognition that religion and belief in God exist as ways people attempt to satisfy or ignore psychosocial needs is at the core of making the transition to a post-theistic world.[1] It follows, then, that those needs, as human needs, will remain relevant in any post-theistic situation as well. Filling the religion gap means identifying, developing, encouraging, and cultivating the kind of social and psychological infrastructure by which human beings can meet their needs without having to rely upon religion or belief in God to do it.

It may not seem obvious that we need to do anything in particular to fill the religion gap, as many people who lack belief also successfully meet these needs on their own. That, of course, neglects the simple fact that making it easier to let go of unfounded beliefs will help more people to do so. The more obvious it is that the religion gap is filled by other means than religion, the easier it will be for people to let go of belief in belief and thus the beliefs themselves.

The data are almost unequivocal, for example, in showing that as economic and security concerns diminish in a society, so too does its religiosity. In an essay about the current decline of religion in the West, philosopher Daniel Dennett commented on this point, writing in *The Wall Street Journal*,

> With hardly any significant exceptions, religion recedes whenever human security and well-being rises, a fact that has recently been shown in numerous studies, but was suspected by John Calvin in the 16th century. He noted that the more prosperous and comfortable his Genevans became, the less dependent they were on church. Presumably, those who deplore the decline of religion in the world today would not welcome the sort of devastation and despair that could give religion its second wind.[2]

This is very likely because as the needs for control are met in ways that do not require a deity, people abandon reliance on a belief in a deity to pretend to meet them. There is a strong correlation between healthy societies and low religiosity on a number of robust socioeconomic health indexes.[3] One thing this suggests is that if we can organize our societies to be effective in this regard and educate people to see the benefits strong, stable, modern democracies afford them, we have a good chance of breaking the need for belief and thus allowing people to let go of what, as Dennett puts it, we've "outgrown."[4]

Consider another example. The extremely low rate of belief in God among members of the National Academy of Sciences would perhaps be perplexing were it not for the fact that being highly adept at the sciences meets many (but not all) human needs for attribution (*nota bene*: being adept at the sciences also cultivates epistemic humility and a demand for having proper justification for beliefs). As scientifically minded people learn to find more and more well-evidenced natural attributions for the phenomena of the world, the notion that the rest of our phenomena have natural attributions—that can be understood and thus brought under some degree of our control—becomes more and more comfortable.[5]

These examples are straightforward in that they illustrate that as the needs met by religion are met in other ways, the reliance on religion, and thus theism, wanes. This is, of course, consistent with the view expressed by psychologists of religion Ralph Hood, Peter Hill, and Bernard Spilka, which I will repeat here because it is of such central importance

> The evidence is that most people in most circumstances initially employ naturalistic explanations and attributions, such as references to people, natural events, accidents, or chance. Depending upon a wide variety of situational and personal characteristics, there is a good likelihood of shifting to religious attributions when naturalistic ones do not satisfactorily meet the needs for meaning, control, and esteem.[6]

Not all of the needs filled by belief in God are so easy to manage as basic attributional needs, social needs, and control needs, of course. The needs to ground and understand morality, to have a sense of purpose, and to cope with death are particularly troublesome, as is the need many people have to understand that which is often called "spiritual." At least in part because our default approach for almost all of the history of the Western world has been to rely upon religion to meet these needs, they seem much harder to handle, but that makes them more important, not less, if our goal is to foster circumstances that render belief in God irrelevant.

Moral Attribution

Moral attribution is particularly thorny. We really need to be working very diligently to understand morality in as close to a scientific way as we can,[7] but more presently, we need to recognize that all of the things we know about moral psychology are immediately applicable to understanding moral communities. What we need to realize most is that moral frameworks are sets of very complex ideas operating on very complicated systems—societies—and so we have every reason to accept that all moral communities face serious limits upon the potential degree of accuracy where it comes to their guesses about right and wrong.

Making such an admission mainstream should encourage conversation and compromise, but we must be cautious in realizing that it constitutes nothing like a call to moral relativism.[8] We have every reason to believe that some answers to moral questions are patently worse than others. Reciprocally, we can also say already that we know that some approaches to determining human values are undeniably better than others.

Of particular importance is that we recognize that above all else, religions are moral communities, and the death of religion will do nothing to prevent people from continuing to form moral communities. It's what people do. Indeed, it may be the most *human* thing about us. A goal in closing this aspect of the religion gap, then, is to help encourage people to invest in their moral communities without being ready to commit to them ideologically.

Where it comes to shifting away from religious moral systems to others, the various approaches labeled *humanism* offer an excellent basis for filling the religion gap. Humanism is an increasingly well-developed system of ethics that centers itself upon the needs of human beings and other sentient creatures, and it expressly endeavors to seek rational, as opposed to religious and supernatural, ways of solving human problems. Humanism stands a strong chance for most people of providing a naturalistic route to moral reasoning once the spell of the religious attributional framework (which provides for many needs, including making sense of morals in a "transcendent," or "beyond me," kind of way[9]) is broken. That most nonbelievers in the world today would also identify as humanists is ample evidence to this claim.[10]

Purpose

Helping people to realize a satisfying sense of purpose in life is also a tricky endeavor because it is intimately tied up with a few core human struggles that we seem to remain poorly equipped at coping with: death and extinction. Becoming lost in the sense of powerlessness attendant to those hard facts of living robs people of the ability to see that the most meaningful purposes in their lives are both clear and present.[11] Satisfaction with life and the capacity to help others achieve it are the human purposes, and the fact that these efforts are necessarily local—as opposed to universal—makes them more poignant, not less. Our purposes in life are defined most significantly in those we care most about.

We each only have so much time in our own lives, and we know with near certainty that some of that time will be dotted with misery. Equally certain is that some of that misery will be overwhelming. Worse, we know it for our loved ones too, and that entails knowing that in the unlikely event that we ourselves avoid the worst miseries in life, those we love most will feel them just as sharply as we make our escape. We will die, and we will hurt before we die. So too with our loved ones, and for many of them, we will be the unwilling source of that pain. This is the macabre canvas upon which the myriad purposes of human lives are necessarily painted, and believe it or not, the hues are truly more marvelous because of it. That we have only so much time to live a wonderful life, and that we know this is true for ourselves and everyone we love, defines exactly why our efforts matter at all.

Our efforts matter because in the light of this collection of facts, harsh and unpleasant as they may be, shines a fantastic opportunity. We can make our lives sparkle, and we can help those we love to do the same. For no matter how many hours of our lives will be spent in despair—and on some level it isn't absurd to measure it in hours since, at present, only the rarest handful among us will live so many as a million of them—we must also know that we possess the capacity to make those we love, including ourselves, tremendously happy in many others. We have the opportunities for love, for support, for help, for good work, and for kindness in every moment, and so realizing our finiteness is a nearly perfect road to understanding the best avenues for human purpose because those moments are the ones that, as they say, truly make life worth living.

Death is perhaps the best lens we have by which we can learn to focus on what matters in our lives and our relationships,[12] and denying it with fantasies of heaven is like looking through the wrong end of the telescope. The way we help people deal with death is to stop denying it, to help people to understand what it means, and to help them understand the way it can center our focus upon what properly matters in life. It is a gift to help people to learn to accept death as a fact of life and to teach them how to use that to better themselves, their loved ones, others, and the world in which we all live, love, and eventually die. The context into which we need to place death is how its acceptance enhances life.[13]

What needs to be accomplished most to help bring about a post-theistic society, so far as death and dying are concerned, however, isn't contextualizing it or finding ways that compete with religion's outright denial of it. We need to keep working diligently to find the best ways we can to cope with the reality of death, and far above that, to cultivate effective ways to help the bereaved learn to care for themselves again.

And note that we have good reasons to believe this is manifestly possible. Consider recent research at Cambridge University by Peter Wilkinson and Peter Coleman on the coping efficacy of religious versus nonreligious belief systems,[14] which found that the strength of beliefs related to coping, not their content, is most relevant in coping with the stresses of aging and death. They write,

> Although a variety of research projects have been conducted on the benefits of religious coping in older adults, no direct comparison between atheism and religious faith has been published. The study reported in this paper tackled this issue by interviewing two matched groups of people aged over 60 years living in southern England, one of 11 informants with strong atheistic beliefs, and the other of eight informants with strong religious beliefs. Five paired comparisons were undertaken to examine the role of the content of the belief system itself in coping with different negative stresses and losses commonly associated with ageing and old age. The pairs were matched for the nature of the loss or stress that the two people had experienced, but the two individuals had opposed atheistic and religious beliefs. The analyses showed that all the study participants—regardless of their beliefs—were coping well, and suggested that a strong atheistic belief system can fulfil the same role as a strong religious belief system in providing support, explanation, consolation, and inspiration. It is postulated that the strength of people's beliefs and how those beliefs are used might have more influence on the efficacy of coping than the specific nature of the beliefs. Further research into the strength of belief systems, including atheism, is required to test and elaborate this hypothesis.[15]

If these results hold water, then we have good reasons to believe that the beliefs about life, living, and dying that are adopted by those who do not believe in God stand every chance of serving as a perfectly functioning coping mechanism for the stresses of life, no religion required.

Spirituality

Where it comes to what gets called "spirituality," we need clarification and honesty more than anything. Part of this means honesty, in admitting that no one has justified reasons for believing in any mysterious energies, realms, or beings. Another part of it means being willing to recognize that the array of states of consciousness, some emotional, that often get branded "spiritual" are often based upon core needs that people have. One of those needs is a sense of significance or for personal context, and another is a need for satisfaction and happiness in life. There are still others.

Finding ways to inspire awe, to slow down the unrelenting race of thought, to have experiences that are considered "transcendent" or "uplifting," to cultivate realistically tempered senses of sanctity and value, to find ways to connect deeply with other people and their world, and so on, without having to ascribe them to nonsense or rely fully upon pharmacology to achieve them is a very worthwhile goal to help people lead more fulfilling, content, and successful lives. It's stupid to pretend that a need for the spiritual isn't important for a lot of people simply because it's so frequently tied to unjustified, mythological, and nonsensical beliefs.

As suggested by neuroscientist Sam Harris in *Waking Up: A Guide to Spirituality without Religion*, borrowing from religion could provide some success in coming up with methods to help people meet "spiritual" needs, although he is right to point out that we should be cautious to do so without having to take a single article on faith.[16] Certainly, religion has succeeded in finding a number of ways to help people meet many of their psychosocial needs, and there are few reasons to think that we cannot borrow from those as we seek better ones. The trick is to figure out what parts of religion attend to what people call "spiritual" needs and then to carve away all of the unfounded beliefs while preserving the effective cores. Harris talks about meditation at great length in *Waking Up*, for instance.

As an analogy, technologists often use biomimicry to engineer fabulous devices because the extremely competitive nature of biological evolution has put a very high premium on efficiency for achieving certain goals. If we think of religion as something that evolved within human societies to help people meet psychological and social needs, we can see that there are great reasons to find out what works from within religions, find out why it works, keep it, and discard the religious nonsense. Religions have proved particularly good at building large communities that provide people with a sense of security, contentedness, and psychosocial context, for instance.

Specific Needs

We have to fill the religion gap not by creating new religions or quasi-religions (or other ideologically motivated moral communities) but by finding better ways to help people meet the psychological and social needs that they use "God" and religion to manage for themselves now. All of the relevant needs outlined in chapter 5 require some attention. It is our challenge in the coming years and decades to continue to build the social infrastructure and body of resources that will allow people to live a fulfilling life without feeling a need to turn to myth to do it. Here, I'd like to outline some suggestions for many of these needs.

Moral Attribution without God

As mentioned, humanism already forms a basis for morality without religion, and so encouraging people to see morals as something that exists between human beings for the benefit of human beings and other sentient life would be an obvious worthwhile effort. This should include fostering and promoting humanist organizations and making them more visible. As humanism gains more and more public acceptance, so does the frequent humanist tagline, "good without God."[17]

It is also important to find ways to help people realize that theistic morals themselves are just human moral frameworks that define religious moral communities, not absolute moral laws given from On High. That is, we need to help people transition from the moral absolutism so often attendant to theistic morals to a position where honesty and humility about our assumptions about right and wrong are central. It is imperative that we help people realize that their moral communities are unlikely actually to know right and wrong with certainty, and that conversation is a necessary component between moral communities with differing frameworks.

This goal must be accomplished not only by fostering humility but also by helping people to ground moral reasoning in the here and now, in something to do with the experiences of sentient beings. In order to really facilitate this goal, we need to create more awareness of how moral communities form, what roles they play in our lives, and how they are a threat to themselves and others if left unchecked.[18] It is beyond question that moving out of the realm of moral squabbling and into moral science is of utmost importance as well.[19]

Purpose (Teleological Attribution) without God

Besides the overwhelmingly important effort of helping people to overcome the denial of death and thus to center purpose within life, of great value to helping people find purpose is helping them to find fulfilling work[20] and to build meaningful, healthy relationships and communities.

Meaning and purpose in life become almost entirely apparent when we facilitate good work and a sense of community. They become even clearer when people identify themselves with their communities. Community-oriented activity that involves rewarding challenge, including group hobbies, is also very helpful in giving people a sense of something worth working for. These could take the form of civic organizations or the forms of things like martial arts, hiking groups, exercise groups and teams, knitting clubs, book clubs, or any other activities groups. Anything that helps us realize that we are connected to other people and engage in our activities partly upon their behalves encourages a sense of not-beyond-me purpose in life. Our friends, families, work, and activities, when we love them, are exactly what we get out of bed for every morning, and that's what purpose in life means.

Phenomenological Attribution without God

Science. Science exists specifically to give functional attributions to natural phenomena. It is *the* set of tools for this job, period. Encouraging public trust and understanding of science is more than sufficient to help most people leave mythology as a tool for understanding phenomena in our world. The sciences (or, rather, the scientific methods) are the absolute best tools we possess for making sense of phenomena in our world, and this is a fact that is already well-known and well-attested to.

Abstract Attribution without God

One of the most useful things philosophers could do is to make it clear that abstract stuff is abstract and that that's fine. Ideas are ideas. They're mental. That's okay. We don't have to take it further than that. That's the level of ideas, and while ideas may give us our only map of reality, they are not reality themselves and shouldn't be confused for it.[21] If we know that ideas are ideas, then we don't have to spend time wondering where they came from or assume they must have been worked into the fabric of the universe by an invisible deity.

On a more practical level, we would benefit from working for political, educational, and economic systems that help people understand that important abstract concepts like justice and liberty are opportunities secured by social contract—not magical properties written into being by "God" itself.[22] Where abstractions like goodness are concerned, coming to understand those via a budding moral science (understanding why what we think of as good is good) would be of immense value. Other abstractions, like beauty, will be best elucidated as phenomena relevant to human nervous systems.

The goal here is to bring the abstract back into the realm of the human, and in this vein, it could be an explicit "arm" of humanism to do so. This goal could be accomplished by celebrating art and music, by investigating ethics philosophically in engaging discourse and scientifically informed lectures, and encouraging civic involvement, in addition to the points already mentioned.

Active Control without God

Any kind of educational systems, formal or otherwise, that legitimately empower people to meet challenges that arise in their lives are of immense value in helping them learn to cope with many of their own problems. In fact, merely engaging in difficult personal challenges can help forge someone into a competent, confident person who is able to meet many of life's challenges head on. Such efforts should be easy to foster and encourage.

Organizing social outlets (and even moral communities—in the forms of something like civic fraternities) with explicit goals of personal growth and development, often via challenging routes, could also be of great use here. Even better would be organizations of these sorts that are committed to philanthropy and civic service because they would provide obvious ways that people are able to come together to help other people in times of need, which is about as good as we can do where it comes to grasping control over many difficult circumstances.

Of course, simply making sure we have functional emergency systems in place also goes a long way. If there's a fire, we know we can do something: we can call the fire department. If there's an outbreak of violence, we can call the police. If a bear wanders into our backyard, we can call animal control or wildlife management agencies. If someone is injured or having another medical emergency, we can call an ambulance. If we need help with a serious emotional problem, we can reach out to a friend, contact a counselor, or, if desperate, call a psychological hotline. These are all things we can do, calling upon systems we can trust to work, to give us a sense of control in an emergency. Keeping all such emergency services well-funded and well-trained makes this system work and is something everyone can contribute to, usually by paying taxes and pressuring local politicians to make sure they are community priorities. We can also learn basic first aid and emergency response on our own.

Further, cultivating the kinds of "spiritual" practices that allow people to realize that not everything needs controlling would also be of significant use.[23] If the other suggestions made here are ways that active control needs could be facilitated, these represent ways in which they could be obviated.

Passive Control without God
The primary imperative where it comes to helping people feel as much of a sense of passive control in life as may be had, in addition to the points raised for active control, comes down to developing highly functional societies and healthy moral communities within them. Working diligently to create political, social, and economic situations in which people know that they can rely upon other human beings, infrastructure, social safety nets, the healthy operation of a mature economy, emergency services, social organizations, and so on, removes the need to rely upon mythological constructs to have a sense that there's some degree of control in life. There is something greater than ourselves that gives us a real sense of passive control already, really. It's us—each other. We should foster that and help make it more obvious.

Where it comes to managing control needs in the rather extreme circumstances that often tend to cause people to turn to desperate hopes against unhappy odds, there is a greater challenge. This is a challenge for individuals and psychologists more than anyone else, although politicians have a responsibility here as well. People need to know there are places to turn, which means qualified people to turn to, when they are in desperate need. Some of these, like emergency services, are public investments.

On the psychological front, we will need trained counselors who know how to help people cope with struggles, and overcoming the stigma (and possibly the expense) of obtaining qualified counseling will be a boon in this regard. The Internet is a home for a vast amount of potential for quick and immediate access to such help, and attempting to find ways to set up low-cost, easy-access, qualified help with major struggles could be something worthwhile.

In any case, we particularly need psychologists who aren't committed to a faith-based tradition, even if they may be informed by it. The problem of faith poisoning psychological counseling is an enormous and abusive one.[24] Those who lack faith respond poorly to faith-based initiatives, however well-intended, and thus those avenues to therapy hold the potential to do as much harm as good if misapplied. Good counselors have a professional duty to provide the best care to the patients they treat, which means setting aside their own beliefs to do that well. If they cannot do so because of either religious commitment or lack of knowledge on how to help people cope without faith-based beliefs, we can count that inability among the harms of the existence of the religion gap itself

Economists and politicians, broadly speaking, are needed specifically because by having a strong socioeconomic infrastructure, we eliminate much of the need for bogus beliefs to be utilized to pretend to satisfy needs for control. Why rely on a magical power or a myth to provide a sense of control when you can know with great certainty that the community that actually exists around you will help keep you safe (and help pick up the pieces when that's simply not possible)? Praying has never stopped a tornado, but communities come together to rebuild homes, businesses, and neighborhoods in the wake of every single one of them. Knowing we're organized to deal with calamities when they arise provides a powerful sense of security without having to rely upon beliefs in mythological powers.

Attachment Needs without God

Creating healthy attachment is a job for parents, mentors, and psychologists. Fostering healthy, secure attachment styles in as many people as possible should help break the need some people have to rely upon a fictional attachment figure like a deity. Good parenting should be encouraged and fostered, perhaps even instructed. Mentoring is a great opportunity, whether social, educational, athletic, or professional. Psychologists should continue to be well-trained and equipped to help those who, for whatever combination of bad circumstances, do not succeed to develop a healthy attachment style or who adopt fictive attachment figures.[25]

Somewhat related, though not specifically an issue concerning attachment, is the way we raise our children for a post-theistic world, and it is incredibly important. Particularly, we must encourage the exact values that we hope to see in the world as it becomes our children's. Openness to belief revision, curiosity, willingness to discuss and compromise, proper humility about what we can and cannot know, and so on, are core values that should be instilled into children as virtues—and virtues they are because they're the surest road to a better world that we have.[26]

Teaching a child that a particular moral community possesses the sole correct avenue to making sense of the world is an incredible failure that must stop. On the other hand, teaching children that there's "nothing either good or bad, but thinking makes it so," that is, complete moral relativism, is almost as bad. There are real places in which we can ground good and bad, and not all attempts at moral reasoning produce equivalent outcomes. Culture and tradition aren't good enough reasons to ignore abuses, and so yet again, we see a strong impetus to raise our children in the direction of these core values that make all necessary conversation possible.

Sociality without God

Community involvement, whether in small groups like bowling leagues, martial arts clubs, service organizations, companies, and the like, or in larger groups like professional, service, or social fraternities, church-like entities, corporations, and so on, provides a great deal of opportunity to create the exact kinds of (moral) communities that provide the sociality and psychosocial contextualizing needs that religion is so often relied upon to fill. To quote Jonathan Haidt in *The Righteous Mind*, "As political scientist Robert Putnam put it, the social capital that is generated by such local groups 'makes us smarter, healthier, safer, richer, and better able to govern a just and stable democracy.'"[27] He goes on to write,

> We humans have an extraordinary ability to care about things beyond ourselves, to circle around those things with other people, and in the process to bind ourselves into teams that can pursue larger projects. That's what religion is all about. And with a few adjustments, it's what politics is about too.[28]

Local groups help us meet our community needs, and any of these approaches can be secular just as well as they could be religious. So, we know that there's no reason whatsoever to feel like there is a demand upon anyone to believe anything that cannot be substantiated in order to have a sense of community belongingness and social support.

Putting an emphasis on community activities, particularly ones in which people are able to socially bind into tightly knit (though not necessarily small) groups—and even moral communities—can help people meet a need that is apparently of utmost importance to human beings. That being the case, something like a secular church could fulfill the need, as churches and the likes have been doing for centuries. It doesn't seem to matter, however, what people are doing so long as a few basic requirements are met.

First, there must be a focus on openness to belief revision wherever the formation of moral communities exists. Moral reasoning will trump fact-based reasoning whenever there is a psychological or social pressure to maintain beliefs,[29] and this must be carefully guarded against. A commitment to willingness to belief revision is the core safeguard there, and this is, of course, a willingness to admit that one's moral leanings are guesses about phenomena (society and culture) too complex to be known with the kind of certainty that morally charged matters often entail. Second, there must be a commitment away from unfalsifiable beliefs; these are of no practical use unless our goal is to protect things we pretend to know but do not know[30] from careful examination. Third, there must be a willingness to recognize our human and sentient kinship with other people and creatures outside of our own moral communities. Some easy examples of these kinds of communities would include secular churches, civic fraternities, social activities clubs, and the many humanist organizations that are arising to meet this very need.

Death without God

As this was already discussed, it will receive only brief treatment here. Considerable resources should be poured into doing what we can to find ways to understand and cope with death without relying upon its denial as a primary mechanism. This will be a job best suited to parents, mentors, writers, and psychologists, but educational resources, supportive communities, and qualified professionals should be readily available to help people cope with this hard reality of life. It should be a well-developed arm of humanism as well. Helping people to learn to realize that life is short and therefore precious seems central to this effort.

Notes

1. Alongside common sense, veritable mountains of evidence, some of it discussed in previous chapters (see any of the copious references to Hood, Hill, and Spilka, to J. Anderson Thomson, Jr., and to Jonathan Haidt, for examples), make the point that religion exists primarily so that people can feel that certain among their psychosocial needs are met, and my contention is that the deity or deities serving as figureheads in these religions are mythological devices believed in specifically to facilitate this goal. Seeing it for what it is and thus breaking the grip of this mythology while salvaging what we can from the structures of religion seems to be a necessary component, then, of breaking free of religious belief.

2. See Daniel Dennett, "Why the Future of Religion in Bleak," *Wall Street Journal*, 26 April 2015, http://www.wsj.com/articles/why-the-future-of-religion-is-bleak-1430104785.

3. Including, for instance, the GINI index. Jerry Coyne has presented this theme a number of times on his blog, *Why Evolution Is True*. For example, see "Income Inequality and the Dysfunctionality of America," 25 January 2012, https://whyevolutionistrue.wordpress.com/2012/01/25/income-inequality-and-the-dysfunctionality-of-america/, and "Why Is Economic Inequality Associated with Religiosity," 21 July 2015, https://whyevolutionistrue.wordpress.com/2011/07/21/why-is-economic-inquality-associated-with-religiosity/. Coyne's primary source is

the insightful *Social Science Quarterly* paper by Solt, Habel, and Grant, "Economic Inequality, Relative Power, and Religiosity."

4. Daniel Dennett, "The Folly of Pretense," *Guardian*, 16 July 2009, http://www.theguardian.com/commentisfree/belief/2009/jul/16/daniel-dennett-belief-atheism.

5. Many argue that scientists are people who are often okay *not knowing* things, but this isn't quite true, even if they have admitted that doubt is better than false certainty. The scientific drive to find out is simply a mature, healthy expression of the natural discomfort that we all have with ignorance, as to be compared with the childish, unhealthy expression of the same known as faith.

6. Hood, Hill, and Spilka, *The Psychology of Religion*, p. 45.

7. Naysayers will insist that this is impossible while simultaneously believing that they have insights into why some moral frameworks are better than others. This, then, would be a classic case of wanting to have it both ways. If one can make a good argument that one moral framework is superior to another, he is also tacitly admitting that there is some way by which we can make evaluative judgments on moral frameworks. Any appeal to evidence to support such an argument also tacitly admits that there is something observable, and thus potentially measurable, upon which such a determination is being made, and little more is needed for a basis for something like a moral science.

8. Above all else, Sam Harris's *The Moral Landscape* is a book meant to bulldoze moral relativism, a point that seems to have been mostly lost in the flurry of wrath from moral philosophers who hated the book for all the wrong reasons. Readers, particularly those who identify as strongly liberal, are heartily encouraged to read it with this particular intention in mind in order to understand why moral relativism is an abject failure.

9. Hood, Hill, and Spilka, in *The Psychology of Religion*, identify the transcendent, or "beyond me" (to quote them) aspect of the way in which religion provides meaning for people to be important. Writing, "a belief in a transcendent and authoritative being, especially when complete sovereignty is attributed to that being (as in the case of Western monotheistic religions), is the basis of the most convincing and fulfilling sense of meaning for many" (p. 16).

10. The American Humanist Association claims that nearly two-thirds of its membership also identify as atheists. See http://americanhumanist.org/paths/atheism, accessed 7 June 2015.

11. See Dan Barker, *Life Driven Purpose: How an Atheist Finds Meaning* (Durham, NC: Pitchstone Publishing, 2015).

12. It is a nugget of folk wisdom, probably with Buddhist origins, that I stumbled upon somewhere that to be truly happy, a person must spend at least an hour a day contemplating death. This is likely to be an exaggeration, but keeping sight of its reality certainly brings what matters in life into very sharp focus.

13. This is not to diminish the current or continued importance or value of grief counseling, which, indeed, is one of the best ways to achieve this goal.

14. Of rather important note, I hold strong disagreement with the authors regarding the phrase "atheistic belief system" in that it is misleading. I would argue that an "atheistic belief system" here is the kind of belief system about life that arises in the nonreligious vacuum when religious beliefs are absent. Such beliefs would include thoughts about death, community, and so on, which are beliefs about life and living, not an "atheistic belief system" in the sense of it being a competing religious position.

15. Peter Wilkinson and Peter Coleman, "Strong Beliefs and Coping in Old Age: A Case-Based Comparison of Atheism and Religious Faith," *Aging and Society* 30, no. 2 (February 2010): pp. 337–361.

16. A full citation to this book was given in chapter 5.

17. "Good without God" is the tagline of the American Humanist Association, for example.

18. Recommend further reading, Haidt, *The Righteous Mind*.

19. Recommend further reading, Harris, *The Moral Landscape*.

20. Again, see Haidt, *The Happiness Hypothesis*, on "flow" and happiness.

21. Readers are encouraged to consider my own *Dot, Dot, Dot* on this point.

22. Civics courses that focus upon helping people to see the reciprocal relationship between the people and the governments that represent them could help tremendously. See Douglas J. Amy, "An Unapologetic Defense of a Vital Institution," *Government Is Good,* published in full at http://www.governmentisgood.com/, accessed 16 May 2015.

23. The reader is encouraged to see Sam Harris's *Waking Up* regarding some of the benefits of a meditative or otherwise contemplative practice.

24. Not only is this a significant problem, including in addiction counseling,

but it's also a big enough problem where a countermeasure has been initiated to handle it. The Recovering from Religion Secular Therapist Project (https://www.seculartherapy.org/index.php), founded and led by psychologist Darrel Ray, exists specifically to address the needs of nonreligious people seeking therapy, many of whom are frustrated to find that many of their options for counselors cannot separate their faiths from their work in a way necessary to provide an adequate therapeutic program.

25. See, for a valuable resource, Lee A. Kirkpatrick, *Attachment, Evolution, and the Psychology of Religion* (New York: Guilford Press, 2004).

26. A growing number of resources exist concerning parenting without having to rely upon religion to do it. Consider, for example, Dan Arel, *Parenting Without God: How to Raise Moral, Ethical, and Intelligent Children, Free from Religious Dogma* (Durham, NC: Pitchstone Publishing, 2015).

27. Haidt, *The Righteous Mind*, p. 282. Haidt cites R. D. Putnam, *Bowling Alone: The Collapse and Revival of American Community* (New York: Simon and Schuster, 2000), p. 209.

28. *Ibid.*, p. 318.

29. Justin P. Friesen, Troy H. Campbell, and Aaron C. Kay, "The Psychological Advantage of Unfalsifiability: The Appeal of Untestable Religious and Political Ideologies," *Journal of Personality and Social Psychology* 108, no. 3 (March 2015): pp. 515–529.

30. The wording in this sentence echoes Peter Boghossian in his *Manual for Creating Atheists*. Boghossian "defines" faith as "pretending to know something you don't know" (p. 24).

CHAPTER 11

GOING POST-THEISTIC

An important part of going post-theistic, as discussed in the previous chapter, is finding ways to help people fill the religion gap without having to rely upon religion or belief in God to do it. This last chapter aims to give some (admittedly vague) sense of what could prove to be fruitful approaches to making the change.

Before beginning, it is important to mention that many of the ways that people can fill the religion gap for themselves are already in existence and well-developed. People who don't believe in God already make ample use of them, and so this effort may be less about coming up with ways to help people fill the religion gap and more about helping them to find what is already there.

In any case, if we want to create a post-theistic society, we have a pressure upon us to help people see how they can make do without their religious beliefs, which is to say to help them find ways to effectively meet their needs without relying upon religious attributions to do it. Broadly, our focus is probably best applied to two types of activities that service the goal of becoming post-theistic: what we could call educational efforts and practical transitional ones. Because I have less to say on transitional efforts, I will discuss them first. Again, the reader is reminded that the goal of this chapter is to initiate a discussion, and so all suggestions here are very general and perhaps even a bit idealistic.

Transitional Efforts

Transitional efforts are practical steps that can urge our society toward being post-theistic. To become post-theistic, we will need to change some things about how we think and do things. I will mention several, and, as many of these topics were covered in the preceding chapters, they will only receive cursory treatment here.

First, our societies have to work hard to become politically and economically stable enough to obviate many of the more desperate turns toward religion, and we need to encourage this kind of change in other societies via ethical political means. Functional modern governments should exist to do everything in their power to secure the lives and rights of their citizens, and those citizens, especially in democracies, have a civic duty to understand their role in making such systems functional, which includes understanding how functional modern governments can and usually do work for the people they represent. This last point, of course, urges us all to carefully and honestly investigate which people our governments represent and to work to make sure it's, as we say in the United States, "We the People."[1]

Also crucial here is the effort of breaking all lingering grip of religion on our political process, which is to say that secularism must be defended where it exists and fostered everywhere else. That will require us to encourage and aid reformers of religion to work from the inside out to help change the beliefs, minds, attitudes, and actions that exemplify and support the most severe and dangerous strains of religious belief—which means working to support these people as much as we can despite any differences in beliefs.

Further, we have to wean ourselves off the pointless and boring arguments, many of which are over philosophical topics or morals, so that these no longer characterize the debate over religion. In fact, nearly the only thing that needs to be said about the intersection of religious beliefs and morality is that each set of religious beliefs represents one particular moral framework out of a vast multitude and establishes one ideologically motivated moral community, leaving moral attribution out of it entirely. Further, instead of wasting time with philosophical-style arguments about religion, we should be taking on projects that address the main reasons people hold their beliefs and thus help them become free of faith. Helping people to uproot their faith-based thinking anywhere we can is of vastly more use than attempting to argue with them and inviting them to reinforce their beliefs via the backfire effect.

As discussed in the previous chapter, we need to continue to help people fill the religion gap, to see that they do not need to rely upon religious beliefs and attributions to understand and navigate the world. A huge part of this effort is captured in the promotion of being openly nonreligious. Projects such as Openly Secular, which encourages and supports being open about being nonreligious, are of great value here, and improving visibility and community involvement of humanist organizations is beneficial for similar reasons.

My last suggestion for a transitional effort will be perhaps my most controversial. We should have therapists and counselors trained to specialize in the challenges associated with leaving behind one's religious beliefs, and we should have lots of them.[2] People leaving their faith traditions are having to completely reconstruct much of the way in which they understand the world, including their own identities, and this is likely to be a difficult process. Trained professionals can facilitate the change via online resources, direct counseling, and, when needed, outreach hotlines.

It may be tempting for some to assume that making such a statement is tantamount to implying that religious belief is a kind of mental illness that needs to be cured, but that is not what is being said at all. Instead, it is merely a statement that a significant shift in worldview is likely to come with some psychological and social challenges that proper therapeutic intervention could mitigate. Importantly, this is *not* a call to train and employ therapists with the task of deconverting believers. Instead, it's merely a recognition that people undergoing the psychological and social struggles associated with undergoing a deconversion could benefit from specifically trained help. Therapists could be of tremendous help for people transitioning from a state of faith-based life to one in which that has been outgrown, and it seems obvious that if this change can be made more smoothly in some ways than in others, then it should be.[3]

It is extremely important to understand the distinction between these two points of view and realize that trying to psychologize people out of their beliefs is almost certainly unethical, if it is even possible. The concern here is to provide professional help to those who are losing their faiths anyway. And note that if the society we currently live in were to suddenly start tipping post-theistic very quickly (as if some critical mass point were passed), we may need a lot of trained facilitators. Preparing for that by training therapists particularly suited to facilitate a transition from religious belief to living without it could be a very prudent step in going post-theistic.

Educational Efforts

The hypothesis underlying the suggestion that we could benefit from educational efforts is that simply that the more people know about how the world works, including their own minds, the more likely they are to accept natural attributions over religious ones. This notion has some support from the observation that so long as their psychosocial needs for attribution, control, and social connection are being met, they will tend to accept naturalistic explanations over religious ones.[4]

Where educational efforts are concerned, two main things matter. First, we need to be creating the right kinds of educational opportunities to facilitate a transition to a world that has left belief in God behind. Second, we need to employ reliable, trustworthy ways for people who want to learn to be able to. For this effort, the Internet is probably our best tool. While there are effective ways to make modifications to our public education systems, including primary, secondary, and collegiate, such changes are slow and difficult to make, and they can be highly political. Some possibilities along those lines will be discussed, however.

High-quality content for the Internet has the advantages of being able to be produced quickly and inexpensively while immediately enjoying a very broad potential audience. The Internet allows creative, entertaining individuals to create a wide array of excellent and inspiring material that is widely and easily accessible to many. We already see people taking such opportunities in hand, and we should see more of it to come.[5]

Take the *Crash Course* series (series, here, is plural), produced by the "Vlogbrothers" John and Hank Green et al.,[6] which covers diverse topics like history, biology, chemistry, and others. These are well-made, highly entertaining, educational, inspiring, and popular, and they are just one highly recognizable example of excellent content production. Similar efforts done on topics that, on their own merits, are deleterious to faith-based belief, effective at increasing public trust in science, and useful for understanding society would be of tremendous use in transitioning from widespread belief to post-theism.

Though I'm hardly an expert in all of the relevant subjects to know for certain, the primary subjects I suspect are most important to fostering a post-theistic world are secular civics, logic and critical thinking, ethics, and cultural studies with a focus put upon comparative religions, though, of course, anything that fosters public trust, interest, and familiarization with science would be of value too. Additionally, any educational resources that could be produced that help people to cope with the hard realities of life—death and extinction particularly—would be strongly encouraged. Furthermore, so long as we can help people avoid crackpots and cranks selling pseudo-mystical woo, I would also suggest resources in personal growth, development, and "spirituality" as being valuable as well.

Specific Subjects

First, consider comparative religions (which would ideally contain units on moral psychology so that cultural underpinnings can be better understood). This subject is the perfect environment to foster an ability for people to take the Outsider Test for Faith presented by John Loftus because it exposes the reality that religion is a cultural phenomenon, not a theistic one. Understanding the cultural underpinnings of religious beliefs helps us see them for what they are, and seeing the cultural basis of religious beliefs in *other* cultures provides a mirror that allows a less-biased view of one's own beliefs. Furthermore, such a course of study fosters understanding for, and thus conversation and compromise with, people with different sets of beliefs, cultures, and moral frameworks.

Instruction in ethics[7] should help people reach a state where they are better able to work out for themselves what right and wrong might mean in terms of what actually matters: ourselves, each other, and other sentient creatures. We do not need to rely upon religious precepts—though we could, where it is applicable, draw from them—in order to make sense of how we might best behave with regard to one another, and educational opportunities in ethics would provide a route to improvement in that regard. Infusing such efforts with moral psychology could enhance matters considerably by providing more understanding of framework-moral behavior versus something a bit more broadly applicable.[8]

Courses in logic and critical thinking can help people become aware that we are naturally bad thinkers in many respects, this properly being part of what we might call "human nature." We are beset by biases and often engage in fallacious thinking, and that's even without the fact that we're often strongly motivated reasoners, which is to say lawyers on the behalf of our own preexisting beliefs and attitudes. These cognitive traps are often ones that lead to faith-based thinking, meaning the sort of thinking that is deliberately *not* critical enough. Studying logic and critical thinking also demonstrates that better thinking is possible and lays some of the necessary groundwork for doing it.

Civics, particularly secular civics, is utterly critical for proper community, society, and government-building efforts. It is also critical to the kind of political engagement that makes democracies highly effective forms of government. People who understand the ways that societies function, and more importantly how they can function when they are doing so successfully, are in an excellent position to help make the kinds of decisions necessary to create the kinds of societies that do not rely upon mythology in order to feel secure or fulfilled. The Nordic countries are an excellent example of highly functioning societies that have little need for beliefs in God, and part of that comes down to a clear understanding of how their society works to make the citizenry safe and secure. An important part of this effort is realizing the importance of secularism for safeguarding the rights of those who will still believe in God along with those who will not.

The other subjects mentioned, such as ways to contextualize and cope with death, personal development, "spiritual" avenues, and so on, are most easily seen as ways that we can close some of the more difficult holes in the religion gap. They therefore require no further elaboration here.

How Do We Do This?

It is conceivable that we could make some of these changes institutionally in the public educational system, with some of these kinds of changes being easier than others to make. I will discuss that shortly. First, though, I want to stress again that creating effective online educational resources is by far the best approach.

As for why, the Internet is an excellent opportunity for almost every reason conceivable: it's faster, it's cheaper, it's accessible (in most parts of the United States and Europe, at least, and expanding rapidly from there), it's subject to none of the political or time constraints that beset formal educational systems, and it's possible that such content will form the backbone of future formal educational systems anyway.

As noted, there are extremely popular channels already in existence that successfully cover, at varying levels of depth, many topics like history, science, and mathematics. Courses directly geared toward comparative religion, civics, ethics, logical and critical thinking, informed skepticism, moral psychology, proven avenues of personal growth, and so on, could easily follow this model and gain rapid success (particularly if some of the current successful purveyors would take up the charge).

Further, some universities already offer some or all of their course content for free online, and many schools cover subjects like these already. With a little effort, these lectures and discussions could be repackaged into something that's easy to get to a massive audience—in this case with the added benefit of top-notch experts in the field delivering the information.

On the other hand, should we want to try to make time for these topics in public education, some or all of these topics could be worked into primary and secondary education or, more easily, into university curricula. The challenges to such efforts will be immense and political in some cases, notably comparative religions. In other cases, the difficulties are more matters of practicalities. At every level, our educational systems are fully burdened with course material as it is, so making these changes would mean attempting to modify existing curriculum or trying to shoehorn in even more material into overfull schedules. Those obstacles aren't trivial. Of course, things can go more easily at the college level, especially where general curriculum requirements are concerned.

Given the intense divisiveness of religion in the modern, increasingly global world, together with all of the difficulties and dangers attendant to that discord, working comparative religions curriculum in may actually prove politically expedient and prudent, at least so long as religious fundamentalists could get over their fear of it. Some provinces in

Canada—notably Quebec, with British Columbia not far behind—seem to recognize this fact, sporting significant majorities of the population in favor of comparative religions being taught at the primary and secondary education levels.[9] What these Canadians seem to realize is that it will be a costly and unacceptable state of affairs for future citizens of our societies to know next to nothing about many world religions.[10]

Where it comes to civics, there is already in existence a weak proxy of this course offered (it is often compulsory) in American high schools, a course often blandly labeled "government." This subject could easily morph back into a more robust course in (American) civics. The key specific change that would accomplish this goal would be to increase the focus on how the varying elements of our government and society work together to create a functional space for all citizens to live and work well.[11] Of course, part of any good civics course is civic duty, something contemporary government classes would do well to stress more seriously in terms of the benefits each citizen enjoys as a result of engaging in civic activity. Like the others discussed here, this course, along with introductory ethics, could easily make for solid general education curriculum in colleges and universities.

Logic and critical thinking courses are a special example because there is a natural place to put them. We require a lot of compulsory mathematics courses in our current educational system that could easily be supplemented or, in some cases, outright replaced with logic and critical thinking lessons. For example, introducing these kinds of concepts—not necessarily formal logic—via puzzles and games could serve as a very strong and useful component of junior high–level mathematics and reasoning instruction, creating a firmer foundation and giving more time for students to mature into subjects like algebra and geometry.

Further, if it comes to being honest about it, few Americans retain *or need* second algebra, geometry, or calculus instruction (scientists, mathematicians, engineers, and economists notwithstanding). Thus, loosening those requirements for courses in practical critical thinking and logic (or computer coding, infused with logic, as it is) could serve as an excellent option for the many students who are not and will not be taking technical paths in their futures. Yet again, nowhere is this more true than at the service-course level in colleges and universities,[12] if the junior high and high school curricula simply cannot be modified in these directions.

Still, we have to recognize that there are various cultural taboos that will not happily tolerate educational changes of these sorts. Besides a general lack of trust by many people anytime the educational system is modified, there are issues with secular civics and comparative religions that run deep. Many American conservatives will see these as overt attempts by the government to attack religion and conservatism (which is rather telling, no?). Consider for a moment the most likely outcomes in places like the Southern United States over the topic of comparative religions, leaving anything including the word "secular" completely off the table.

On the one hand, we could certainly expect public outcry to the notion that schoolchildren will actually learn what other religions might teach in an academic and comparative fashion. If the possibility that school children might actually learn what Muslims, Hindus, and Buddhists[13] actually believe won't scare people enough on its own, the fact that teaching comparative religions in an evenhanded way is not a First Amendment violation will be widely and loudly missed.

On the other hand, were we to see comparative religions taught in primary schools in the American South, we have to wonder how many zealous evangelical Christians would eagerly misuse such a course as a platform to preach their faith, to name just one group that is common in that area and demonstrably prone to doing it. The answer, however illegal such behavior would be, is almost surely not zero—think again of the ongoing squabbling about teaching biological evolution in that region, which often reaches state-level legislative bodies and courthouses.

This problem would be considerable, but it wouldn't be insurmountable. Requiring qualified teachers to teach the subject would help, and safegaurding the effort via legally capable watchdog agencies committed to secularism (like the Freedom From Religion Foundation) would help more. A fear of the potential for abuse is a reason to find ways to mitigate and minimize it, not a reason to abandon worthwhile projects.

Of course, anything that might happen in any of these regards requires us to make a commitment to having qualified instructors for these kinds of subjects (and the kind of pay and working environments that attract them and keep them in their jobs). This is a statement that should go without saying, however, and so it requires very little elaboration. Still, as I noted, I do not think that our best efforts are likely to be spent in trying to revamp our mandatory educational system unless that is happening at the level of general curriculum in colleges and universities.

This Is NOT "Atheist" Education

It would be extremely poorly advised, not to mention flatly wrong, to refer to any of these efforts as some kind of "atheist" educational system.[14] Courses like civics, ethics, logic, critical thinking, and comparative religions might be identifiable as topics many "atheists" are interested in—along with biology, physics, psychology, and just about every other field of inquiry[15]—but that's only a reflection of the underlying fact that the religions aren't actually true. These topics themselves are extremely beneficial and neutral, so if they discourage religious belief, it's only incidentally to the fact that religious beliefs are mythological cultural objects, not facts about the universe. In fact, these topics would benefit the religious as well in that they would provide a way for them to hold their beliefs more rationally. Those religious people who are unable to argue for the teaching of logic and critical thinking are tacitly admitting that their own worldviews aren't being held accountable to logical and critical analysis, a horned dilemma for them, for sure.

More importantly, this isn't about teams. "Atheism" is dead because theism makes no sense. It's not needed in the sense of a brand for educational channels or efforts. Branding anything with "atheism" not only fails to recognize this incredibly important point, but it also puts it into a box that is less likely to be opened by the people who most need to see it. We don't need to talk about "atheism" anymore. There are just people, some of whom suffer from the acceptance or reliance upon more bad ideas than others—any brand of theism being a particularly noteworthy example.

To see the contents of this chapter or book as anything like "atheist" indoctrination is an error, and the mere fact that people might think that it is (or should be) says a lot about *why we should avoid branding anything with atheism and should, in fact, stop acting like atheism is a thing at all.* All that is being advocated here is an attempt to foster the kinds of circumstances—educational, social, transitional/support—that we should expect naturally to typify a post-theistic society and to facilitate the change to one as it occurs on its own. Nothing like indoctrination would help or should happen.

A Last Point

In Peter Boghossian's *A Manual For Creating Atheists*, he advises that we *avoid facts* when having discussions intended to help people uproot their faiths.[16] Research seems continually to be showing that often, more facts fail to persuade most people and, often, cause them to entrench themselves further in erroneous beliefs.[17]

Thus, it simply isn't likely to be the case that the simpleminded answer that "more education" will successfully help people change their beliefs. Beliefs of these kinds are often held at the moral level, and being held there, they are likely to override countervailing facts and opinions.[18] When these sorts of beliefs aren't held for moral reasons, they're often held in response to an attempt to meet or ignore various psychosocial needs that, I think we can all agree, often run more deeply than the need to be *right* about our beliefs.[19]

It seems to be the case that more education often will neither change people's moral commitments, nor reliably dent their faith (since faith-based beliefs are often regarded with 100 percent confidence, among other reasons). This resistance to facts is why developing techniques that help us uproot faith-based thinking and that destroy the absolutism of moral reasoning are essential to the process of going post-theistic. People who are genuinely curious almost always benefit from more education in ways that are positive. It is up to us to work very diligently to help people find the psychological and social space that they need to become genuinely curious.

Notes

1. This isn't entirely intended to be a call for populist politics, but it's almost beyond doubt that many of the ills of the societies of the Western world are intimately related to a troubling plutocratic trend over the past few decades. Governments have a remarkable track record of representing who or what pulls their strings the hardest, and we should bear this in mind as we engage in politics. For instance, Islamic theocracies represent those with the most influential views of Sharia. Christian theocracies in days gone by were hardly different, representing the interests of the Catholic Church or the Church of England. Governments that represent moneyed interests usually do well by them, concentrating money and power in their hands. Populist democracies, by extension, should likewise do

well by the general populace, and as the data already discussed show, reducing the political and economic disparity in a population has a remarkable effect at reducing reliance upon religious beliefs as well.

2. That there is a rather significant demand for such a thing is amply proved by the response to Sarah Morehead's Recovery from Religion Hotline, which was nearly overwhelmed with demand in just its first month of operation. People leaving religion face a number of challenges for which support would be of great use, and this hotline is a step in the right direction. For more, see Tarico, "Controversial Recovering from Religion Hotline a Hot Commodity."

3. For more information, see Recovering from Religion and the Secular Therapy Project, spearheaded by psychologist Darrel Ray, http://recoveringfromreligion. org/.

4. Hood, Hill, and Spilka, *The Psychology of Religion*, p. 45.

5. Of course, people wishing to push religious beliefs are well aware of this fact as well, and they already produce content to this end, but as philosopher Daniel Dennett has pointed out, religion cannot hide the truth and the primary reason is the Internet. We have good reasons to believe, then, that despite the ability to disseminate misinformation, the dissemination of legitimate information will be effective at creating the kind of doubt that causes people to revise their beliefs (as per philosopher Peter Boghossian's Street Epistemology method). Legitimate sources tend to have the distinct advantage of comporting with each other, which should encourage their ability to undermine religious beliefs. See, for example, Dennett's interview with Andrew Aghapour. "Churches Can No Longer Hide the Truth: Daniel Dennett on the New Transparency," *Religion Dispatches*, 4 May 2015, http://religiondispatches.org/churches-can-no-longer-hide-the-truth-daniel-dennett-on-the-new-transparency/.

6. See https://www.youtube.com/user/crashcourse.

7. Ethics, here, as a field should be distinguished from moral philosophy. In fact, recent fascinating research by Eric Schwitzgebel demonstrated that moral philosophers may not tend to be more ethical than average. See Eric Schwitzgebel, "Do Ethicists Steal More Books?" *Philosophical Psychology* 22, no. 6 (2009): pp. 711–725. Instruction in ethics should take a more practical approach than moral philosophy and simply challenge students to work out ways in which they legitimately can behave better in everyday situations. Getting moral philosophers on board and moral relativists out of the way would be of huge use here.

8. Lest this appear grandly idealistic and impractical, consider the initiative called Philosophy for Children, run in the United Kingdom by the Society for the Advancement of Philosophical Enquiry and Reflection in Education (SAPARE). The SAPARE mission statement reads, "We train teachers in Philosophy for Children which encourages children to think critically, creatively, collaboratively and caringly. We help children, particularly those facing disadvantage, to become lifelong learners." Their goal is expressly to bring exactly these kinds of topics into public education, and it is modeled after a similar effort that exists in the United States. For more information, see http://www.sapere.org.uk/.

9. Douglas Todd, "Is BC Brave Enough to Follow Quebec's World Religion Curriculum?" *Vancouver Sun*, education blog, 19 July 2013, http://blogs. vancouversun.com/2013/07/19/is-b-c-brave-enough-to-follow-quebecs-world-religion-curriculum/.

10. Of note, even if this sort of course cannot be squeezed into current primary or secondary education in other locations, there is a great deal of space for it by reorganizing what constitutes a basic general education at the university level.

11. See Douglas J. Amy, *Government is Good*, http://www.governmentisgood. com/. This seems to be a missing part of our American civics education, judging by the huge gap between the amount of trust Americans tend to extend to government and how much it deserves.

12. In at least one university in which I have worked, during the time of my appointment there, the logic course offered by the philosophy department ceased to serve as a satisfactory replacement for service-level mathematics. Scuttlebutt in the mathematics department indicated that the philosophers wanted out of the challenge, but that formal logic once stood as an acceptable means to satisfy general education mathematics requirements, we see that it could do so again.

13. And this is to name only three non-Christian religions, which also implies that it isn't specifically naming all of the other Christian denominations, like Catholicism, any of the Orthodox sects, Lutheranism, Anglicanism, and so on, that the predominantly Protestant American South abhors nearly as much for reasons that might actually be even more nonsensical.

14. This section exists only because of an expectation of many angry objections that I am openly calling for "atheistic" reforms to our educational system. I am not. I am making calls to educational reforms that could help strengthen societies and help break the grip of faith. If any religion can be maintained without the need of faith, they should delight in these suggestions and rally behind them.

15. Theology is left off this list because it isn't a real field of inquiry.

16. Boghossian, *A Manual for Creating Atheists*, pp. 71–73.

17. As discussed previously, this is covered under what is known as the backfire effect. See Brendan Nyhan and Jason Reifler, "When Corrections Fail: The Persistence of Political Misperceptions," *Political Behavior* 32, no. 2 (2010): pp. 303–330.

18. Justin,P. Friesen, Troy H. Campbell, and Aaron C. Kay, "The Psychological Advantage of Unfalsifiability: The Appeal of Untestable Religious and Political Ideologies," *Journal of Personality and Social Psychology* 108, no. 3 (March 2015): pp. 515–529.

19. This point, that we're not necessarily committed to having correct beliefs, is one of my all-time favorite ironies in the entire discussion of religion, provided by the theologian and philosopher of religion, Alvin Plantinga, of Notre Dame. Plantinga formulated an argument against metaphysical naturalism (the view that all that exists is the natural world) called the "evolutionary argument against naturalism (EAAN)." The basic thrust of the EAAN is that if we have naturalism as a baseline worldview and evolution as the kind of process it is, there is no particular reason to believe that we should favor correct beliefs over beliefs that simply seem to work. It is more than a bit humorous, then, that the prevalence of superstitions like Christianity, which Plantinga attempts to defend with tremendous Sophistication™, is the perfect refutation to the backbone of his own argument. It seems, indeed, that we do not have a real need for correct beliefs, as the long-standing success of Christian superstition amply demonstrates. (Of course, the mere fact that holding them increases the probability that one will assess situations correctly and behave accordingly indicates that an evolutionary bias for being able to generate them could be a beneficial trait for a sentient creature to possess, refuting Plantinga further.)

CONCLUSION: THE FUTURE OF REASON

The last part of the subtitle to Sam Harris's 2004 *End of Faith* is "*The Future of Reason*." Harris was right: the future of reason lies upon the other side of the end of faith. In order to get to the end of faith, at least in the religious sense, we need to learn how to get rid of God. The easiest way to get rid of God is to realize that we've all been wrong about that word, and the ideas behind it, all along.

When we see theism as mythology—when we realize the complex web of psychological and social factors for which the deity is employed—in that very instant, we get rid of God. Faith, of course, remains, and, even without belief in God, it will continue to remain in various articles, such as beliefs in heaven or in reincarnation or in cosmic justice, and in social, moral, and political assumptions (these being absolutely redundant). The future of reason depends upon ending faith, and that is something we can work for, but where faith in God is concerned, it all dissolves in the exact moment we realize that we've been talking about the topic in the wrong way all along.

The analogy provided earlier to Poseidon as a mythological representation of various aspects of oceanic dynamics remains poignant. Fluid dynamics is hopelessly complicated, and anywhere in the ocean that we may be, there are influences and forces above, below, and far away that are difficult to know and still nearly intractable to work with. Some two thousand years ago, these complex factors were impossible for mariners to grasp, and so they invented Poseidon. Similarly, the fabric of our social and psychological lives is complicated, murky, and altogether mysterious. This difficulty, though, like the sea, does not render the psychosocial milieu so far outside of our own cogitation that we require the employment of a mythological figure, God, to come to grips with it. We can understand

241

that something real is going on, something that has absolutely nothing to do with a supremely powerful agent, whether loving, angry, or just temperamental.

Theism is mythology. It is not philosophy. It is not really even a worldview because it looks to a fantasy as a method of attempting to characterize the world.[1] Treating theism on its own terms is a mistake that commits the error that gave the title to this book: it gets "God" wrong.

Since theism isn't even worth considering on its own terms, as it gets its central object wrong in the central way, atheism as a counterpoint to it is unnecessary. When atheism gets treated as its own kind of thing, it becomes both ridiculous and likely to be harmful to the ultimate goal of leaving God behind as a society. That war has been waged, and intellectually, it is over. Culturally, however, we still have our work cut out for ourselves, and though the task is not small or easy, the best hope we have for leaving God behind as a society is in exposing theism for exactly the mistake that it is.

"God," as a set of ideas, is an important concept for humanity, and it has helped and continues to help billions of human beings attempt to live better lives by allowing them to fulfill many of their core psychosocial needs (and to ignore others). Pretending that when believers talk about "God" that they do not know what they are talking about is condescending and unfair. It isn't that they don't know what they're talking about; it's that they're talking about a mythological construct that embodies what they really mean.

When believers talk about "God," they are saying that they have psychological and social needs that they do not know how to meet, and the myth of theism allows them to meet some of those and ignore others. These needs are for morals, for sense of self, for understanding the world, for control, for purpose, for context, for something larger than themselves to cope with or deny death, and for community. We can do better by these needs without religion and without belief in a mythological God. These needs can be met, and they can be met well and without reliance on Iron Age folklore. That's obvious, and so the challenge that lies ahead of us constitutes little more than the incredible effort of connecting those dots for as many people as can be done.

Understanding what "God" means could cut through theism completely, but there are obstacles to this. Most notably, faith is an almost insurmountable barrier because it, almost by definition, makes itself unquestionable. Given that, we must uproot faith. We must take techniques like Peter Boghossian's Socratic questioning, Street Epistemology, and John Loftus's Outsider Test for Faith and help people with them. This means we must study to understand how people make their moral judgments and commitments and then dig into how they justify those beliefs until they are able to become open enough to reconsider them. We must do so recognizing how central these beliefs are *to how people understand themselves*. Patience, honesty, caring, and a healthy respect for the dignity of human beings is completely necessary throughout this entire process, as is a full commitment to being willing to admit that we, ourselves, very well may be wrong (and surely are about a lot of things!).

Meanwhile, we must commit ourselves to defending, strengthening, and spreading secularism. We must encourage reform of dangerous religions from within. We must identify the projects worth engaging in and do those, forsaking those with less worth, even if they appeal to our own senses of self (as defined in the increasingly identifiable moral communities branding themselves as "atheism"). We must work to fill the religion gap—to find and encourage ways to meet the needs met by religion without having to rely upon it—while recognizing that artificial attempts to do this will not succeed. We must work along pathways that service the goal of getting rid of God. Then we will be able to go post-theistic.

This is possible. Knowing that "God" doesn't mean what people think it means clarifies the entire discussion and improves our approach. If we have a sense of where we're going, a sense of where we are, and a sense of what the terrain between is like, charting a course will be straightforward. Our charge is to do just that, no longer wrong about God.

Notes

1. Theism may better be described as an "unworldview" as, classically, God is unworldly.

ACKNOWLEDGMENTS

I should start my acknowledgements for this book with my friend Chris, who talked with me tirelessly about God and belief when I first decided to write. Besides being a wonderful resource and excellent sounding board for ideas, he has a tremendous talent for suggesting books that he thinks people may find interesting or useful. So it was that he recommended that I read *The Happiness Hypothesis* by psychologist Jonathan Haidt. He said I might find it "interesting" and that it is "thought-provoking."

It is, and so I have to acknowledge Haidt's contribution to my thinking as well—very strongly. It was while reading *The Happiness Hypothesis* and some of his other work that I ran across three core concepts that truly incubated this book. First and second, I learned about psychosocial valuation and, through that, about the aspect of it that Haidt serendipitously, for me, referred to by the term *divinity*. Third, I went on to learn about his moral foundations theory, which he developed together with Craig Joseph. Those three ideas were the pieces I was missing in my long quest to understand the term "God."

My friend Chris deserves more thanks, though, too, as he recommended Haidt's *The Righteous Mind*, one of the most important books currently in print, and a lovely psychology of religion textbook, by Ralph Hood, Jr., Peter Hill, and Bernard Spilka, to whom I'm also thankful. These two books, especially the textbook, filled in many more pieces of the puzzle I had already started to put together and proved absolutely invaluable resources. They really became the backbone of my thoughts about the meaning of the term "God," a core that was fleshed out further by J. Anderson Thomson, Jr., to whom I also owe appreciation and acknowledgment.

I heard of Thomson through my friend and colleague Peter Boghossian, who has been by far the person deserving the most of my gratitude. He's been everything from friend to collaborator to editor to a de facto agent for me, and he has always been overwhelmingly encouraging about this project. He also generously wrote the foreword and helpfully connected me with my publisher, Kurt Volkan, who has been both enthusiastic and extremely supportive in all regards. Kurt, therefore, also is someone to whom I'm deeply grateful.

Thanks are due also to John W. Loftus, who strongly inspired me and who has been a great supporter of my efforts from the beginning, and to Jonathan MS Pearce, who helped me refine my understanding of God as an *idea* instead of a being, and who did some wonderful editing of the manuscript with me. Jonathan was also instrumental at helping me finish my last book and was the one responsible for getting me in contact with the late Victor Stenger in the last few months of his life. Vic composed a foreword for my previous book and challenged me in a way that improved my writing significantly. He will be missed, and yet he too is thanked.

Many other people deserve a great deal of my appreciation as well, including some who will earn it after it is too late to add them here. I will refrain from mentioning any more specifically except for two, however, and trust that any and all who have reached out to me—for discussion, to challenge my thinking, to suggest resources, or to help me make this work more visible—should know that they all deserve it. Of the two I will mention specifically, the first is Sam Harris.

Sam Harris is, more than Haidt or Hood, Hill, or Spilka, the real intellectual force behind this book. No other thinker has led me to think clearly about difficult concepts like morality and the notion of a deity more than has Sam Harris. As readers will find, this book, for whatever original thinking it may contain, bills itself as a callback to roots placed in the ground by Harris more than a decade ago, all the way back to *The End of Faith* and some of his earliest high-profile writing. It also restates (and hopefully amplifies) a call he made in 2007, that *atheism* needs to go right alongside theism. Much of this book was composed standing upon the surprisingly broad and square shoulders, if only figuratively, of Sam Harris, and for that I owe him great thanks.

And secondly, among those I want to name directly, and lastly of all I'll mention, I thank my wife—for putting up with me while I chased my dream of writing.

ABOUT THE AUTHOR

James A. Lindsay is an author and outspoken atheist voice who holds degrees in physics and mathematics, including a doctorate in the latter. Motivated by a love of knowledge and learning, along with his life experience of growing up and living in the Southeastern United States—on the buckle of the Bible Belt, as they say—he writes and speaks in an attempt to clarify our religious and cultural landscape and by doing so to help heal the related harms. He has been published in *Scientific American* and is the author of the detailed book *God Doesn't; We Do: Only Humans Can Solve Human Challenges* and *Dot, Dot, Dot: Infinity Plus God Equals Folly*.